MEDIEVAL
MERCENARIES

MEDIEVAL MERCENARIES

The Business of War

William Urban

Foreword by Terry Jones

GREENHILL BOOKS, LONDON
MBI PUBLISHING COMPANY, MINNESOTA

Greenhill Books

Medieval Mercenaries
The Business of War

First published in 2006 by Greenhill Books, Lionel Leventhal Limited, Park House,
1 Russell Gardens, London NW11 9NN
www.greenhillbooks.com
and
MBI Publishing Co., Galtier Plaza, Suite 200, 380 Jackson Street, St Paul,
MN 55101-3885, USA

British Library Cataloguing-in Publication Data

Urban, William L., 1939–
Medieval mercenaries : the business of war
1.Mercenary troops – Europe – History – To 1500
I.Title
355.3'54'094'0902

ISBN-13: 978-185367-697-0
ISBN-10: 1-85367-697-7

Library of Congress Cataloging-in Publication Data available

For more information on our books, please visit
www.greenhillbooks.com, email sales@greenhillbooks.com
or telephone us within the UK on 020 8458 6314.
You can also write to us at the above London address.

Edited and typeset by Palindrome
Maps drawn by Derek Stone

Printed and bound in Great Britain by Creative Print and Design (Wales), Ebbw Vale

CONTENTS

ILLUSTRATIONS

Endpapers: Flemish School, Predella with the Taking of Jerusalem, Ghent
Museum voor Schone Kunsten © 1990, Photo Scala, Florence

FOREWORD

I n 1980, I wrote a little about the mercenary armies of the fourteenth century and how their proliferation throughout Europe was regarded by contemporaries as a catastrophe on a par with the Great Plague itself. It seemed then as big a threat to civilisation as the Atom Bomb does to us today: a Sword of Damocles hanging over us all...a genie that has been let out of the bottle and that can never be put back in.

Well, I can only say that I wish I'd had this book back in 1980.

Bill Urban's *Medieval Mercenaries* puts the events of the fourteenth century into a vivid historical context. He provides an astonishingly clear overview of the whole subject of mercenaries and he does so with tremendous authority and wit.

It makes a thrilling read.

Starting with the professional armies of Rome, he traces the rise of mercenary troops in the tenth and eleventh centuries, until their dominance of the battlefield during the Hundred Years War. He writes amusingly about the way Renaissance Italians turned the business of war into a minor art form, realising that both victory and defeat were equally unwelcome to the professional soldier: defeat bringing death and victory unemployment.

Bill Urban also provides a review of the literary treatment of mercenaries from Chaucer to Mark Twain's *A Connecticut Yankee At The Court Of King Arthur* and Conan Doyle's *The White Company*.

His conclusion is that though mercenaries seem like the problem they are, in fact, merely a symptom. And I would agree with that.

However, I also feel that the real business of war is less to do with the institution of professionalised armies and more to do with those who employ them. It is true that, in the fourteenth century, the ordinary professional soldiers got out of hand, forming themselves into freelance armies during periods of peace, and bringing death, destruction and mayhem to large swathes of Europe.

But in England, by the late fourteenth century, the real perpetrators of war were not the common soldiers, but the barons. Men like Thomas of Woodstock, Duke of Gloucester, and Thomas Beauchamp, Earl of Warwick, needed warfare because their only hopes of gaining wealth and expanding their retinues lay in prosecuting the war with France. The ruin, death and destruction that this brought upon the civilian population meant nothing to such men, just so long as they profited from the chaos. To these two must be added Richard, Earl of Arundel, who although wealthy enough himself not to need to go to war, seems to have been of such a bellicose nature that warfare was his natural preoccupation.

These were the men whom the French writer and crusade activist, Philippe de Mézières, described as 'great Boars, black and bristling, sons of that mighty Black Boar who so many times…destroyed the vineyards of France.' (*Le Songe du Vieil Pelerin* I, 117)

The barons adamantly opposed Richard II's policy of peace between France and England out of their own self-interest and in despite of the interests of the people. Perhaps little wonder that Philippe should characterise King Richard as 'a miraculous white boar' working for the common good.

Today the situation seems pretty similar except that there is no miraculous white boar on the horizon as yet. The hawkish barons have been replaced by the revolving door between the military–industrial complex and the policy-makers – the precise mechanism that President Eisenhower warned about in his departing speech to the nation. In the twenty-first century war has been firmly and publicly espoused by administrations on both sides of the Atlantic.

As always, there are pretexts put forward for waging war…didn't Attila the Hun claim he was invading Europe in order to rescue a damsel in distress? She happened to be the Emperor's sister Honoria, who had smuggled out her ring to Attila and begged him to rescue her from a life of boredom!

Today other pretexts are found that are no less flimsy, but who cares as long as there is profit to be made out of warfare? It is not the mercenaries themselves, however, who propagate a state of perpetual conflict, but their employers – the politicians connected to the construction, servicing and arms industries, who stand to make handsome bonuses and future incomes out of a thriving war economy. The deaths of hundreds of thousands of innocent people count as little to these people as the misery of the peasantry did to the barons of the fourteenth century.

As long as there are people and companies who make vast profits out of war, war will continue to plague our world. But we should not blame the mercenaries and the professional soldiers – they are merely the messengers of death.

Terry Jones, 2006

PREFACE

I T IS TIME for a survey of medieval mercenaries that describes how they created – in Juhan Kreem's elegant phrase – the business of war. Although textbooks often pass over mercenaries, they were present throughout the medieval era. Moreover, the textbooks and surveys have neither the personal details that make narrative history interesting and exciting, nor analyses of what mercenaries actually did. These deficiencies are part of what this book intends to address.

A second intent is to examine the popular literature that has created our imagined world of medieval mercenaries. If it is true that what we believed happened is almost as important as what actually did take place, then no study of this era would be complete without looking at authors who made the literature of medieval war popular. Just as no discussion of Italian mercenaries can be complete without referring to Machiavelli, no portrayal of the Hundred Years War can ignore Shakespeare, Conan Doyle and Mark Twain.

A third intent is to investigate how it was that, in an era when money was short and oaths were long, mercenary soldiers were so important. The importance of mercenaries varied from place to place and time to time, but they were rarely of no consequence whatsoever.

PRELIMINARY OBSERVATIONS

Mercenaries were needed because although medieval societies tried to rely upon feudal oaths and local militias, these were often insufficient. Also, neither knights nor peasants complained when strangers risked their lives for them in moments of crisis. Inquiries about personal morals, respect for the law, body odour and so forth tend to be kept short when survival is at stake.

What employers wanted were mercenary *units*, groups ready for combat from the moment they arrived, not individual warriors of questionable background. Such units were thus a service commodity.

Employers often wanted to command the army, but not all had the talent or experience. Mercenary generals offered some hope of battlefield success. Hope at a price, of course. And at a risk. No one could guarantee that the new employee would perform as expected, or even that he would not attempt to take over the business. Outsourcing has its risks.

Mercenaries also negotiated like unions, picking the most awkward moments to demand an increase in pay. As a student of mine once said of strikers in Paris who had shut down the entire transportation system, 'Don't they know that is inconvenient?'

Employers were also beseeched by idealists to avoid armed conflicts, the argument being that war itself was questionable morally and in practice. If abandoning a disputed point was sufficient to make peace, giving way might be the cheaper and wiser course. Of course, hard-headed advisors would point out that if neighbours concluded that a peaceable lord was an easy mark, then bullying could be expected. Fighting had some benefits, even if the war was likely to be lost – the lord who fought back was at least likely to be respected, and therefore left alone.

These aspects of medieval military practice tend to be forgotten. But historical truth is what people remember, as W. C. Sellar (1898–1951) and R. J. Yeatman (1897–1968) remind us. Their *1066 and All That; A Memorable History of England, comprising all the parts you can remember, including 103 Good Things, 5 Bad Kings and 2 Genuine Dates* (1930) said that history is not what you thought it was, but what you remember. What you can remember, for example, is the date 1066. Not what it signified. Moreover, they said:

> The Norman Conquest was a Good Thing, as from this time
> onwards England stopped being conquered and thus was able to
> become top nation.

This parody of the Whig School of history is also worth noting, because it is so much like modern political correctness, which discourages the writing or reading of military history. According to the Whig School, every person and every action is judged Good or Bad according to whether the cause of parliamentary democracy and the middle class was advanced or retarded. Political Correctness makes similar judgments based on a combination of excessive politeness and tender-heartedness. Thus it occasionally seems that hurting people's feelings is worse than killing them. There is also a tendency to believe that if war is good for business, that is sufficient reason in itself to hate war.

In this the adherents of political correctness share an important attitude with the medieval Church – that making a profit from someone else's need is immoral. Thus, the merchant who rushed grain to a war-ravaged land sinned as much by making a profit as the mercenaries who looted and burned it.

Several decades later another humourist-historian gave us an additional insight into mercenaries. Richard Armour (1906–89), the author of *It All Started with Stones and Clubs. Being a Short History of War and Weaponry from Earliest Times to the Present, noting the Gratifying Progress made by Man since his First Crude, Small-Scale Efforts to Do Away with Those Who Disagreed with him* (1967), wrote:

> The Vikings landed in the British Isles, sailed up the Seine to Paris, and traveled even as far as Russia and Constantinople. Whether the Vikings fought simply for the love of fighting, as some historians contend, or were primarily interested in loot, is a matter of conjecture, but there is no reason to believe that the two reasons are mutually exclusive. The Vikings proved that in war you can combine fun and profit, with travel thrown in as a bonus.

More seriously, the bottom line is this: in the Middle Ages rulers generally recruited professional warriors only for emergencies, did what they could to control them, and ultimately dismissed them. The alternative to hiring mercenaries was to suffer defeat, and defeat meant more than turning the cheek to receive another slap. I have been asked many times, rhetorically, 'What do wars really settle'? 'Nothing', I now respond, 'except who owns the land, who works it, what taxes and services will be demanded, what languages are spoken, what religions are followed. Other than that, perhaps not much'.

When important values are at stake – who lives, who dies, who flourishes, who suffers – one can understand hiring mercenaries. Some will do more for less justification.

Mercenaries were more than a gang of toughs. Nobles were mercenaries, too. As Maurice Keen says in his authoritative work, *Chivalry*, 'In terms of motivation, calculation and conduct the line between gentlemen and mercenary was simply too difficult to draw with precision'. Hence, this book will examine the old contention that gentlemen, even today, are too grand to soil their hands with commerce, especially with the business of war. As one who teaches in a small but good liberal arts college in the American Midwest, I am aware of a widespread academic tendency to pour scorn on programs which prepare students for employment – students should be *educated*, not *trained*. One extension of this argument is that ROTC (Reserve Officers' Training Corps), which *trains* volunteer students to be officers, should be abolished. I occasionally ask, 'Where is a democratic nation to develop its future officers?' The response is usually a shrug – meaning 'not here' – but occasionally I get an answer that suggests that armies are no more necessary than police.

I can live with that. But only in a conversational sense, a willingness to humour overly excitable colleagues, not as agreeing that muggers will disappear as soon as governments do. This book will show that every society has individuals who will take advantage of disorder to indulge their worst instincts.

Also, if Sellar and Yeatman are correct in saying that history is not what you thought it was, but what you remember, I hope that readers will look at modern fictional accounts of medieval history with new appreciation and all movies with scepticism.

No one likes mercenaries. Yet everyone has used them. Advancing the awareness of this widespread practice of the past and the present should be justification enough for a book on mercenaries and the business of war.

William Urban
Lee L. Morgan Professor of History and International Affairs
Monmouth College (Illinois)

MAPS

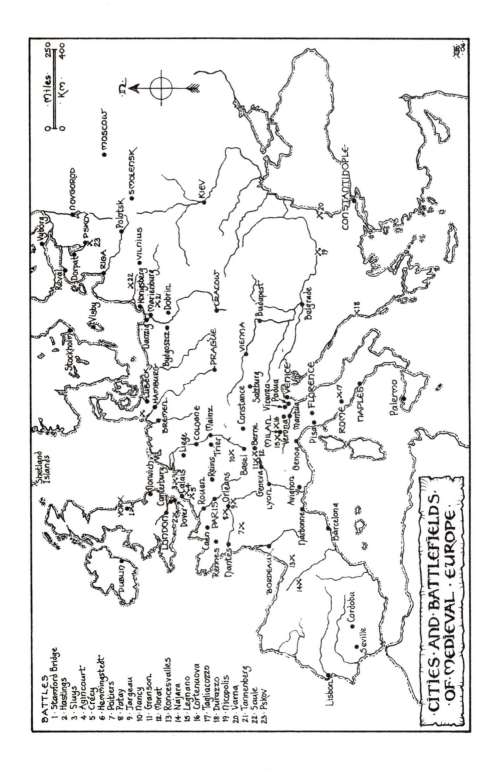

CITIES·AND·BATTLEFIELDS·
OF·MEDIEVAL·EUROPE·

BATTLES
1· Stamford Bridge
2· Hastings
3· Sluys
4· Agincourt
5· Crécy
6· Hemmingstedt
7· Poitiers
8· Potay
9· Jargeau
10· Nancy
11· Granson
12· Morat
13· Roncesvalles
14· Najara
15· Legnano
16· Cortenuova
17· Tagliacozzo
18· Durazzo
19· Nicopolis
20· Varna
21· Tannenberg
22· Saule
23· Pskov

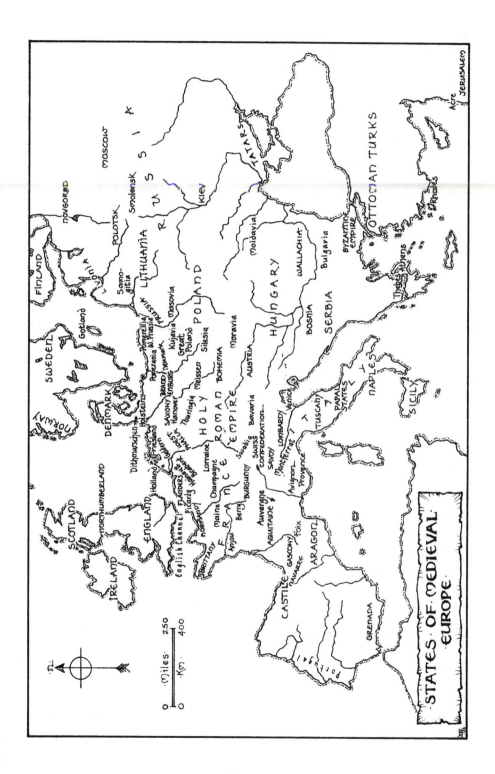

STATES OF MEDIEVAL EUROPE

19

1

EARLY MEDIEVAL MERCENARIES

THE CONNECTION BETWEEN mercenary and employer is money. Early Germanic tribesmen might serve in Roman armies, but for their own wars they relied on promises of booty, oaths of loyalty and ancient tribal traditions. Mutual protection was also important, and coercion, too. It is a mistake to think of the German tribes as composed of pure racial or linguistic groups – tribes dissolved and reformed repeatedly, often with only a mythological connection to the royal family; clans were not limited to blood relatives and those who married members, but were practical means of assuring mutual aid and protection. Although in moments of danger blood might be thicker than water, oaths to give aid were thicker yet – and since some of these groups were little more than bands of brigands, we could say, 'thick as thieves'.

We can look upon the late Roman legion alternatively as a mercenary force or professional army. The commanders recruited young barbarians, trained them, and made them loyal to themselves; they left alone Roman citizens and serfs, who were too important to the economy to be wasted in service along the frontiers – they were needed to produce crops and pay taxes. No taxes, no food = no army. When the defences of the western empire collapsed, the government there lost much of its ability to collect taxes, after which it could not raise armies to restore the frontiers and internal order. In the east, in contrast, in that part of the Roman state we call the Byzantine Empire, vast areas remained untouched by rampaging invaders. This made it possible for the emperors to restore agricultural production in devastated regions, and thus to survive for many centuries to come.

Constantinople was the heart of the Eastern Roman Empire, and although the emperors and people there all spoke Greek, they still considered themselves Roman. The city remained Greek-speaking until 1453, then Greek in spirit even longer; and more than a few Greeks today believe that it should be Greek again.

The emperors' Roman predecessors had hired Germans because they considered them good warriors and likely to be loyal. This lasted until the Germans took over the government of the western empire themselves. Then Byzantine emperors replaced their Germans with a new farmer-soldier class and a wide variety of hired barbarians. The emperors were very practical on military matters. Most of all they advised flexibility, which could be achieved by selecting the right mix of mercenaries for each war.

Byzantine armies were models of efficiency and organisation. The emperors raised competent generals to command, men who had been formally trained in strategy and tactics; and who had modern technologies such as Greek fire to call upon. The military manuals advised commanders to study the enemy's army, then raise forces appropriate for countering its strengths and playing upon its weaknesses; the central striking force was often composed of mercenaries – the Varangian Guard being the most famous.

Byzantine wealth naturally attracted the attention of greedy neighbours – pagan Persians, Muslim Arabs, Bulgars and Russians who eventually adopted Byzantium's Orthodox faith, western Christians and ultimately Muslim Turks. The Byzantine armies fought off all but the last, and even then were able to delay the final Turkish triumph for centuries.

VIKINGS

The western counterpart of the Byzantine Empire was created by Charlemagne and eventually became known as the Holy Roman Empire. Roman institutions, however, were few – principally maintained by the Church – and this Frankish state soon collapsed under the weight of Muslim, Hungarian and Viking attacks. The rulers of the successor states parcelled out lands to men who could provide military protection and supervise basic governmental services. Such a primitive system was viewed with disdain by Byzantines.

In turn, western Europeans who prided themselves on once having been associated with Rome, or at least with the name Roman, looked upon the

Vikings as simple barbarians. While there was some truth to this assessment, it was also misleading. In many ways – in literature, art and maritime technology – the Vikings were a very sophisticated people; they also possessed a vitality that seemed to be lacking elsewhere.

In the ninth century Scandinavians overran many of their neighbours' territories. While Danes went to southern England and Normandy, and Norwegians to Scotland, Ireland and Iceland, the Swedes went east, sailing up rivers into what is today Russia, then transferring to rivers leading down to the Islamic and Byzantine worlds. Most took along goods for sale – usually human beings collected along the shores of the Baltic and North Seas; later Vikings served in the famed Varangian Guard.

At Saint Olaf College in Northfield, Minnesota, one dining room is (or used to be, in an era when it was acceptable to portray Vikings as warriors rather than as merchants, settlers and explorers) decorated with a large map of medieval Europe, with the Viking raids indicated by little burning buildings. The area of Poland is blank because while the Vikings left enough survivors elsewhere to record their depredations, their devastation of the Polish coast was almost total. (Some scholars see a connection between the words Slav and Slave, reflecting the huge numbers of Slavs who were sold down the Russian rivers.) This slave trade was one basis for the prosperity of the Scandinavian economies. Male slaves often ended up as eunuchs, the women as servants and concubines.

Viking warriors served Scandinavian kings as bodyguards and tax collectors, but the best pay and the most alluring off-duty attractions were to be found in Constantinople.

THE VARANGIAN GUARD

In 987 the Byzantine emperor Basil II (976–1025) asked Vladimir of Kiev to lend him some 6,000 warriors. From that time on, Basil's armies were invincible; when he crushed the powerful Bulgarian state, he became known as 'the Bulgar killer'. He advanced the borders of the Byzantine state to the Danube River in the north and into Syria in the east. Scholarly opinion is divided as to Vladimir's ethnic origins. Russians say that he was a Slav; almost everyone else thinks he was a descendant of Viking immigrants. It doesn't really matter. What is important is that from that time until 1204, when western crusaders captured Constantinople, the Varangian Guard was there to defend imperial interests.

As time passed the guard was recruited from ever more distant regions – first Russia, then Scandinavia, and finally England and Iceland. The decline in Viking recruits after the Christianisation of Scandinavia perhaps reflects the desire of the Viking kings to live in peace. They had overrun England and parts of France and Ireland and wanted more than anything to collect taxes peacefully. Ending the raids would also reduce the likelihood of potential rivals earning a military reputation. As a result, young men looking for work as mercenaries had to travel far. And Constantinople was, if anything, far away.

Except for critical moments during rebellions and foreign invasions, the Varangian Guard rarely left Constantinople; the name apparently came from the oath they had taken, but this, like many details passed down by oral tradition, is unclear. The Scandinavian mercenaries had their own barracks not far from the imperial palace, conveniently located for protecting the imperial person and his family. They were also employed to suppress the riots that could be anticipated at major sporting events and for arresting nobles and religious leaders who incurred imperial wrath.

The commander of the Varangian Guard ultimately became a kingmaker. The best example was Harald Hardrada (1015–66), himself king of Norway after 1047, a tall but well-proportioned warrior with long blond moustaches and one eyebrow permanently arched. He had, according to the appropriately named *King Harald's Saga*, fled Norway after rebels had killed his half-brother, Saint Olaf, in 1030. Harald made his way to Byzantium, found employment with the emperor, and was soon the Guard's commander. For several years he often won battles or concluded sieges by cleverness and cunning rather than sheer physical prowess; he was known for his ruthlessness, his pride and his long memory for insults. His saga by Snorri Sturluson, found in the *Heimkringla*, is filled with tales of his valour and enterprise.

One anecdote concerned the Varangians' freedom from direct control by the Greek commander of the army, which fundamentally meant that Harald could keep his men out of dangerous situations. The decisive dispute that settled the matter did not occur in the face of the enemy, where Harald could be accused of disloyalty, disobedience and cowardice, but on the march. One evening the Vikings arrived first at the assigned campsite, where they chose the most comfortable place to spend the night. When the commander arrived, he ordered the Varangian Guard to move so that he could pitch his own tents there. Harald challenged his right to give this order, since the

Varangian Guard was solely under the command of the emperor and empress. When the dispute reached the point that each side was pulling out its weapons, Harald suggested that the two commanders draw lots, the loser to withdraw his claims both to the campsite and the larger question of command. The commander agreed, on condition that the two lots to be drawn would be identical except for the mark made by the two men. When the commander had made a sign on his mark, Harald asked to see it so that he would not accidentally duplicate it. The Greek showed him his lot, after which Harald made his mark and put it in the container from which a trustworthy referee would draw one lot. However, the instant that the marker was drawn, Harald snatched it from the referee's hand and threw it far into the water. The Greek objected, saying that now nobody would know who had won. Harald, however, said that all they had to do was look at the remaining lot; they would see that the Greek's mark was upon it; therefore, the one that had been drawn and then thrown away had to be Harald's.

Harald did not trust the emperor to safeguard the treasure he was accumulating, but sent it immediately to Jaroslav of Novgorod for safe keeping. He sacked four towns in Sicily and Africa, each time by a clever ruse. The last city was far too large and well defended to take by storm; the only chance to get into the city was by trickery. Harald started by spreading the word that he was ill, then that his condition had worsened, and lastly that he had died, after which his men requested permission to bury Harald inside the city's church. The monks dutifully came out to take the coffin, but the Vikings arranged to drop it right in the gate, thus preventing the defenders from closing it when the rest of the army charged.

A later expedition took Harald to Jerusalem, then even further east so that he could bathe in the Jordan. Although normally only half-Christian in spirit and actions (he later had two wives at one time), he donated great riches to the churches in the holy city. No point in not buying eternal life insurance when the opportunity presented itself.

Harald's plans to leave Byzantine service was not good news to the emperor, Michael IV (1034–41), who would have difficulty replacing him, and even less welcome to the fifty-five-year-old empress, Zoe, who was rumoured to have lusted after his handsome body. Michael was acting on politics rather than potential romantic affairs when he confined Zoe to a convent, but it was a mistake. Michael died suddenly and unexpectedly – as had Zoe's first husband, Romanus III, in 1034. Zoe returned to the palace, married her husband's incompetent and unattractive nephew, Michael V, thereby placating those who insisted on a male ruler.

In the complicated power struggle that followed Harald threw his support to Zoe, whose best claim to exercise power was being the niece of Basil II and for a knowledge of perfume manufacture unrivalled until the twentieth century. She seems to have put her knowledge of chemistry to the process of invigorating her husbands, then 'devigorating' them. Her efforts to become pregnant at an advanced age reflect better on her determination than her understanding of biological principles. Michael V eventually tired of the effort. He had first been her lover, then her husband, and finally he wanted to be emperor on his own. He packed Zoe off to a convent.

Michael might have got away with this if Zoe had not been so popular, if he had been more able or if he had cultivated the support of the Varangian Guard. But arresting Harald on charges of misappropriating public funds was one mistake too many. Michael V was overthrown in 1042 by a conspiracy involving dynastic loyalists, careerist politicians and the Varangian Guard. Harald restored Zoe to power, then blinded her husband and sent him to a monastery.

The episode fits perfectly into the stereotype of 'Byzantine politics' — a court characterised by jealousy, secrecy, complex plots and universal corruption. It was the perfect environment for an ambitious mercenary general to rise to prominence. Had Harald's royal blood been Greek rather than Norwegian, he could have become emperor; perhaps, despite his being a foreigner, he could have married Zoe and ruled as long as she lived. But that seemed a poor career move. He said no.

Zoe, resenting rejection, began to listen to Harald's enemies. Soon Harald heard the call of Norway, where the usurper had become unpopular; the moment seem right for a Christian to sit upon the northern throne again.

Harald, having assessed Zoe's governing abilities as minimal and her physical attractiveness even lower, escaped from the great city and sailed for home with legendary quantities of moveable wealth, reputedly taking with him for a short while the empress's niece, who was ready to marry him. Harald tarried in Novgorod on his voyage long enough to woo Jaroslav's daughter, Ilsabe – 'the golden lady in Russia'. As Snorri wrote in his rhymed story:

> The warlike king of Norway
> Won the match of his desire;
> He gained a king's daughter
> And a hoard of gold as well.

Such was the literature that inspired future generations of Scandinavian youths to dream of fame and fortune, earned as mercenaries abroad.

SAXON ENGLAND

The Saxons had conquered England from the Romano-British in the fifth and sixth centuries, effectively eliminating them as a factor in language, religion and government, leaving behind only the semi-mythical stories of King Arthur to commemorate the long and bitter struggle. The Saxons in their turn fell victim to the Vikings in the ninth and tenth centuries, but with less dire results; when Danes and Norwegians overran most of the British Isles, they only forced the Saxons, Scots and Irish to pay tribute.

The most important Viking physical presence was in eastern and central England, in the Danelaw, where they gave new vigour to the economy, especially to the town of York. Saxon resistance to the Vikings in the west led to a union of the petty kingdoms under King Alfred (871–99), who hired the first English mercenaries, Frisian sailors who had their own reasons for disliking Danes and liking regular pay; later kings hired professional guards called *housecarls*. Eventually all Saxons accepted Danish sovereignty as long as the king remained far away. King Canute (1016–35) is remembered more for his self-deprecating wisdom than his empire stretching all the way to Estonia.

When the Saxons achieved independence again, they did not dismantle the fiscal apparatus for collecting tribute money. This income made the Saxon king rich despite England being a comparatively poor country. Similarly, the Northmen who gave their name to Normandy made that region more important than its natural resources should have allowed.

The Norman Conquest of Saxon England began with a dispute about which of six men would be the successor of Edward the Confessor (1042–66); only three, however, had the military resources to be serious contenders– William the Bastard, Harold Godwinson and Harald Hardrada, who had become King of Norway in 1047.

The saintly king's vow of chastity had disrupted the smooth transfer of power that was the chief virtue of hereditary succession. The three leading candidates had equally good claims on the crown. However, Harold Godwinson, earl of Wessex, was at Edward's deathbed. According to Snorri, Harold bent over Edward's mouth, then stood up to call on all witnesses to testify that the king had named him his successor. There were many sceptics, men who were used to politicians' wiles; among them was Harold's own brother, Tostig.

Harold was the son of Godwin, who had governed England for Canute. Godwin had selected Edward as king during the last succession crisis, and had dominated the compliant ruler with one significant exception, when Edward had exiled him temporarily. Godwin returned, but died in 1053 before he could guarantee the succession to his son Harold. This son was the favourite of the *Witan*, the Saxon assembly, which was actually in session when Edward passed away. Harold Godwinson was known to most of the *thanes*, as the Saxons called the landed warrior class, because he had carried out many of the tasks associated with daily governance after his father's death, and his sister had been Edward's chaste and loyal wife. He met two of the four characteristics set by the Witan for the next ruler: he was a man of character and ability, and he was English. Forty-four years of age, he was at the height of his physical and mental powers. However, he was not of royal blood and the king had not indicated his wishes, not even on his deathbed, except perhaps in Harold's ear.

Awkwardly, Harold's brother, Tostig, the eldest of Godwin's five sons, thought that he had the better claim to be head of the family and, hence, king. Edward's favourite, Tostig had been sent north to defend the borderlands against the Scots in 1065, but his men had provoked a rebellion among the very people they were to protect. The rebels killed his closest associates, seized the treasury, and marched south to demand that the king give them a better governor. Tostig, who had been hunting when the crisis arose, accused Harold of provoking it. Harold, in the presence of the king, swore that he was innocent of any involvement. Edward, unable to raise troops to put down the rising, reluctantly ordered Tostig into exile. This was a mistake.

Tostig went to first to Denmark, hoping to persuade King Sven II (Canute's grandson, king 1047–76) to support his cause; but that monarch said that he too old and feeble for such an enterprise (he was forty-six). Then Tostig sailed to Norway and approached King Harald Hardrada. For fifteen years Harald had been making annual raids into Denmark, but recently he had made peace with King Sven. Now Harald was bored. Moreover, he was touched to the quick by Tostig's taunt that he had fought hard to possess Denmark, but would not accept England when it was being handed to him. More to the point, Harald's warriors were probably short of cash after two years without an opportunity to loot somebody. Still, many Vikings were aware that one Saxon housecarl would be equal to two Norwegian yeomen, and that there were many of them, all wearing mail armour and wielding large axes. Others scoffed at this – Vikings were unbeatable, they boasted, and they had almost always bested the English.

Tostig's original plan was to become king himself, but King Harald was not willing to undertake such a venture for only a little money. Besides, he probably enjoyed taunting the petitioner (his nickname means 'hard bargainer'); for a Viking a bare-knuckles negotiation was almost as much fun as a brawl, and it could last longer, without anyone being actually killed. When Harald asked Tostig why Norwegians should fight to make one brother king of the English rather than another, when no Englishman could be trusted for anything, Tostig changed the argument: he said that Harald should become king himself; for his part, Tostig was ready to settle for the governance of Northumbria, with perhaps an appointment to rule England whenever Harald would be absent (which would be most of the time). Harald, satisfied with this proposal, soon had an army ready to sail.

King Harald entered the tomb of St Olaf, trimmed the holy corpse's beard and nails, then threw away the key. When he joined the fleet of 200 warships and more supply vessels, an aged woman saw ghostly carrion birds perched on every prow; she remarked that they were awaiting the prince's feast. The old troll had it right in at least one respect: the warriors on board had an appetite for a rich meal of human flesh and bones. She was also right in suggesting that Harald would be the chief course. But Harald, certain of his 'luck', was unmoved. He was turning his back on Norway; his future was in England, at least what would be left of it by the time his warriors were sated. He was fifty years old, plenty of time left for more adventures, for greater ambitions.

The third candidate was William, duke of Normandy (1035–87). The Norman nobles were descendants of Viking immigrants, but their blood had been mixed with that of French counts and knights and they had enthusiastically adopted the language and customs of their subjects. In a way the Normans combined the best and worst traits of both their ancestral culture and their adopted one. Most importantly, they could never stay quietly at home. War was their natural environment, and when a feud was not available locally, they sought a conflict out abroad.

Some wild young Norman knights had already gone to Italy in 998 as mercenaries. William's father, Robert the Devil, had encouraged more of them to go south, out of his hair and into somebody else's. Just as well. When he became a pilgrim and set off for the Holy Land, he named his illegitimate son William his successor, hardly anticipating that he himself would die on the journey. That the seven-year-old William survived to adulthood was a miracle. His upbringing must have been the most arduous training in statecraft on record, and even at age eighteen, when he announced that he would assume the government personally, he had to subdue a dangerous revolt by his vassals. Henceforth he kept his knights employed at foreign wars, encouraging even more to go to southern Italy. The most prominent of the Normans there – Robert Guiscard (†1085) – made himself master of Naples and assisted his brother, Roger (†1101), in conquering Sicily. They became the protectors of the Papal States against the Holy Roman emperor and provided many volunteers for the First Crusade. The ties with Normandy would remain important for several generations; this gave French monarchs excuses to intervene there from the thirteenth century on.

William's claims to the Saxon throne were shaky. Once in the past, he said, Edward had promised to name him king. Sometimes William suggested this was in 1042 before Edward had left Normandy to become king himself, when William was a teenager; sometimes it was during a meeting in 1051, when William visited the king during Godwin's exile – there were many Normans at the court at that time. William's claim was reinforced in 1064, when Harold found himself in Normandy, either on a diplomatic mission or driven ashore by storms. According to William, Harold swore to become his 'man' (the act of *homage* from the Latin *homo*) and then to do all that he could to assure that William would be elected king. Storytellers disagree as to where this oath was given and of what it consisted.

What might have happened was that Harold used this promise to secure his pre-eminent position in the government just as Tostig had done with Harald Hardrada – a oath of fealty that cost nothing but would secure him from disaster should Edward recommend William to the Witan as the next king. In the meantime, William could boast of his future prospects: he was now only a duke, but soon enough he would be a king.

Strangely, when William heard of Edward's death, he had only one question of Harold: would Harold marry William's daughter as he had promised? Harold, however, had both a long-term mistress and an intended bride. He was not willing to give up either for an under-aged fiancée. Instead, Harold moved quickly to obtain election by the Witan and be crowned. When he heard of the mobilisations in Norway and Normandy, he ordered his army to assemble.

The core of Harold's force were the *housecarls*, professional soldiers equipped with mail armour, shields and axes. The mass of troops came from the militia, called the *fyrd*, most of which was composed of thanes, landowners who were willing to fight enthusiastically in defence of their homes; warriors of the lower classes were meagrely armed and of indifferent spirit.

William called an assembly of his vassals in the spring. His proposal to build a fleet to transport the army to England was not well received. Vikings had never hesitated to board ships to attack enemy lands, but Vikings were foot-soldiers. Normans fought in mail armour from horseback, hurling spears and slashing with swords; no one had experience in transporting large numbers of warhorses in Viking-style vessels. The lack of space meant that there would be too few rowers to guarantee reaching the English coast if the winds were not favourable; any contrary breeze would drive many vessels far off course, which would not have been a disaster for an ordinary merchantman, but no merchantman was ever loaded with knights and their mounts. Also, by the time a fleet could be ready to sail, it would be autumn, and the weather would be unpredictable. If a summer crossing of the Channel was a daunting prospect, an autumn crossing was positively frightening.

William tried to persuade his vassals not only to agree that his cause was just, but also to promise to bring twice as many men as their feudal contracts stipulated. They balked at that. They were willing to perform their feudal duties, but they made it clear that it was up to him to recruit the army.

The duke's efforts to recruit his peers failed equally miserably. Neighbouring counts and dukes saw no advantage in assisting him to become even more powerful; already he was a regional bully, a menace to everyone. He had more success with the pope, who was eager to 'reform' the English church, that is, to force it to accept recent doctrines that increased papal authority. The pope declared William's venture holy (the term 'crusade' was still unknown), with spiritual benefits for everyone. This may have been meant as a warning to the German emperor, who was extending his authority over the Holy Roman Empire by using church resources, but the pope was not ready to tip his hand there yet. First England, which paid the lucrative 'Peter's Pence' to the pope, then the rest of Christendom.

Last, William sent out a call for volunteers. Warriors flocked in from all parts of the French kingdom, mostly young knights, probably younger sons who had little chance of inheriting enough land to maintain their noble status. In lieu of pay, he promised to give them estates now held by Saxons — as it was often put, 'to rely on the duke's generosity'. When that news reached England, the Saxon thanes realised that they had to stand by Harold or lose everything.

Most notable among William's allies were Bretons. They composed an entire wing of his army at the battle of Hastings. Brittany was a major breeding ground of mercenaries from that time on.

THE BATTLE OF STAMFORD BRIDGE

Harold perceived that Duke William was a greater threat than the Norwegian monarch. His subjects had agreed with him, the fyrd even remaining at the Channel for six weeks beyond the term required by their feudal obligations. But there was a limit to what could be expected of vassals, and by mid-September it seemed obvious to everyone that it was unlikely that William could launch a fleet; no sane man would attempt to sail from Normandy in the face of a north wind and worsening weather. Moreover, there was hardly any food left along the coastline to feed the army. Harold had barely sent the fyrd home when news arrived that King Harald Hardrada had landed in the north.

The Norwegian king had actually sailed in mid-August, but he had stopped in the Shetland Islands and in Scotland to recruit more troops. Therefore, he did not arrive on the English coast until mid-September. He first captured York, using a feint to lure the militiamen from behind their ditch, then striking so hard that his men were able to walk across the ditch on Saxon bodies without wetting their feet. Three days later York surrendered, after which the king announced that he would hold a public meeting at Stamford Bridge; there he would distribute rewards to his followers and to those Saxons who surrendered in time. King Harald then relaxed, apparently believing that Harold Godwinson was far away on the south coast awaiting the arrival of the Normans.

Harold Godwinson, however, was no longer on the Channel. At the head of his housecarls he made an incredible forced march northward, the last 200 miles in five days, arriving at Stamford Bridge without warning. King Harald and Tostig were not even properly armed when they saw an army approaching – fine shields and shining coats of mail, with weapons glittering like ice. Was it local Saxons coming to surrender? It couldn't be a hostile force – Harold could not have arrived so swiftly. Still unsure who it was, Tostig recommended retreating to the ships. But Harald Hardrada believed that he and a handful of men could hold the oncoming foe at the bridge. It was a matter of pride. And a Viking belief in fate. And in luck. Harald sent messengers to his men at the ships, urging them to hurry forward, then took up his position at the bridge.

According to Snorri's tale, Harald's black horse stumbled as he rode around to inspect his troops. Nimbly he darted to his feet, saying, 'A fall is fortune on the way.' As Harold of England saw this, he asked who the big man with the blue tunic and beautiful helmet was. Told that it was Harald, he commented how large and strong he appeared, but that it appeared that his luck had run out this day.

When Tostig asked Harold how much English land he would give King Harald to go away, Harold replied, 'seven feet' to be buried in, seven feet because he was unusually tall. Tostig was another matter. Harold offered him Northumberland, but he refused to pay Tostig's supporters for their service. Some of Tostig's troops were Flemish mercenaries, who needed paying. Tostig, his honour touched, refused; surprisingly, he did not reveal Harold's identity during the negotiations, because the Vikings would likely have slain him then and there, ending the war before it started. Harald did not know his opponent by sight, but when he asked who had spoken so well, Tostig told him it had been Harold. The Norwegian king commented that he was a little man, but that he stood proudly in his stirrups.

In such a way battle was chosen over compromise. Each knew that it would be an unusually bloody affair, with men with axes chopping away grimly at one another. But from Harold Godwinson's point of view, speed was important – he had a tactical advantage and the greater numbers. Delay would work only for King Harald, who must have been watching the horizon for sign of his men.

As the Saxons came on, King Harald raised his banner, called 'Land-waster', then fought like a mad-man, a berserker, until he was hit by a chance arrow in the eye or throat. Harold then offered to spare Tostig, his men, and the surviving Vikings, but they replied that they would rather die than surrender to Englishmen. And so they did. Tostig fell after defending the royal standard bravely, together with most of the Vikings who had exhausted themselves in hurrying to the fight in full battle gear.

It had been a costly victory. The Vikings had fought to the death. Harold's troops were completely exhausted, and many were wounded. But they had less than a week to recover before news came that William had landed in the south.

THE BATTLE OF HASTINGS

The Bayeux Tapestry pictures the events of the invasion from the Norman point of view. William's crowded ships made the crossing without difficulties, the men and horses spilling out on to *terra firma*, happy that no hostile force was there to attack before they had recovered from seasickness, fright and exhaustion. The troops then spread out to loot and burn. It was what the mercenaries had looked forward to from the beginning.

Harold made his return from York to London in only four days, resting his army there while awaiting reports from his scouts and asking William what terms he would accept to return home. William reminded Harold of his earlier oath, then demanded that he be recognised as king. Harold chose to fight.

There were reasons for Harold to delay. Time was on his side in every way – his housecarls would have been more rested – each day more troops would have joined his army, and once all England was mobilised, he might be unbeatable; even without waiting for the warriors from the northern shires, his army would soon outnumber William's decisively. On the other hand, Harold learned only now that he had been excommunicated by the pope! Perhaps it was best to strike at William's forces quickly, before this fact sank in among the pious Saxons of England. Also, he did not want to abandon the rich southern shires to his opponent, who might establish an effective base there and become impossible to root out. Those who knew the Norman skill at constructing castles were not willing to throw away their lives in hopeless assaults later. Better to fight now.

Harold may have wanted to drive William out of England, but he understood that footmen had to stand on the defensive against horsemen. Therefore, he could not simply march south and attack. His strategy had to be more subtle. He chose a ridgeline near Hastings, a place that William had to pass to break into open country or give up his campaign. Harold may have had about 8,000 men, slightly more than William, but his army had fewer archers and no cavalry. Harold's men stood in deep ranks, relying on their shields for protection, on their spears and axes for victory in close combat. William wanted a mobile battle, using his archers and horsemen to overwhelm the Saxons at first one point, then another.

The decisive moment came when William's cavalry charge failed and in its disorderly retreat caused some infantry units to flee the field rather than be trampled by the warhorses. One wing of the Saxon army, overly excited by their success, ran down the hill in pursuit. William rallied his cavalry, then expertly cut off that body of Saxons from their comrades on the hill and slaughtered them. On a level ground Norman horsemen were invincible.

The remaining Saxons remained immobile at the crest of the hill, undoubtedly appalled and disheartened by the disaster they had witnessed, William reorganised his forces, pointed them toward the Saxon position, then charged. The Norman assaults were beaten back again and again, but there was no way for the Saxons to turn the repulses into a rout. All afternoon the fighting continued, with the Saxon army slowly being ground down. At last, surrounded at the top of the hill, the Saxons scarcely had room to swing their axes or the strength to do so. But any warrior who moved out from the shield wall to gain space to strike at his foes became a target for the Norman archers.

As the archers saw that the Saxon shields – some round, but others a distinctive kite-shape – were catching most of their missiles, they raised the trajectory, so that the arrows came down at a steeper angle. According to the Bayeux Tapestry, two possible interpretations of Harold's death are possible: one that an arrow passed through his visor, giving him a fatal wound; or that he was cut down by a horseman. In either case, Harold's death was decisive: the surviving housecarls and thanes fled for their lives.

William was no longer 'the Bastard'. Henceforth, he was William the Conqueror.

NORMAN ENGLAND

William did not occupy England swiftly. He had lost too many men, and there were strong cities and fortifications still in Saxon hands; moreover, many of his men fell ill, and he was unwell, too (making one wonder what the outcome would have been if Harold had delayed combat for another week). But there was no one to organise resistance. Harold, Tostig and two other brothers were dead. God seems to have spoken on the question of who was the rightful monarch. The churchmen recognised William as king. After that there was no going back.

The Normans' roundabout advance on London left a wide trail of death and destruction that led to further collapse of Saxon will. Those Saxons who could sought to ingratiate themselves with their new ruler, but few were able to do without forfeiting most of their property. Many fled the country.

William built a number of powerful castles, the most famous being the White Tower in London. So strong that it could only be taken by starvation, and then only if the attackers controlled the Thames as well as the land, the Tower loomed over the eastern part of the city, its garrison always ready to swarm out in defence of royal interests. Such a garrison might well be composed of mercenaries, men who would have little or no sympathy with the merchants, artisans and workmen of London – middle- and low-class scum who were nature's chosen victims, the lawful prey of those who understood how to better themselves in the opinion of the world and in material possessions.

As William turned his attention to raising the money necessary to finance his military occupation of the country, he lost whatever potential he had for reconciling the Saxons to his governance. But that was irrelevant: William had to pay his troops, and therefore his subjects had to pay him. He succeeded well in the south, where the bulk of his forces were concentrated and where the richest lands lay. No one dared complain, at least not loudly – the mercenaries may not have spoken English well, but they understood when Saxon voices sounded resentful.

DANISH INTERVENTION

William was less successful in the north, whose cities and towns had lost comparatively few men at Hastings. His earls easily occupied the major cities, but usually found them abandoned. The inhabitants were not far off, in the hills, and soon enough they swooped down on the newcomers, wiping out several careless Norman garrisons.

A critical moment came in 1069, when King Sven arrived with an army of Danes, Poles, Saxons and Frisians. Most were undoubtedly mercenaries. He had good reason to expect a warm reception. After all, the money to raise his army had come from the north, where almost everyone wanted to see a return of the good old days of King Canute – an absentee ruler who, nevertheless, saw to the preservation of peace and order.

The Danish campaign began well. In the spring Sven joined with the Saxon army of resistance, captured York and massacred the first Normans to oppose him. But afterward, as he looked at the sacked and burned city, Sven realised that he lacked supplies for the winter. Returning home was his best option. Perhaps he could return in the spring.

William had meanwhile hurried north, surprising two Danish forces and slaughtering them. Then, once he realised that Sven was sailing away, William began to deal with the king's Saxon allies. Leaving behind small garrisons to hold the castles, he went into the hills. Although the Saxon warriors probably evaded his forces most of the time, the peasantry could not. William slaughtered farmers and their animals, burned houses, barns and fields, and made it impossible for anyone to plant crops for the coming year.

The next year there was massive starvation in the north. There was almost nobody left to resist William's subsequent punitive expeditions – brutal plundering raids known as the 'Harrying of the North'. There was no point to another Danish intervention.

Only the last great rising, that of 1075, threatened William's grasp on the crown, and that only because some of his most trusted vassals were involved. Thenceforth even the most resolute Saxon rebel understood that the only way to survive was through abject surrender.

✕

A RYE TURN OF FORTUNE

William's unsuccessful efforts to pacify the north without depopulating it may be due less to his inability to pay mercenaries from the sparse crops than from the overlooked fact that climate makes harvests in northern England and Scotland unpredictable. Frenchmen were unwilling to eat what local farmers could raise most easily – rye. Hence, according to William Kapelle of Brandeis University, French culinary tastes were responsible for William's failure to prevail in the borderlands – his men were simply unwilling to stay where the bread was so, so brown. The reputation of English cookery has never recovered.

It was not that the northerners hated Normans particularly: they had rebelled against Tostig, too. They wanted to govern themselves in their own rough way, with the strongest speaking on behalf of everyone. How could the king guarantee his own authority and still bring quiet to the north? Henry I (1100–35) resolved this problem by offering a few Normans estates there, then leaving the rest to their Saxon owners. This provided a combination of stability and fighting power. Everyone had to worry about the Scots, the king must have thought, let the Saxons wear themselves out fighting them.

SCUTAGE

Despite England's possessing some of the best records of the Middle Ages, it is still not fully understood how vassals provided garrisons for the royal castles and troops to serve in royal expeditions. In theory, lords and knights were supposed to serve in person, but in practice this was not always possible. The warriors who had fought at Hastings eventually grew old. Garrison service was often unpleasant and boring.

The king, not eager to hear complaints from his vassals, allowed them to provide replacements. Or better yet, he allowed vassals to substitute money payments. But even vassals willing to appear in person with their men found that it was awkward to take skilled farmers and artisans away from work. Most likely they hired common soldiers to replace militiamen, and mercenary horsemen in place of knights.

But there was another force at work. That was the practice of vassals paying the king an additional tax, *scutage* (meaning 'shield money'), in place of military service. The kings liked this system. In peacetime the money went straight into the Exchequer; in wartime they could hire strong, healthy young men rather than rely on vassals who might be aged, infirm or lacking in enthusiasm.

One result of this innovation was to separate the military function of English knights from their honorific and monetary roles. Future kings would require well-to-do commoners to become knights, whether they wanted to or not. Their duty, as the king saw it, was first to pay the fees that accompanied the ceremony, and second to pay scutage. Whether they ever appeared in person, equipped for battle, hardly mattered.

This ambiguity toward the nobility of knighthood was common elsewhere in Europe. The term *miles* and *knight* were not always synonymous with *noble*. Modern scholars who attempt to codify the rules of feudalism often end up describing the usages of northern France. That can be misleading.

Still, the rest of Europe often looked to France for models of behaviour and culture, but perhaps most of all the warrior classes, who viewed with envy French knights' privileges and prestige. Rulers were more likely to copy only the art and architecture. This was especially true in England. Despite the kings being more French than English, they had no desire to import bad habits from the Continent.

Knights of the shires occasionally participated in tournaments, served as justices and tax-collectors, and voted for representatives to Parliament. But it was royal officials, such as the sheriffs, who organised regional defence and recruited young men for service abroad. The knights of the shires might have degenerated totally into pheasant- and fox-hunting elites if the practice of primogeniture had not produced in each generation younger sons with only two career options: the Church or the battlefield.

The younger sons had to do *something*. Some became mercenaries.

POSTSCRIPT TO THE BATTLE OF HASTINGS

In one of history's most bizarre ironies, the battle of Hastings was fought again in 1081 in Albania. When the Saxon survivors of the disaster of 1066 realised that William the Bastard was going to confiscate all their lands and honours, they resisted fiercely. By 1069, however, when King Sven withdrew from the island, they understood that their cause was lost. Many Saxon nobles gathered whatever they could quickly on to ships and sailed into exile. Under the leadership of an otherwise unknown thane named Siward, 350 ships made their way to Constantinople, arriving while the city was being besieged by a Turkish army. The Saxons immediately set to work, fighting with their customary skill and determination. The new emperor, Romanus IV (1068–71), was so impressed with their valour, skill and dedication that he rewarded some of their number with estates and enrolled others in a special unit of the Varangian Guard and stationed them on the Albanian coast, an area in danger of being lost to Norman knights and mercenaries from the kingdom of Naples. Fifteen years after the battle of Hastings, Saxon and Normans met in battle at Durazzo, the Adriatic terminus of the old Roman road leading across the Balkans to Constantinople.

The Normans were serving under Robert Guiscard, who was undermining the already shaky position of the new emperor, Alexius Comnenus (1081–1118). Constantinople seemed ripe for plucking, its armies having been crushed by Turkish forces and most of its Asiatic territories lost.

The Saxons seemed to be Comnenus's last hope. He was confident that if they followed the Byzantine army manual and maintained discipline, that they would prevail. However, according to a widely read account by the emperor's daughter, Anna Comnena, the warriors from distant 'Thule' unwisely charged up a steep hill to get at their ancestral enemies and, exhausted by the effort, were mercilessly slaughtered. The Byzantine Empire survived the disaster, but only barely. From 1081 on, the emperor lost city after city, province after province, to Christian and Muslim foes. In the end all he could think to do was to appeal to Pope Urban II for help in recruiting mercenaries and volunteers. Such a request hurt him to the uttermost depths of his Orthodox Greek soul, to ask the hated Roman pontiff for aid. But he had no choice.

Pope Urban II, for his part, dared not ask the Germans to help – he was involved in a life-and-death struggle with what later generations called the *Holy* Roman emperor. Instead, he went to France and asked for volunteers to liberate Jerusalem. Thus, out of a request for mercenaries to rescue Constantinople emerged the First Crusade!

Two partly mercenary armies had fought it out at Hastings and Durazzo, with much more than money at stake. It was an ancestral feud, and once the Saxon ruling class was finally and truly exterminated, England was destined to remain dominated by Normans until the fourteenth century, when at last Norman and Saxon fused together to create a new language and a new nation – England.

William and his successors understood well how to use art, poetry and pageantry as royal propaganda. With all these means they encouraged youths and even experienced warriors to imagine service in a royal army as a step to wealth and higher status; this was not confined to Englishmen (however that term applied), but to all who saw mercenary service as honourable, profitable and (probably) temporary.

THE GOLDEN AGE OF ENGLISH MERCENARIES

For many years British medievalists quarrelled about what constituted the essential nature of English feudalism. What many overlooked was that the foreign rule of the Normans could be maintained only by the use of hired troops; that is, mercenaries. This was to affect everything, from the Exchequer to the strategies and tactics of war.

William the Conqueror's descendants continued to fill out their armies with mercenaries. But where to get the money? The royal estates were insufficient to his needs – too much land had been given to relatives, vassals and the Church, on the promise they would provide warriors when necessary. This had not worked. The kings relied on taxes to pay bureaucrats and soldiers.

Although we read more about mercenary horsemen than about infantry, most mercenaries seem to have been foot soldiers. Infantry was superior to cavalry in several respects: training was easier, equipment was less expensive, and infantry were well suited to fighting in hills and woods. They were indispensable for garrisons. Moreover, some knights were more interested in preparing for tournaments than battle; time spent on garrison duty was time wasted. The importance of mercenaries became obvious during the most senseless of all English conflicts, the civil war between Stephen (1135–54) and Matilda (Maud, Holy Roman empress 1110–25, who claimed the throne of England 1135–47). This was known popularly as the time *when God and His angels slept.*

This struggle provides the background for the twenty-one murder mysteries by Ellis Peters (Edith Pargeter, 1913–95), all centring on the fictional Welsh monk, *Brother Cadfael.* Beginning in 1994 Derek Jacobi began starring on BBC as the medieval monk-detective. To date thirteen episodes have been filmed. As Ron Miller says on the *Mystery* website of Cadfael, 'He's what Sherlock Holmes might have been if born 750 years earlier and bottle-fed on a good deal more of the milk of human kindness than Conan Doyle ever gave him.'

But Cadfael was also a worldly-wise man. Before he entered the monastery to do penance for his sins, he had been a well-travelled warrior. It comes as no surprise to him that the mercenary soldiers he saw in the civil war were less than gentlemen.

In the sixteenth of her Cadfael series, *A Rare Benedictine* (1979), Peters tells us something about her humble hero's crusading and seafaring past, and how he became a monk. It was an autumn day of 1120 when Lord Roger was returning from the war in Normandy that Cadfael was introduced as a 'blunt and insubordinate' Welshman who was, nevertheless, 'experienced, and accomplished in arms, a man of his word'. Somewhere, in the Holy Land or elsewhere, he had 'imbibed the code of arms and wore it as a second nature' (actions the reader had best not attempt to imagine).

In *The Potter's Field*, Peters described King Stephen's hiring Flemish mercenaries, 'feared and hated by the civilian population, and disliked even by the English who fought alongside them'. But while the Flemish fought on both sides and would change employers readily, so would the barons and earls. Before long the communities nearest to the nest of pillagers pretending to be Maud's supporters were glad to have the Flemish protection.

The problem here, as was almost universally the case, was that Stephen and Maud lacked the money to pay all their troops. However, the civil war gave them an advantage over other monarchs who found themselves similarly embarrassed at pay-time – they could confiscate their enemies' estates and give them to their supporters. Historians often treat gifts as special favours to lords who were already rich, but it was also important in paying off mercenary leaders. How the mercenary leaders chose to pay their troops was *their* problem.

Some mercenaries settled permanently in England on the estates given to them for their services. Most probably just took their money, found a likely town and opened a bar or inn. Others bought a small farm, married and hired labourers. Yet others, like Cadfael, must have entered the Church, the universal refuge for the aged, the ill and the repentant. A few went home, others dared not appear in the native parishes. Very likely we can discern in names we encounter daily the origins of some of these men: Brett (Breton), Fleming (Flanders), Holland, Berry, French, Ireland, Scott and Welch.

Novels such as Ellis Peters's form our modern view of medieval life and war every bit as much as do the best historians. This is partly because the novelists read carefully and deeply, but more because they reach a much wider audience. The best historians occasionally appear as 'talking heads' on documentaries, but it is the scriptwriter and the director who determine what the audience sees. This is especially true in movies, where the poor technical advisor's wisdom comes in a distant second to the needs for additional conflict, drama, mystery and a simplified storyline.

Mercenaries had become a part of medieval warfare. If the profession was a poor career choice – disease, injury and death being common fates – it was, nevertheless, an alternative to poverty and boredom. As Kenneth Fowler says in *Medieval Mercenaries*: 'War was a lottery, and although the stakes were dangerously high, they were still worth the gamble'. It was a young man's business, but it could be a lord's career.

2
EARLY ITALIAN MERCENARIES

MEDIEVAL ITALY

By the year 1000 secular rulers in Italy were hiring mercenaries to fight against Arabs, Greeks and local enemies; so were the many bishops and abbots, who were more numerous there than anywhere else in the Roman Catholic world and who, as clerics, were not permitted to bear arms. Since many territories were too small to raise armies of any significance, mercenaries were the answer to the rulers' needs; this was true of the pope's situation, too. But finding dependable leaders for these bands was not easy: the example of the Normans warned against bringing in ambitious foreigners; vassals would be tempted to enrich themselves; and even entrusting one's army to an uncle, a brother or nephew was not without some risk.

As Italian cities made themselves independent of lords and bishops, they found themselves in the same situation as the prelates. They had to prevent former rulers from regaining power, suppress banditry and piracy, and defend markets from competitors. Cities, growing rich from the expansion of trade in the eleventh and twelfth centuries, became increasingly important in regional politics – they could better afford to pay mercenaries than could counts or bishops.

Records are probably misleading regarding the earliest mercenary army, because the first to be mentioned was only in 1159, raised by Pope Alexander III to fight Friedrich Barbarossa, the Holy Roman emperor (1152–90) who was hoping to incorporate Italy more fully into his domains. Barbarossa had valid reasons for claiming the territories of Charles the Great (Charlemagne), who in 800 had ruled the lands comprising modern Germany, France and

Italy; Barbarossa believed that he could assert that claim effectively in Italy, because many nobles and more than a few cities there promised to assist him in his efforts, if he would help them against local enemies. All this and more is found in Umberto Eco's *Baudolino* (2002), a creative effort to tie the exotic places of medieval imagination to actual events of twelfth-century Italy.

Barbarossa ultimately failed, defeated on the battlefield. But he miraculously won back most of his losses at the conference table – if not territories, at least recognition of his rights as Holy Roman emperor. His opponents could not keep armies in the field. Civic armies were excellent for defending their own cities, but were unable to fight at a distance from their homes. Thus, the staying power of feudal armies once again proved their worth. Barbarossa might have come to dominate Italy totally if he had not taken the cross for the Third Crusade in 1189 and drowned in a small stream shortly before entering the Holy Land.

Germany immediately erupted into civil war, and Italy returned to its chaotic petty feuds. The imperial territories were held together by Barbarossa's son, Heinrich VI (1190–97), who married the heiress to the immensely rich kingdom of Sicily. Then he, too, died, leaving a young son who would grow up to be Friedrich II von Hohenstaufen, the greatest employer of mercenary forces of his era. Friedrich II's most significant innovation was to hire Arabs and Berbers – Muslims! This was easy because Sicily still had a significant number of Arab inhabitants from the days when they had ruled the island. Friedrich's Norman ancestors had conquered them, but had not dispossessed them or forced them to become Christians. Therefore, they were well disposed to Friedrich from the beginning.

GUELPHS AND GHIBELLINES

For generations Italians and Germans had been divided into two great parties. The party of the emperors was named after the dynasty that ruled for most of the twelfth century, the Hohenstaufens; Italians, whose pronunciation of German left something to be desired, turned *Waiblingen* (the district most associated with the Staufen dynasty) into *Ghibelline*. The party of the popes was named after the Hohenstaufens' principal rivals in Germany, the *Welfs*; Italians called them *Guelphs*.

Italian nobles tended to support the Ghibellines, churchmen the Guelphs;

the rising commercial centres, uneasy about demands for more taxes, tended to side with the opposite party of their nominal ruler. But it was a more complex system than it appeared. Alliances would dissolve and reappear. Existing party alliances would be reordered to maintain a balance of power. In addition, popes tended to be suspicious of every emperor, even emperors whose family was Guelph by tradition, because all emperors eventually had to take Ghibelline positions or be reduced to ciphers taking papal orders. When this happened, the popes did not hesitate to make Ghibellines their ally. True believers were encouraged to trust to their betters' judgement. Papal infallibility, broadly defined, became a political argument long before it was declared a matter of faith in a more limited sphere.

Although everyone had assumed that bishops and abbots would be both ambitious and corrupt, there was always a pious but unrealistic hope that popes could rise above earthly temptations. From the late twelfth century on, however, as popes sought to control central Italy and to dictate policies to all secular rulers, their opponents became ever more sceptical about papal intentions.

POLITICAL CRUSADES

The public wanted to believe in the popes. The holy fathers were, after all, one after another, heads of Roman Christendom. They held, everyone believed, authority derived from Peter, the first of the apostles, bestowed directed from the Son of God himself. The authority included the keys to heaven and hell, the power, if need be, to save sinners or condemn saints. While in practice it was unlikely that any pope would excommunicate a saint, an interdict stopped all religious services – baptisms, confessions, blessing marriages, and last rites – thus punishing the innocent along with the guilty.

In addition, the Donation of Constantine gave the popes secular authority over the lands surrounding Rome (the Papal States) and, theoretically, the entire western Roman Empire. This claim had to be defended by papal armies. Although emperors were sceptical about the legitimacy of the document, they could not prove it a forgery. Thus, most Roman Christians believed that it was genuine until a Renaissance scholar demonstrated that it could not have been written in the fourth century.

Technically speaking, while many popes had authorised or ordered the use of armed force, none had declared a crusade against a Christian before the late twelfth century. That was because the concept of granting a plenary indulgence (the full remission of sin) to crusaders had come into existence barely a century before. If a pope could promise crusaders that, should they be so unlucky as to die on crusade, they would enter immediately into the kingdom of heaven, the next logical step was to promise warriors who fought for the pope in Italy the same rewards.

In 1066, three decades before the first crusade, Pope Alexander II (1061–73) had provided William the Conqueror with a consecrated banner to carry on his invasion of England. Still, it was not until 1199 that a pope declared a formal crusade against a Christian ruler. Pope Innocent III (1198–1216) created that precedent to raise an army against Markward von Anweiler, a prominent lord in the Romagna and the March of Ancona. Similarly Innocent recruited volunteers against Conrad von Uerslingen to recover Spoleto, Assisi and Sora. Though well meant – Innocent could argue that a pope needed the means to enforce his edicts – the potential for abuse was enormous. And where potential existed, actuality would soon appear. Abuses followed quickly, followed by increased scepticism concerning papal motives.

Mercenaries had also become common in crusader armies. As initial enthusiasm for holy war faded, practicality took its place.

FRIEDRICH II VON HOHENSTAUFEN

Friedrich Barbarossa's death on crusade in 1190 caused his German sup-porters to stream home to protect their possessions from attacks of Welfs and perhaps even the pope. Richard the Lionheart, assuming leadership of the remaining crusaders, soon offended the French and the remaining Germans. As revenge, the French attacked Normandy and the Germans took Richard prisoner when he tried to slip through Austria in disguise.

Friedrich Barbarossa's son, Heinrich VI, employed Richard's ransom to hire a huge army of mercenaries for an invasion of southern Italy and Sicily, the inheritance of his Norman wife. The pope could hardly object, but he was frightened by Heinrich's swift successes; he was now surrounded by imperial territories, virtually a prisoner and certainly in no position to oppose Heinrich's wishes. God, however, came to his rescue in the form of a mortal illness, sweeping away both Heinrich and his wife, leaving only a three-year-old son, Friedrich, who was committed to papal protection lest he be murdered by one of the many Germans and Italians who feared that he would unify the Holy Roman Empire with Sicily, making the whole into a centralised, Ghibelline state.

Young Friedrich alone among the monarchs of Europe had potential to surround, and then engulf, the papal states. Still, Pope Innocent III was unwilling to murder him. He persuaded himself that it was safe to leave Sicily and Naples under the control of a governor till Friedrich attained his majority, then to use him against any bullying by the Holy Roman emperor. In the meantime, the electors of the Holy Roman Empire, wanting a mature ruler, chose Friedrich's uncle as German king. Innocent decided to tame this emperor-elect by supporting a Welf challenger. This was unsuccessful, but soon the successful Hohenstaufen was assassinated because of a personal quarrel.

Innocent III, though a strong figure who humbled kings and launched crusades, was unable to persuade the Welf emperor to follow his dictates, either; as a result, he had to replace him. The only viable candidate was the young king of Sicily, Friedrich.

Friedrich, meanwhile, had learned some valuable lessons by observation and experience. He had been tutored in languages, literature, science and statecraft, but his highly original mind took him far beyond conventional lessons. He looked deeper into issues than almost any contemporary. Perhaps this was because he had survived only by understanding what his guardians really meant when they spoke and by adopting appropriately subservient behaviour; if dissembling came naturally to him, so too did believing that others were doing the same. He learned to look for unconventional men to protect him from assassination and to assist in governance; he wanted nobody around who would be likely to betray him or who would report to his enemies or even listen to them.

Friedrich surrounded himself with Muslim bodyguards, who later became the nucleus of his mercenary army. Some of his most loyal followers would follow his example, but not to the extent of learning Arabic as Friedrich did, nor dressing in flowing robes, being attended by African servants or being accompanied by sufficient concubines to make up a harem. His wives he married, impregnated and abandoned in swift succession. All this astounded contemporaries, who quickly dubbed him the *Stupor Mundi* (the wonder of the world). Young Friedrich, preternaturally aware of the self-serving motives of his various guardians, played whatever role they wished to imagine for him. They never conceived that in a few years they would be seeing in him the Anti-Christ himself.

Friedrich crossed the Alps into Germany in 1215 to be elected German king, the necessary first step to becoming Holy Roman emperor. At the time he seemed only a beautiful and talented young blond hero, skilled in the physical and mental graces, but willing to defer to his elders' judgements. Poets, girls and patriots were thrilled; and when, having re-established stability to his long disordered northern kingdom, he re-crossed the Alps to be crowned emperor in Rome, he was accompanied by volunteers and mercenaries to repress a rebellion in his Sicilian kingdom.

Honorius III (1216–27) could hardly prevent the emperor making himself master of his own lands, but he was frightened by the speed and thorough-ness of Friedrich's invasion. The papal court was soon flooded by exiles and reports that the emperor was becoming a very dangerous man. The pope was an honourable man, who wanted to find compromises, but his cardinals and Guelph allies pushed him to crush this young upstart while there was still time. Honorius tried bring the emperor to heel, but failed. Everything Honorius did antagonised Friedrich and persuaded many of his supporters that the pope was determined to ruin their every effort to create a stable secular government. Honorius's successor, Gregory IX (1227–41) was not a man of similar good will; instead, he would use every opportunity to harass Friedrich in Sicily and in Germany. Friedrich's supporters came to see in Gregory the very personification of evil that the pope claimed to see in the emperor.

The crisis came when Friedrich failed go promptly on crusade. The Fifth Crusade became stuck in the mud of the Egyptian delta in 1219; and when almost the entire crusading force was killed or captured, Friedrich was blamed. The emperor's vow had been conventionally vague, a statement of good intent that he would fulfil at a convenient moment. Under intense papal pressure, Friedrich gathered a fleet and an army in 1227, and boarded ship for the Holy Land. However, when an epidemic broke out, he turned back and put his men on land to recover. Although military experts understood that sick men could not fight and that crusaders in the Holy Land already would not welcome the arrival of plague ships, Gregory IX was in no mood to tolerate excuses: he excommunicated Friedrich.

Contemporaries were not immediately alarmed. Popes excommunicated emperors all the time. The common assumption was that Friedrich would either hurry to Rome personally to apologise or send emissaries who would offer political concessions until the pope was satisfied. But Friedrich simply loaded his men back on to their vessels and sailed to the Holy Land. Friedrich, after all, had married the heiress of the kingdom of Jerusalem and might lose that land if he delayed coming to its defence. Once in the Crusader States he met an unexpectedly hostile reaction from churchmen and local nobles. Apparently they were aware of how strictly Friedrich ruled in Sicily, and the pope had told his legate to recommend a combination of cool politeness and insults.

Friedrich surprised everyone by negotiating directly with the sultan, speaking in Arabic. He suggested a peaceful solution to the situation, a joint Muslim-Christian state ruled by the sultan's brother and Friedrich's sister. She turned down the opportunity to end the war, but the Arabs were charmed by the emperor's worldly practicality; they quoted him as saying that the world had been taken in by three great deceivers: Moses, Jesus and Muhammad. The sultan returned Jerusalem to Christian rule and signed a peace treaty. The Christians were outraged; the new state was indefensible, and in any case Jerusalem should have been won by force of arms.

After two years Friedrich boarded his ship under a shower of rotten fruit and vegetables and sailed for home. When he arrived in Sicily, he discovered that pope-inspired rebels had tried to seize control of the kingdom. He was not in a good mood.

Friedrich recruited mercenaries to restore order, and his plausible threat to invade the Papal States brought him a cease-fire with the pope in 1231 and a removal of the excommunication. Consequently, when he made his impressive state visit to Germany in 1235–7, he had few difficulties in removing a son who had attempted to rule independently and then reforming the constitution along lines that had worked so well in Sicily; he also made his relatively unsophisticated northern subjects aware that they had a more magnificent ruler than they had ever imagined: Arab bodyguards, camels, leopards on golden chains; a patron of poets who could quote in numerous languages, an expert on falcons and women, and the master of the memorable phrase; widely travelled, conversant with kings, churchmen and anchorites; multi-lingual and multi-cultural; a figure who had bent powerful men to his will. It seemed that nothing could stop him.

Pope Gregory determined to make something out of that nothing, and the instrument was fear of Friedrich's plans to impose the same order on northern Italy that he had in Sicily and less perfectly in Germany. The heart of Gregory's coalition was Milan, the most populous and wealthy city in

Lombardy, but its limbs were composed of the many tiny states to its east and south – Venice, Padua and Florence. Here party loyalties were still important. It remained to be seen whether Friedrich's imperial vassals and mercenaries could reinforce local Ghibellines sufficiently to overwhelm the Guelph-papacy alliance.

EZZELINO DA ROMANO

Ezzelino was the same age as Friedrich, born in 1194, a fact that the emperor might have appreciated, since he was a student of science, which in those days meant being knowledgeable in astrology. Friedrich would have been even more interested in Ezzelino's ruthless efficiency and courage; also perhaps his hairy body and black hair, which led the popular imagination to believe that he was the son of Satan; alternatively that he was part dog. The crudeness of these charges suggests the vile nature of political invective in this era; and perhaps the fear and hatred that Ezzelino inspired among his enemies.

Ezzelino's small ancestral estate was sufficient to provide opportunities for moving up in the world, but it was hardly equal to the rival d'Este family. His grandfather had gone on crusade, his father was a famous womaniser and competent warrior. Ezzelino had a younger brother, Alberico, and sister, Cunizza, who was as beautiful as Ezzelino was ugly, at least according to troubadours, especially the one who later became her lover. The popular explanation for Ezzelino's appearance was that the devil had raped his mother. Rape, at least, was a socially acceptable explanation. Submitting voluntarily was unimaginable.

Ezzelino had viewed young Friedrich von Hohenstaufen at a distance on his triumphal 1215 journey to Germany, noting that the future seemed to be his. Unfortunately, Friedrich was accompanied by the d'Este. There was no way for a da Romano to obtain as much as an introduction.

The d'Este, bolstered by their new imperial connections, began pressing their neighbours to acknowledge their regional hegemony. With many noble families and wealthy cities seeking to avoid d'Este domination, the da Romano family quickly became prominent among those in the opposing ranks.

Ezzelino's first military action was in the siege of a d'Este castle which had been used as a base for attacking commercial travellers to and from Padua. Soon after this had been successfully concluded, Ezzelino's father, though still in the prime of life and in good health, took holy orders. At the same time the elder d'Este died. At the heads of the respective families were Ezzelino, now twenty-six, and Azzo VII d'Este. It was assumed that Azzo would escort Friedrich von Hohenstaufen through northern Italy after he crossed the Alps, but it was Ezzelino who met him. Ezzelino's newly raised mercenary army outnumbered Friedrich's forces significantly, a fact that seems to have impressed and worried imperial advisors, but Ezzelino was satisfied with making Friedrich's acquaintance and taking him south to meet his next escort. Friedrich, who undoubtedly appreciated the seriousness of the situation, marked Ezzelino as a man to watch, perhaps a man to draw to his side.

Not long afterward Ezzelino married the daughter of a prominent local Guelph family, and Cunizza was given to his wife's brother. Quite likely Cunizza's looks were the key to this arrangement; certainly his were not. No children came of this or any of Ezzelino's other liaison with women, a fact noted by popular rumour. The alliance was important in that it involved Ezzelino even more deeply in the feuds against Azzo d'Este that took an unexpected turn when Cunizza's husband changed sides. Ezzelino's response was to encourage a good-looking troubadour, Sordello, to entice his sister to run away. Sordello's poems praising his new love had already circulated widely, enraging her now cuckolded husband, who demanded assistance in this matter from his d'Este allies. To make matters worse, Ezzelino paraded his famous sister at his court, but kept his wife practically a prisoner; presumably she survived on short rations and no sex.

Cunizza, however, unexpectedly married Sordello. Ezzelino, furious that such a valuable asset would be thrown away on the altar of love, arranged for an annulment. While Sordello fled for his life, Cunizza quickly found new lovers.

That winter Ezzelino attacked Verona by surprise. The defenders had assumed that the heavy snow was sufficient protection against any army, but Ezzelino gave his mercenaries shovels and put them to work. Attacking at dawn, they captured that vital city, then moved on Vicenza, the crossroad of all important traffic to and from the mountain passes. Making his brother governor of Vicenza, Ezzelino was now in a position to negotiate with the Ghibelline forces.

FRIEDRICH II'S NORTHERN CAMPAIGNS

Friedrich faced a new coalition of enemies in the north of Italy – the Lombard League, organised by the pope and led by Milan. Victory here was essential, lest he be cut off from the money and men he was raising in Germany. The old lines of family and civic alliances were being redrawn, and Ezzelino was as willing to renegotiate his loyalties as anyone. No surprise then, that when Gregory IX excommunicated the emperor in 1227, he extended the ban to Ezzelino as well. When Friedrich sailed on to the Holy Land, the Ghibelline position in Lombardy practically collapsed. Ezzelino was forced to relinquish his gains until 1235, when Friedrich made his triumphal march to Germany. As the imperial forces retook Verona, the d'Este proclaimed their loyalty to Friedrich, but it was Ezzelino who received credit for making the roads safe for Friedrich to travel across a traditionally hostile region.

Immediately attacked by Azzo d'Este, Ezzelino sent a hurried message to Friedrich which persuaded the emperor to reverse his march – arriving just in time to rout the d'Este. The lines were now firmly drawn: Ezzelino was the emperor's man in the north. As such, he became a special target of Guelph and papal propaganda.

When Ezzelino advanced on Padua, the citizens were so divided on what to do that they began fighting one another; the d'Este duke, attempting to sally out the gate, was repulsed and followed back into the town. Ezzelino assigned Arab mercenaries to guard the gates, then took numerous hostages to guarantee the loyalty of the citizenry. He subsequently made himself *podestá* (governor) of Verona, Padua and Vicenza. Friedrich, who returned to Italy in 1237, was very pleased, but he needed the largest possible coalition for his decisive confrontation with the Lombard League – therefore, he invited the d'Este family to join his forces, too.

Friedrich recruited German and Hungarian mercenaries, and even warriors from southern France (where the notorious Albigensian heresy had held sway until recently crushed by the inquisition and crusaders from northern France). The pope denounced these troops, claiming that Italy was his by virtue of the Donation of Constantine and, therefore, he could forbid anyone to enter it. Friedrich mocked him, laughing that the pope was preventing the Holy Roman emperor from travelling through the Holy Roman Empire. In late September he invaded Lombardy.

Ezzelino's charge broke the Milanese at the battle of Cortenuova in

November 1237. As a reward, Friedrich gave the hero one of his illegitimate daughters as a wife. Ezzelino was still married, legally at least, but church ties were not important to the emperor in his present mood; and Ezzelino was not inclined to dispute his judgement. Friedrich then arranged for Alberico's daughter to marry the son of Azzo d'Este. That, he hoped, would guarantee peace in the north; and to make sure that this da Romano woman did not run away, he sent the newly married pair to southern Italy on a diplomatic mission; that is, as hostages.

The emperor spent 1238 in Padua, entertaining lavishly. He ordered Ezzelino to return the confiscated d'Este cities – the d'Estes were, after all, traditionally Ghibelline and, more important, still powerful. But that was only a formality, since Friedrich II had carefully garrisoned the cities with Saracen troops. Meanwhile, Pope Gregory IX was fuming and fusing; the aged pope, now over ninety, knew that Friedrich was waiting only for him to die so that he could dominate the electoral conclave and assure the selection of a churchman who would bow to imperial wishes. The pope, therefore, struck while he still had the ability to do so; in the spring of 1239 he excommunicated Friedrich and released all his supporters from their vows of fealty.

Not satisfied with the results of placing the emperor under the ban, Gregory IX preached the crusade against him, too, ostensibly for atheism and heresy. Calling him a 'self-confessed heretic' and identifying him as the 'blasphemous beast of the Apocalypse', Gregory called a general council to meet in Pisa in 1241 to debate measures for dealing with this criminal.

The imperial coalition fell apart. The Lombard League reorganised themselves. Azzo d'Este slipped away to join the papal army, followed by many local nobles – even by Ezzelino's own brother, Alberico, who could read the stars as well as the superstitious emperor. Friedrich turned to his only remaining loyal follower, Ezzelino, and named him imperial vicar for the northern regions. The time for a policy of moderation and forgiveness having passed, Ezzelino began executing nobles caught in plots – atrocities that were repaid upon Ezzelino's supporters. The only enemy Ezzelino could not find in his heart to punish was his nephew, Cunizza's son, who was now a handsome and likeable member of the Guelph party. Ezzelino divorced his wife, but this did not harm his relationship with Friedrich, who picked up and discarded women casually himself.

Then came a respite. Friedrich captured many of the prelates travelling by sea to the council, then the long-awaited death of Gregory IX was followed by a two-year interregnum. Friedrich blocked the convocation of cardinals until mid-1243 in hopes of persuading the desperate churchmen to accept a compromise. But he had overreached himself. He acquired in Innocent IV (1243–54) one of the most relentless men ever to occupy the papal throne, and a member of a Roman family whose lands he had laid waste. Moreover, Catholics throughout Europe were concluding that the emperor was in the wrong and out of control.

Innocent not only resumed the war in Italy, but he stirred up rebellion in Germany; his candidates to replace Friedrich as emperor were not powerful figures, but they encouraged others to seize imperial prerogatives, and soon they had routed the imperial forces. The pope excommunicated Friedrich II, declared him a heretic and enemy of God, and proclaimed a crusade against him and his allies. He mobilised all the forces of the Church – bishops, abbots, friars – to bring down the now shaken emperor.

Friedrich marched back and forth, sure of the loyalty of his mercenaries, but he could not trust vassal, cleric or city. He besieged the strategic city of Parma, only to meet total defeat. After that he fled to Sicily, leaving the struggle for northern Italy to Ezzelino. His vicar could do little to reverse the imperial fortunes, so he spent as much time as possible entertaining his new wife. Balthazar's feast!

THE COLLAPSE OF FRIEDRICH'S EMPIRE

Friedrich had avoided marching on Tuscany, perhaps from having received a prophecy that he would die in Florence. In late 1250, however, ill from dysentery, he asked where he was. Told that the village was called Florence, he lost heart and died. His illegitimate son Manfred succeeded him in Sicily, his young but legitimate son Conrad claimed Germany. But the pope was not ready to compromise: he was determined to wipe out the Hohenstaufen brood.

Innocent IV offered to forgive Ezzelino's past crimes, to confirm his present holdings, and to enjoy future benefits if he would switch sides. But Ezzelino, though alone in the north, mistrusted this pope. At the least, he knew, papal favour would go to his enemies, and they would see to his destruction. So Ezzelino refused.

The pope's subsequent denunciations were furious; every past crime was dredged up and new ones invented, and if it were not for the hyperbole that marked this notorious era, one might believe it. The pope accused Ezzelino of castrating boys, cutting off the breasts of girls, starving entire families. No names. Only more inventive crimes.

This gave Ezzelino an excuse for robbing churches and monasteries to pay his troops.

Conrad IV, the son of Friedrich II, entered Italy in 1252 and revived Ghibelline fortunes temporarily. Negotiations dragged through 1253, ending finally in a papal excommunication and condemnation. Conrad started his offensive with a fine army and a full treasury, but malaria struck him down in May 1254. When papal forces seemed on the verge of full victory, Manfred brought Saracen troops from Sicily into the fray and swept away the Church's mercenaries.

The passing of Innocent IV changed nothing; Alexander IV (1254–61) was just as determined to wipe out the Hohenstaufen family and their supporters. The new pope won over Alberico da Romano, then organised a new military alliance headed by Azzo d'Este.

In the summer of 1256 Ezzelino marched against Mantua, knowing it to be lightly garrisoned, but unaware that a papal army was only waiting for him to reduce the forces guarding Padua. When Ezzelino heard that his commander in Padua had made a series of errors (first draining the moat, then accidentally setting fire to the main gate, and then fleeing, causing the panicked troops to run for their lives), he hurried back and took revenge on the citizens, executing hundreds, perhaps even 2,000 soldiers he had taken prisoner.

This persuaded Alberico to change sides again.

Ezzelino captured Brescia after defeating the papal army and capturing Alexander's legate. However, in September of 1259, when he went to the aid of the Ghibelline faction in Milan, he arrived too late – the Guelphs had detected the conspiracy and crushed it. On his retreat, he found a critical bridge in enemy possession, and then was attacked by Azzo d'Este while fording the river. Hit in the Achilles' tendon by an arrow, he fell much as did the Greek hero. He died eleven days later in captivity, perhaps of his wounds, but more likely from a lack of food and rest – as prisoner he refused the first and was denied the last.

Alberico was next. Besieged in a small castle for six months, he surrendered only when half his men were dead, the supplies were exhausted and no help was in sight. That at least saved his surviving mercenaries. Alberico was forced to watch his wife and daughters burned alive, his six sons executed and dismembered, then he was tied to four horses and ripped to pieces.

Cuzzina was taken in by the generous people of Florence. Dante, an important member of the Ghibelline party there (and thus later exiled for life) gave both Ezzelino and Cuzzina immortality in the *Paradiso* of his *Divine Comedy*:

In quella parte de la terra prava	In that part of sinful Italy
italica che siede tra Rēalto	which lies between Rialto and
e le fontane di Brenta e di Piava,	the sources of the Brenta and Piava
si leva un colle, e non surge molt' alto,	A hill rises, but not very high,
là onde scese già una facella	from which a firebrand descended
che fece a la contrada un grande assalto.	to assault the countryside.
D'una radice nacqui e io ed ella:	I was born of that same stock.
Cunizza fui chiamata...	I was called Cunizza...

The firebrand, of course, was Ezzelino.

When the pope moved against the Hohenstaufen supporters in Germany, imperial authority there disappeared so completely that even papal allies were appalled. Friedrich II had brought down with him many who had seen him as national hero, as the best hope for national unity. Those who hated him could rejoice, temporarily, but it was a celebration over the ruins of both Italy and Germany.

SUMMARY

Papal policy achieved its next great victory when a French army under Charles of Anjou defeated Friedrich's indolent and unready successor in Naples, Manfred, in 1266, killing him and many of his German and Saracen troops in battle, then hunting down his children. In 1267 came the valiant but poorly planned campaign of Conradin von Hohenstaufen, Friedrich's grandson. Though excommunicated and then opposed even by many Ghibellines, Conradin managed to get his tiny army across the Alps, and make his way to Naples; on the way he befriended many Guelphs, especially in Florence, giving him hope that he could make a permanent reconciliation with family enemies. However, in the summer of 1268 his German–Italian–Arab–Catalan army was defeated by Charles's French mercenaries at Tagliacozzo, when his troops dispersed to plunder the French camp; he was captured and, after a mock trial, beheaded. His fate was mourned widely as a miscarriage of justice, but there was no remedy for the catastrophe to the Ghibelline party. The pope prevented the electors of the Holy Roman Empire from selecting a German king for an additional five years, until he was assured that the choice would be a weak ruler. There was no evidence that this last legitimate Hohenstaufen would have governed like his ancestors, but the pope was unwilling to run any risk – better to wipe out the entire family. This was hardly a morality superior to that of the mercenaries, and it could not be enforced without mercenaries.

Charles of Anjou (1226–85) was among the most ambitious and dislikeable personalities of the era, but he was the best champion the Church had. He attempted to eliminate the Ghibelline party in Italy, started wars with Aragon and Byzantium, and invaded North Africa; with a strong base in Provence, it seemed likely he would dominate northern Italy. But his dreams were rudely disturbed by the Sicilian Vespers (1282). The uprising was not completely a surprise – Charles provoked rebellions wherever he ruled – but no one expected to see a great-grandson of Friedrich II on the Sicilian throne. King Pedro III of Aragon (1276–85), who had married one of Manfred's daughters, came close to stripping Charles of all his domains. Dante later placed Pedro and Charles among the Negligent Rulers in Purgatory, singing in heartfelt accord. To judge by the severity of their sins, they are still there.

In contrast, Dante depicted a handsome and smiling Manfred, confident of salvation because neither priest nor pope can frustrate God's love. They could prevent his burial, but not his eventual entry into heaven. If his daughter will pray for him, the allotted time to wait (535 years, that is, thirty for each year of disobedience to the Church) will be shortened.

3
THE 'CLASSIC' MEDIEVAL MERCENARY

TERRITORIAL RULERS WANTED warriors who were young, skilful, ready to obey orders…and numerous. Vassals often failed on all four counts, especially the last one. Therefore, rulers turned to mercenaries.

A mercenary soldier is obviously one who fights for pay. Strictly speaking, to say *mercenary soldier* is a redundancy. Mercenary comes from *mercer*, meaning to buy and sell. *Sold* is the German word for money; *solde* in French. Both words have their roots in the word for a silver coin, a *solidus*, which ultimately goes back to the Latin word for salt, which Romans used for paying *sal*aries ('worth his salt'). Consequently, the word *soldier* implies an individual who hires out his talents, much like a common workman. We only need the two words together now because the evolution of governmental institutions later transformed irregular hired warriors into a professional class. Warriors who fought because of personal obligations, such as knights, were referred to as one's *men* or one's *vassals*. Today soldiers are committed to serve a *nation* no matter whether they are volunteers or in a professional army. A soldier no longer changes employers and rarely goes on strike for higher wages.

Philippe Contamine, in *War in the Middle Ages*, restricts the term mercenary to warriors who are 1) specialists, 2) stateless, 3) paid. This narrow definition eliminates almost everyone who leaves a record of his existence beyond pillage and plunder.

John Schlight, in *Monarchs and Mercenaries*, suggests: 1) They work only for pay; they are usually ignored in chronicles and other records, but when mentioned are called mercenaries; few are identified by name. Most are infantry from poorer areas of the country and are recruited by professional warriors who then make the contracts with employers. 2) A mercenary is employed by an acknowledged lord and is protected by the laws of war; if captured he can be ransomed or he can offer to work for the victor. A highwayman or thief, in contrast, usually operates in small bands and can be dishonourably hanged if caught. 3) He is a foreigner.

Kenneth Fowler, in *Medieval Mercenaries*, his study of the Great Companies of the mid-fourteenth century, is less willing to put mercenaries outside established society. While conceding that some *routiers* (members of free companies, that is, working for themselves) rose from obscurity, most had 'chivalrous backgrounds or pretensions'.

This book will use a broader definition: a mercenary hires his military talents out for pay. Often he takes employment with minimum concern for the morals, ethics or cause of the paymaster, but usually there is some political affinity that draws the two together. Mercenaries who survive what might be called their apprenticeship were probably more skilled than most knights and militiamen, but they often had homelands and even more often complained about not being paid.

It is not always easy to tell who is a mercenary soldier. For example, how should we characterise these examples?

1 A vassal who remains in service past the customary term required (often forty days) and is reimbursed for his expenses. Is he fighting for pay?
2 A knight who serves in a household for pay, but does not hold a fief. Is he a bodyguard or a mercenary?
3 A knight who holds a tax fief, i.e., he takes a share of the taxes rather than the income provided by peasants or burghers. He is certainly not what we think of as a typical vassal.
4 A knight who holds a money fief, promising to appear with a certain number of soldiers whenever summoned. His followers will certainly be mercenaries by Contamine's definition, but is he?
5 A man who is selected (or pressed) for service by a royal commissioner. Is he a draftee or a mercenary? What if he stays on past the time required?
6 Two lords are in a royal army – one is performing feudal service, the other receiving pay. Is their practical relationship with the king or each other affected?

The records regarding mercenaries improve with the passage of time, but records in and of themselves prove little. It is only in the study of campaigns, particularly in looking at the length of service provided by the knights and infantry, that we can determine the importance of hired soldiers. One rule of thumb is: *vassals go home for holidays, mercenaries fight on.*

LORDS AS MERCENARIES

According to Jean Froissart, when King Edward III (1327–77) decided to go to war in 1329, he asked his brother-in-law, the earl of Hainault, who might be willing to join him. The earl suggested the duke of Brabant, the bishop of Liege, the duke of Geldern, the archbishop of Cologne and some lesser nobles: 'These are the lords that can, in a short time, furnish greater numbers of men-at-arms than any I know; they are very warlike themselves, and, if they choose can easily make up ten thousand men completely armed and equipped; but you must give them money beforehand, for they are men who love to gain wealth.'

Barbara Tuchman summarised this attitude: 'Knights pursued war for glory and practiced it for gain.' Maurice Keen cited the well-travelled Ghillebert de Lannoy as informing his son that there were three honourable ways to acquire the wealth needed for a noble life: service at court, a good marriage and war. Keen noted wryly that thrift 'is a notable absentee from Lannoy's list'. And he warned us that, though the sources emphasised the lifestyle of the rich and beautiful, this worked its way down the social scale until it provoked a reaction against the *parvenu*, the newly wealthy upstart who flaunted his riches without taste or breeding. This snide emphasis on ancient breeding and lineage provoked one lawyer to retort that 'nobility without riches is like Faith without Works'.

The medieval compromise, Keen said, was to emphasise virtue. While we cannot measure virtue well – that is an internal attribute – we can see the heraldic devices, coats of arms and extravagant gestures. Honour could be earned in the tournament, great honour in a siege, and yet greater honour in battle. Dishonour was the greatest punishment that society could inflict.

Since it was not honourable for a knight or noble to fight for money, subterfuges were necessary to disguise this. Some have accepted these subterfuges at face value, but we might do well to remember Huizinga's summary in *The Waning of the Middle Ages*, that, 'Thus a blasé aristocracy laughs at its own ideal. After having adorned its dream of heroism with all the resources of fantasy, art and wealth, it bethinks itself that life is not so fine, after all – and smiles'.

In short, mercenaries were not commoners only, but powerful nobles as well, and not all were foreigners.

GERMAN MERCENARIES

German feudal customs differed from French and English models. In France birth determined who had the right to become a knight and who did not; in England individuals of sufficient wealth were required by the king to undergo an expensive ceremony of knighthood, whether they wanted to or not, whether they were trained at arms or not. In Germany there was little connection between nobility, knighthood and wealth. One was noble by being born noble, and powerful noble vassals served more powerful noble lords, but at the bottom of the feudal pyramid were *ministeriales* (*Dienstleute*).

A *ministerial* was a man-at-arms and served a lord. But, holding little or no land, he was more an employee than a vassal. Like English and French knights, he often served as judge in the local court, carried out judicial punishments, collected taxes and, in time of war, served with a horse and armour; but, unlike English or French knights, he could be replaced at any time. Whenever he suggested that his services entitled him to be considered noble, his betters reminded him that his ancestors had been commoners or even serfs. That was a blemish that no soap could wash off. The positive side of this was that a sturdy young man could become a *ministerial*, then, if his lord was pleased, become a knight (a *Ritter*). Also merchants and artisans – familiar with weapons from protecting themselves and their property while travelling and from service in the city militia – occasionally became knights. There was no impossible barrier to *limited* upward mobility in Germany. While most ministeriales remained men-at-arms, all had a plausible dream of becoming a knight. Some became mercenaries.

The best of the mercenaries in the Holy Roman Empire came from the kingdom of Bohemia, mostly Czechs, but also German-speaking knights who had settled in the mountains and woodlands. These warriors fought in every conflict north of the Alps and put their earnings into the hundreds of castles that survive today in the Czech Republic.

LOW-BORN MERCENARIES

When commoners became mercenaries, it was usually as foot soldiers. Lacking equipment and training, significant social advancement was difficult, but Jean Froissart, the great chronicler of the early Hundred Years War, showed that it was not impossible:

> Poor rogues took advantage of such times, and robbed both towns and castles; so that some of them, becoming rich, constituted themselves captains of bands of thieves; there were among them those worth forty thousand crowns. Their method was to mark out the particular towns or castles, a day or two's journey from each other; they then collected twenty or thirty robbers, and, traveling through by-roads in the night-time, entered the town or castle they had fixed on about daybreak, and set one of the houses on fire. When the inhabitants perceived it, they thought it had been a body of forces sent to destroy them, and took to their heels as fast as they could. The town of Donzere was treated in this manner; and many other towns and castles were taken, and afterwards ransomed. Among other robbers in Languedoc, one had... [held] the lord of Cobourne... in prison until he ransomed himself for twenty-four thousand crowns paid down. The robber kept possession of the castle and dependencies, which he furnished with provisions, and thence made war upon all the country round about. The king of France, shortly afterwards, was desirous of having him near his person; he purchased the castle for twenty thousand crowns, appointed him his usher-at-arms, and heaped on him many other honors. The name of this robber was Bacon, and he was always mounted on handsome horses of a deep roan color, or on large palfreys, appareled like an earl, and very richly armed; and this state he maintained as long as he lived.

Froissart continued to note that it was not unusual for other bold thieves to become rich and famous:

> There was one of the name of Croquart, who was originally but a poor boy, and had been page to the lord d'Ercle in Holland. When

this Croquart arrived at manhood, he had his discharge, and went to the wars in Brittany, where he attached himself to a man-at-arms, and behaved very well. It happened, that in some skirmish his master was taken and slain; when, in recompense for his prowess, his companions elected him their leader in the place of his late master; he then made such profit by ransoms, and the taking of towns and castles, that he was said to be worth full forty thousand crowns.

Employers were often in a hurry to raise mercenaries. Take the case of the Spanish merchants who had arrived in Flemish ports in 1349 only to learn that an English fleet was lying in wait for their ships to sail home. The Spaniards had no choice but to reinforce their crews locally.

The battle was hard-fought, but at length the English captured several vessels and disposed of the surviving crews and mercenaries by throwing them overboard. Presumably they searched the corpses and captives carefully first, on the assumption that the men had been paid before the combat began. Froissart, ever the gentleman, does not say. *Gentlemen never talk about money.* They take it, but they never talk about it.

CLERICS AS MERCENARY COMMANDERS

Some military commanders were clerics. As for example, Henry Despenser, bishop of Norwich, who was, according to Froissart, 'young and eager, and wishing to bear arms, never having done so but in Lombardy with his brother'. It was still early in the Great Schism, when he found himself suddenly entrusted by the Roman pope, whom the English supported, with the responsibility of raising an army of crusaders and guiding it to Avignon, to capture the pope supported by the French. According to *The Chronicle of Henry Knighton* he raised an immense sum of money from the sale of indulgences, and fine ladies competed to lavish him with jewels and silverware. And, while most of his troops were mercenaries, volunteers also flocked to his service. Among them was the young squire in Chaucer's *Canterbury Tales*:

And he hadde been somtyme in chyvachie
In Flaundres, in Artoys, and Pycardie,

And born hym weel, as of so litel space,
In hope to stonden in his lady grace

In short, the fashionably dressed young man had gone to war to impress his girlfriend, not to save his soul. Nor to serve the king. Bishop Henry Despenser gathered his fine array together in April of 1383. According to Froissart:

> There were in the pay of the church, and under the command of this bishop of Norwich, several good knights of England and Gascony...in the whole, about five hundred lances and fifteen hundred other men; but there were multitudes of priests, because it was an affair of the church, and had been set on foot by the pope. The men-at-arms were punctual in laying in their stores, and the king gave them a passage from Dover and Sandwich. Their purveyances were at those places about Easter; and all who were desirous of going on this expedition, which was sort of a croisade, marched thither in small bodies. Before the bishop and the captains embarked...they were summoned to attend the king's council, where they solemnly swore, in the presence of the king, to fulfill the object of the expedition, and that they would never make war on, or harass any country or men who acknowledged pope Urban, but only those who were under the obedience of Clement.

The bishop disembarked his forces at Calais and awaited the arrival of the English marshal, who failed to appear. Without that reinforcement there was no possibility of marching alone straight through France to Avignon, so he asked his subordinates whether it would be practical to attack France or Flanders. One responded:

> 'Sir, you know on what terms we have left England: our expedition has nothing to do with what concerns the wars of kings but is solely pointed against the Clementists. We are the soldiers of pope Urban, who has given us absolution from all faults if we destroy the Clementists. Should we march into Flanders, notwithstanding that country may now appertain to the king of France and the duke of Burgundy, we shall forfeit our engagement; for, I understand, that the earl of Flanders and all the Flemings are as good Urbanists

as ourselves; besides, we have not a sufficient army to enter Flanders, for they are prepared and accustomed to war, having had nothing else to do for these last four years. They are a numerous people, and it will be difficult to march through so strong a country. But if you are determined on an expedition, let us march into France, there we shall find our enemies.'

The final recommendation, however, was to attack Flanders, which he promptly did. So easily did the venture shift from being a questionable crusade to a questionable act of English policy. But there was even worse to come, the bishop's men taking bribes to surrender a key fortress. The *Westminster Chronicle* denounced the whole affair as infamous and an 'everlasting humiliation to Englishmen'.

It is no wonder that Chaucer's squire did not earn his spurs on this expedition. No Englishman came away with honour. As for the French, they got roaring drunk on captured wine.

THE DRUNKEN AND DISSIPATED MERCENARY

Let us not make the mistake of valuing mercenaries too highly. For every army composed of competent fighting men, we see many more resembling the unit raised by Pistol in *Henry V*, Act III, where a serving boy describes his three masters:

> As young as I am, I have observed these three swashers. I am boy to them all three: but all they three, though they would serve me, could not be man to me; for indeed three such antics do not amount to a man. For Bardolph, he is white-liver'd and red-faced; by the means whereof 'a faces it out, but fights not. For Pistol, he hath a killing tongue and a quiet sword; by the means whereof 'a breaks words, and keeps whole weapons. For Nym, he hath heard that men of few words are the best men; and therefore he scorns to say his prayers, lest 'a should be thought a coward: but his few bad words are match'd with as few good deeds; for 'a never broke any man's head but his own, and that was against a post when he was drunk. They will steal any thing, and call it purchase.

Shakespeare might well have had an ancestor who literally 'shook a spear'. More important, he knew the low value of the mercenary armies of his own day and happily drew on them to show that England's heroes were great partly because they had to achieve victory against both superior odds and the low quality of their own officers and men.

Thus it was that, at the point where the Middle Ages became the Renaissance, then the modern world, Shakespeare presented the mercenary far differently from the medieval chronicler Jean Froissart. The mercenary became a low-born comic figure, ineffective on the battlefield and in the bedroom, ungrammatical, unshaven, untrustworthy even in peacetime and unreliable in war. These varied pictures – the mercenary as hero, the mercenary as entrepreneur, the mercenary as criminal, the mercenary as buffoon – are also worthy of study.

4

CHIVALRY

THE WORD CHIVALRY – from the French *chevalier* (horseman) – had from its earliest days an association with *cavalry*, but it implied more than fighting on horseback. A *miles* (knight) was the embodiment of prowess, loyalty, generosity, courtesy and manly bearing – that is, nobility. Maurice Keen, in his highly regarded book *Chivalry*, says that it is 'an ethos in which martial, aristocratic and Christian elements were fused together'. It inspired generations of young noblemen – and commoners who emulated them – to admire the paragons of fourteenth-century military virtue, the *paladins*. It was for this audience that Jean Froissart wrote:

> To encourage all valorous hearts, and to show them honorable
> examples, I, John Froissart, will begin to relate…that whereas
> various noble personages have frequently spoken of the wars
> between France and England, without knowing anything of the
> matter, or being able to assign the proper reasons for them; I, hav-
> ing perceived the right foundation of the matter, shall neither add
> nor omit, forget, corrupt, nor abridge my history: but the rather will
> enlarge it, that I may be able to point out and speak of each adven-
> ture from the nativity of the noble king Edward of England, who
> so potently reigned, and who was engaged in so many battles and
> perilous adventures, and other feats of arms and great prowess,
> from the year of grace 1326, when he was crowned in England.

As Froissart boasted, there were many who attempted to describe the chivalric glories of what later generations would call the Hundred Years War,

69

but none was as successful as he would be. A cleric, easily liked and trusted to put his patrons in a good light, he moved easily from court to court, recounting his tales and adding to the stories he was writing down in colloquial French. Since many English nobles and knights believed themselves to be as authentically French as their Continental counterparts, he could admire English and French heroes impartially, nor was he required to bear arms against any of them. He knew the language of chivalry and he understood the literary tastes of his era perfectly.

Froissart had his heroes. This was, in part, a continuation of literary tradition, the *chanson d'geste* – stories that can be traced back to the *Song of Roland*, which celebrated the death of the hero at Roncesvalles, fighting overwhelming Muslim enemies, but too proud to summon Charlemagne to rescue him. But it was also a literary device – a plot line that could tie numerous stories together, a place to return after concluding one of his numerous digressions.

He introduced his readers first to the young English king, Edward III, whose grandfather had been the redoubtable Edward I of *Braveheart* fame; in the movie Edward I (1273–1307) was the king who gave the phrase 'out the window' new meaning. For better or worse, the public knows history more from movies than from reading, English–Scottish history especially. (As a guide in the National Gallery in London told me, 'Mel Gibson has a lot to answer for.') Edward I was among England's greatest rulers. Crusader, conqueror of Wales and Scotland, reformer of the court system and the national administration, Edward brought an end to fifty years of weak rule and disorder. He had also protected English business interests threatened by French aggression (or, in the French view, Flanders being brought back into the French kingdom); it was inevitable that Edward III would take a similar interest in Flanders.

Edward III was Froissart's greatest hero, but not the only one:

> Although he, and also those who were with him in his battles and fortunate rencounters, or with his army when he was not there in person, which you shall hear as we go on, ought to be accounted right valiant: yet as of these there is a multitude, some should be esteemed supereminent. Such as the gallant king himself before named; the prince of Wales, his son; the duke of Lancaster; Sir Reginald lord Cobham; Sir Walter Manny of Hainault, knight; Sir John Chandos; Sir Fulke Harley; and many others who are

recorded in this book for their worth and prowess: for in all their
battles by sea or land, in which they were engaged, their valor was
so distinguished that they should be esteemed heroes of highest
renown – but without disparagement to those with whom they
served. In France also was found good chivalry, strong of limb and
stout of heart, and in great abundance; for the kingdom of France
was never brought so low as to want men ever ready for the
combat. Such was king Philippe of Valois, a bold and hardy knight,
and his son, King John; also John, king of Bohemia. And Charles,
count of Alençon, his son; the count of Foix...and many others
that I can not at present name; but they shall all be mentioned in
due time and place; for, to say the truth, we must allow sufficient
bravery and ability to all who were engaged in such cruel and
desperate battles, and discharged their duty, by standing their
ground till the discomfiture.

In contrast, the warriors to the north of England were not as interested in
the concepts of chivalry. Honour, yes. Duty, yes. But chivalry was expensive
and Scotland was poor. Chivalry was represented by the extravagant gesture,
and Scots were practical. In Scotland you inherited your enemies or you
earned them, but forgiveness and forgetfulness were virtues that experience
had shown to be dangerous. Froissart wrote:

The Scots are bold, hardy, and much inured to war. When they
make their invasions into England, they march from twenty to
four-and-twenty leagues without halting, as well by night as day; for
they are all on horseback, except the camp followers, who are on
foot. The knights and esquires are well mounted on large bay
horses, the common people on little galloways. They bring no
carriages with them, on account of the mountains they have to
pass in Northumberland; neither do they carry with them any
provisions of bread or wine; for their habits of sobriety are such,
in time of war, that they will live for a long time on flesh half
sodden, without bread, and drink the river-water without wine.
They have, therefore, no occasion for pots and pans; for they dress
the flesh of their cattle in the skins, after they have taken them off;
and, being sure to find plenty of them in the country which they
invade, they carry none with them. Under the flaps of his saddle,

each man carries a broad plate of metal; behind the saddle, a little bag of oatmeal; when they have eaten too much of the sodden flesh, and their stomach appears weak and empty, they place this plate over the fire, mix with water their oatmeal, and when the plate is heated, they put a little of the paste upon it, and make a thin cake, like a cracknel or biscuit, which they eat to warm their stomachs: it is therefore no wonder, that they perform a longer day's march than other soldiers. In this manner the Scots entered England, destroying and burning everything as they passed.

While the Scots apparently ate an early form of pizza, the English were less adaptable – they suffered real hunger during their campaigns across the northern border. Both sides burned villages, stole animals and mistreated any people they came across. The war was interrupted by truces, but never quite ended. Not even the death of King Robert Bruce (1306–29) brought peace long; he had brought ten years of English rule over Scotland to an end, and not even Edward III could reverse his achievement.

SHAKESPEARE

Wars were formal events, begun with an elaborate challenge that presumably satisfied the Church's definition of a Just War. Froissart described how far this varied from a genuine effort to seek reconciliation of differences:

[T]he king of England...sent memorials and remonstrances through Germany, or wherever he expected to gain assistance. The duke of Geldern (who was nephew to the king of England, being the son of his sister, and thus cousin-german to the children of the king,) and the duke of Juliers, were at that time true and loyal Englishmen: they had been very much affronted by the manner of the king of France sending his challenge by a servant, and rebuked the king for it, highly blaming both him and his council for this unbecoming form of sending it. They said, that war between such great and renowned lords as the kings of France and of England should have been declared by proper messengers, such as dignified prelates, bishops, or abbots. They added, that the French had not followed this usual mode, through pride and presumption. These lords sent their challenge to the king of France in a handsome manner, as did several other knights of Germany. It was their intention immediately to have entered France, and to have done such deeds there as twenty years should not efface; but their schemes were broken by means they did not expect, as you will hereafter find recorded in this history.

Shakespeare's audiences were still very much aware of these wars. They were not confused by references to alliances of French and Scot, as Westmoreland's advice in *Henry V,* Act I:

> But there's a saying, very old and true:
> > If that you will France win,
> > Then with Scotland first begin.
> For, once the eagle England being in prey,
> To her unguarded nest the weasel Scot
> Comes sneaking, and so sucks her princely eggs;
> Playing the mouse in absence of the cat,
> To tear and havoc more than she can eat.

Exeter then notes, 'It follows, then, the cat must stay at home'. That is, no war with France. Shortly afterward the ambassadors of France enter, presented a gift from the dauphin (the heir to the throne, then regent for the mentally unbalanced king), then warned Henry to stay out of France.

The king, who, according to Shakespeare, was only fifteen at the time, chose to ignore the warning and inquired into the gift. Exeter said drily, 'Tennis-balls, my liege'. Henry's response to this began calmly, but soon rose to dramatic fury. He addressed the French lords:

> But tell the Dauphin, I will keep my state,
> Be like a king, and show my soul of greatness,
> When I do rouse me in my throne of France:
> For that I have laid by my majesty,
> And plodded like a man for working-days;
> But I will rise there with so full a glory
> That I will dazzle all the eyes of France,
> ...

Tell you the Dauphin, I am coming on,
To venge me as I may, and to put forth
My rightful hand in a well-hallow'd cause.
So, get you hence in peace; and tell the Dauphin
His jest will savour but of shallow wit,
When thousands weep, more than did laugh at it.

Henry was actually twenty-six when he became king and an experienced military commander, but authors are permitted to take some license in making stories tauter.

Shakespeare gave us Henry V as a hero, but he added Pistol as a captain of mercenary troops. That is an important point – even the best of the English commanders, leading the best of the English armies, had to hire mercenaries. Thus, in a very real sense, the heroic was combined with the profit-motive, the patriot with the amoral killer, the pure sense of honour with the most cynical expressions of profit and pleasure. Even the royal favourite with the blustering fool.

YOUNGER SONS

The practice of primogeniture, that is, passing down property and titles to the eldest surviving son, resulted in a ready supply of mercenaries. Many younger sons were educated for the clergy, but there was such likelihood that the eldest son would die young that at least one of his brothers would be trained as a knight, too – 'An heir and a spare'. Or sometimes more.

The plight of the younger son was pitiable. Unless he was willing to hang about his brother's house, unmarried and probably unmarriageable, perhaps hunting and drinking, his only hope was, as Maurice Keen reminds us, in knight errantry. This did not mean a quest for the Holy Grail, but service in a crusade or as part of some great lord's retinue. Or as a mercenary. Wages were one attraction, loot another, and then there was pure adventure, but even more important was pride. Service in arms kept the status of the knights above the merchants and rich peasants, and even proud clerics. A young noble, even one who could not afford the ceremony of knighthood, could not imagine another profession than military service.

The example of William Marshal (1144–1219), the fourth son of a minor noble, was always before the eyes of ambitious young men. William became the associate of four kings of England and regent for Henry III (1216–72). William's start was that of a tournament champion, then as a mercenary collector of prisoners and booty, later a crusader and finally a wise councillor. He married well and was named Earl of Pembroke.

Abolishing primogeniture would not have resolved the problem. It might have alleviated it for a generation, after which the problem might have become worse. Everyone, eldest sons included, would have had to fight for lands, titles and prestige instead of inheriting them.

This was the spirit that Shakespeare described in *Henry V*, Act II:

> Now all the youth of England are on fire,
> And silken dalliance in the wardrobe lies:
> Now thrive the armourers, and honour's thought
> Reigns solely in the breast of every man.

THE FREE COMPANIES

Free companies were private armies that made war on their own, ravaging one territory after another. The technical French name for them was *routiers* (bands), which to the English ear suggests moving around the countryside. Indeed, when faced by effective resistance, they would volunteer to move on, to sack some traditional enemies' lands, if not attacked. This would save lives on all sides except those of the next victims.

The paradox was, as Keen notes, that no one wanted to hire mercenaries, but everyone had to – or lose the war. Then they became impossible to dismiss safely. Once these companies were no longer paid, they became dependent on pillage for survival.

Not even the Church was safe. Especially not the pope, who in the fourteenth century had acquired a reputation for greed and parsimony. Thus Avignon, the papal residence on the Rhône River, came to represent the portal into the mercenaries' paradise. In 1365, Froissart reported:

> There was at the time a king in Hungary [Louis the Great
> (1342–82)] who was desirous of having their assistance, and would

have given them full employment against the Turks, with whom he was at war, for they had done him much mischief. He wrote, therefore, to pope Urban V [1362–70], who was then at Avignon, and who would gladly have seen France delivered from these companies, and also to the king of France and to the prince of Wales. He wished to enter into a treaty with their leaders, and offered large sums of money to them and a free passage; but they would not listen to it, saying, that they would not go so far to make war. It was told them by their oldest captains, who were well acquainted with the country of Hungary, that there were such narrow passes, if they should in any combat be engaged in them, they would never be able to get out, but must infallibly be cut off. This report frightened them so much, that they had not any desire to go thither.

The pope developed a plan to send the companies to pillage elsewhere. As unchristian as this proposal might have been, even churchmen had to think of their own welfare now and then. Still, there were many who criticised those who employed mercenaries, often chastising them right to their face, as in this August 1366 incident described by Froissart. Two French emissaries approached Sir John Combes, the governor of Montauban, a town belonging to the Prince of Wales on the border of Gascony, to complain about the mercenaries there:

'They are robbers and pillagers, who have severely oppressed the kingdom of France. And you, sir John, if you had become courteous to your neighbours, ought not thus to have supported them in their robberies of poor persons, without a shadow of justice; for these are the causes that give rise to hatred between the great. If you do not therefore drive them out of your fortress, you are neither a friend to the king nor kingdom of France'.

'My lords,' replied the governor, 'it is true there are men-at-arms in my garrison, whom my lord the prince has ordered thither, and whom I retain for him. I am not therefore inclined to send them away thus suddenly. If they have given you any cause of displeasure, I do not see from whom you can right yourselves; for they are men-at-arms, and they will support themselves in their usual manner, either on the territories of the king of France or on those of the prince.' The lord of Narbonne and sir Guy d'Asai made answer by saying: 'They are indeed men-at-arms, but of such a sort that they cannot exist without pillage and robbery, and have very unbecomingly trespassed on our boundaries, for which they shall pay dearly, if we could but once meet with them in the open plains. They have burnt, stolen, and done many shameful acts within the jurisdiction of Toulouse, complaints of which have been made to us, which if we suffer to go unpunished, we shall be traitors to the king our lord, who has appointed us to watch over and guard his country. You will therefore tell them from us, for, since we know where their quarters are, we can find them, that they shall make us amends for their proceedings, or they will fare the worse for it.'

The governor was at a loss to give a suitable answer – he could not turn the mercenaries out, nor could he control them; on the other hand, he did not want to start a war. After five days the mercenaries sallied out for another raid, only to find a large French force lying in wait. There was a terrific battle, which resulted in the French routing the mercenaries and pursing them back to Montauban. Once in the town, however, the French knights found themselves attacked by the townspeople and even the women dropping heavy objects on them; finally Gascon reinforcements arrived to defeat and capture the French knights (who were later released for the payment of a 'moderate' ransom).

Such English and Gascon blackguards ravaged the beautiful fields and villages of France through the Hundred Years War. The least sign of disorder, civil war or foreign invasion brought them forth in great numbers. War is terrible, it is said, but war not fought to a decisive conclusion is even worse. This war of the ungovernable against the ungoverned was rightly considered the worse fate a country could endure long before the philosopher Hobbes found the words to justify *The Leviathan* – the powerful state that could provide protection against outside attack and domestic disturbances.

No one disliked the appearance of the Leviathan more than the medieval mercenary. In the place of the free companies and the free soldier came the royal army and the police.

THE LEVIATHAN IN ACTION

There was only one Leviathan in the Middle Ages – the state of the Ottoman Turks that had taken Constantinople (Istanbul) for its capital in 1453. Learning from their subjects and, in fact, often using privileged slaves to manage the state, the Ottomans created a government that was effective, responsive and for a long time relatively just. But the Ottomans rarely relied on goodwill alone – their subjects understood that resistance or insults would be swiftly followed by brutal punishments; not paying taxes promptly was both an act of resistance and an insult. Theirs was far from a pacifist state, since it institutionalised raids into Christian lands for slaves, animals, and training the army, but it was also more than a military machine. It was a multinational, multiconfessional state where each faith governed its own members under Ottoman supervision and nobody was allowed to attack anyone else; it was a state that encouraged trade and commerce, learning and comfort, a state where Voltaire's characters in *Candide* could tend their garden, secure in the knowledge that whatever happened at the top of the government, common people could get on with life. The Yugoslav novel by Ivo Andrić, *The Bridge on the Drina* (1945), described the Ottomans' alternative world to that of feudal Europe. The Ottomans had the best army of the era, and its main striking force, the Janissaries, was composed of slaves trained to be soldiers and administrators. The slaves were Christian boys taken from their parents as tax – in Andrić's novel from a small town in Bosnia; all became devout Muslims, and they often ruled the sultan as much as he ruled them.

There were several Christian rulers who attempted to concentrate power in their hands. None succeeded, though Friedrich II had come close. A few had some success in northern Europe – the Teutonic Knights in Prussia and the dukes of Saxony and Brandenburg. In Italy there was Milan, the once proud independent republic that was ruled by the Visconti family after 1277. The most industrialised state in Italy and the richest, Milan had an armaments industry that assured Visconti mercenaries first class weapons.

Petrarch, the first humanist philosopher of the Renaissance, lived in Milan between 1353 and 1361 as a guest of the Visconti; in return he acted as Milanese diplomat to the pope and Holy Roman emperor. Among his many lasting innovations was legitimising scholars becoming active in politics; much later Leonardo da Vinci continued this tradition – from 1482 to 1499 he painted and now and then designed engines of war of improbable usefulness.

The most memorable Visconti came late. Gian Galeazzo (1378–1402) inherited a share of Milan from his father Galeazzo, then murdered his uncle Bernabò in 1385. The international cry of outrage was muted by Bernabò's reputation as a cruel tyrant, and stifled by Gian Galeazzo's royal connections. His sister Violante had been married to Lionel, a grandson of King Edward III; nine years after Lionel's death in 1368, she married the marquis of Montferrat. Gian Galeazzo's own first wife had been Isabella of Valois, the sister of King Charles V of France. Eight years after her death, he married Caterina, the youngest daughter of his uncle Bernabò.

Gian Galeazzo's successor was his son, Giovanni Maria (1389–1413), who was assassinated in May of 1413. Then came Filippo Maria (1392–1447), who had executed his first wife in 1415 because of alleged infidelity and apparently never consummated his union with his second spouse; his only love was a mistress who bore his only child, Bianca Maria, whose marriage to his mercenary general Francesco Sforza (1401–66) legitimised Sforza's seizure of power in 1450.

These first examples of the all-powerful state were so totally negative that the lovers of liberty were less willing than ever to trust their fate to an absolutist ruler. It was better to risk the free companies.

BLOOD AND MORE BLOOD

The Church was no better at providing leadership. Critics denounced the popes' involvement in power politics, and, indeed, several pontiffs are better understood as Renaissance princes than as inheritors of Peter's spiritual authority. If only the cardinals would elect a saint, pious folk cried, someone who would reform the Church. But saints did no better than consecrated sinners.

St Catherine of Siena (1347–80), for example, was fixated on blood, even seeing the stigmata, the five wounds of Christ on her own body – a gift invisible to others. She became immensely popular through her fasts, her visions and her eagerness to tell political leaders what they should do. St Catherine's solution to the presence of mercenaries was a crusade. She appealed to John Hawkwood, the most famous of the English mercenaries in Italy, with soothing words, she talked sweetly to the pope, she wrote letters to the wives (!) of prominent men, and she was relentless – she would talk until her listeners fell asleep. Yet she stiffened the backs of popes and kings, she drove them to support the concept of church reform, and she gave new life to popular religious enthusiasm. Nevertheless, she could not persuade the mercenaries to give up their easy life in Europe and march on Jerusalem where they would most likely perish. Perish unpaid.

John Hawkwood was once met at the gate of Montecchio by two friars who wished him peace. According to Keen, he responded, 'May God take away your alms. Do you not know that I live by war and that peace would be my undoing?'

Against this St Catherine could do nothing. She became the patron saint of unmarried girls. Together with St Francis, she also became the patron saint of Italy. No wonder the poor peninsula suffered so. Against such other-worldliness what could hard-thinking realists like Petrarch and Machiavelli do?

Contemporary society valued prowess too highly. Neither saints nor poets nor political scientists could change that.

BLOOD AND ROSES

Huizinga's famous summary of late medieval life – that it smelled of blood and roses – resonates today. Pride, violence, luxury, treachery, religious ecstasy and foolishness were to be seen everywhere in medieval France and England. Chivalry had gone mad with excess and boredom, it had taken refuge in dreams and fantasies. Froissart was the chief representative of this phenomenon. In his day readers were immensely interested in heroic figures – real men who combined the attributes of champions and warriors. Today our heroes reek of blood and roses, and boredom and steroids.

A later generation took refuge in Romances, imaginative literature with magic, supernatural creatures, exotic locations and exaggerated emotions. This illustrated how far from the original concept chivalry could evolve. At the same time books of manners became popular. In the strange way that human beings behave, sometimes the less we practise a noble idea, the more we honour it. And vice-versa.

Thorstein Veblen's searing condemnation of upper-class superficiality in

The Theory of the Leisure Class – its glorification of war, sports and conspicuous consumption – applies fully to the late Middle Ages. This is the problem that Voltaire addressed in *Candide*, praising work as the only sure cure for mankind's three besetting sins – poverty, vice and boredom. Voltaire knew what he was talking about – he only had to look around eighteenth-century French society to see the degenerate remains of a noble class that looked down upon work as something unworthy of a gentleman.

Huizinga concluded his chapter on chivalrous ideas by saying of the bored aristocracy that, having prettified their values with every available resource, they looked at the product and smiled – ironically. So should we.

5
THE HUNDRED YEARS WAR
PART ONE

THE BEST ONE-PARAGRAPH summary of the Hundred Years War is by Eric Christiansen, a British historian with a dry but rapier-sharp wit:

> The Hundred Years' War was a series of wars conducted from 1339 to 1453 on many different levels, which were rarely combined into one conflict. At the top, kings of England, France and Castille locked horns over claims ranging from possession of one tenth of the French kingdom to the whole of it. At the bottom, teenage thugs beat the brains out of villagers for the sake of a mule and a change of clothes. That was not a pretty sight; but knights and ladies at the top did their best, with tournaments, feasts, festivals, and processions to make their wars look good whenever they could. The contrast has not been ignored by historians and novelists, and will presumably always horrify those who believe that cruelty and civilization are incompatible.

Christiansen's elegant and funny review of Jonathan Sumption's *The Hundred Years War*, volume 2, will delight those who appreciate traditional narratives. The war, as irrational as it was, was an important event and mercenaries were central to its beginnings, its tragic twists and turns, and to its two anti-climactic conclusions.

ORIGINS OF THE WAR

England was in disorder when Edward III became king. His father Edward II (1307–27) had enemies who claimed that he was incompetent as a warrior, an administrator and as a husband. Rumours had swirled around his sexual orientation, which in the England of those days mattered. Edward II had relied on the Despenser family for advice and *more personal* services, but their policies had not been successful. His unhappy wife, Isabella, had gone back to France, raised a mercenary army, and with the help of her lover, Roger Mortimer, had invaded England. She smothered her husband (malicious rumour had described a more imaginative fate – a white-hot poker in the rectum) and then crowned her teenaged son.

Meanwhile, France was on the move, continuing a long-term policy of whittling away at English possessions in Gascony, the German states to the east, Flanders to the north and Brittany in the west. The war in Flanders especially worried the English, since that could affect the English trade in wool. Also the French king had supported the Scots in their wars with Edward II, occasionally attempting to send his incomparably trained and equipped knights to support them. Since French aid to the Scots might prove fatal to the English monarchy, Edward III's advisors suggested that his French cousin might benefit from a reminder that France had problem neighbours, too.

This sounded good, but in reality Edward III had little with which to counter French encouragement of the Scots. To be sure, three French kings having died in short order, their sister, Edward's mother, had a stronger claim to the French crown than her uncle, Philippe VI of Valois (1328–50), who had been passed over earlier as lacking the talents necessary for a monarch. Philippe bargained away royal prerogatives in return for his vassals' support; then he relied on extending the Salic Law (against a woman governing) to her son. Under less tense circumstances this exclusion would have been relatively unimportant. But at this moment, youthful Edward III seized whatever weapon was at hand – if he could defend his French possessions only by claiming all of France, he would claim everything necessary. Later he would even try to be elected Holy Roman emperor.

Alas for Edward, he had few means of supporting his legalistic quibble. In point of fact, he could not put nearly as many knights into the field as Philippe. In theory, every able-bodied man in England between sixteen and sixty was to present himself for military service, but in practice royal commissioners, usually local knights, would enlist troops according to the categories needed – so many archers, so many spearmen, so many knights. This was, in Sumption's words, 'taxation in kind', but since the draft fell on so few men, it was not unpopular – moreover, 'some probably relished the chance of wages and plunder'. Local communities paid for their immediate expenses, but the king provided pay on campaign. One result of this system was a higher percentage of infantry than was common in France, and a higher quality of foot soldier. Many of the newly recruited knights and soldiers lacked experience in war, but an even great problem was the lack of strategic vision and proper tactics.

These all came to Edward III in his wars with Scotland. In a few years he would transform a nation despised for producing feeble warriors into a mighty military machine. But that could not be imagined when the Hundred Years War began.

France was meanwhile undergoing strains far more severe than contemporary observers noticed. Neighbours were fearful and jealous, royal authority was diminished by the system of relying on powerful vassals to carry out policy, and the economy was depressed by taxes and inept royal policies. The king's armies were large, but paying the troops was not easy. Despite high taxes, little money made its way into the king's treasury – much went to ecclesiastical lords, relatives and the pockets of government officials; and the rich cities of Flanders had managed to drive away both the king's tax collectors and his armies. Efforts to raise money from the king's remaining subjects were unpopular and only temporarily effective.

The technical reason for war was Edward's refusal to do homage for Gascony (Aquitaine, Guyenne and other lands). As Edward's mother put it, the son of a king does not bow to the son of a count and promise to 'be his man'. This was the opinion of the well-informed Florentine chronicler, Villani, who noted Edward's refusal to go through the ritual of handing over his lands to his lord, then receiving them back as a generous gift. But Villani added a more important motive: the French desire to take Gascony and all the English possessions.

At the end of 1330 Philippe had learned that Edward had just overthrown his mother's government and executed her lover. This was a moment of opportunity – it might take years for Edward to put England back into order. A French army immediately invaded Gascony.

Initially Edward chose to resist indirectly. By giving aid to the count of Flanders and the Flemish cities, and hiring at great expense a host of

German lords, he could keep the French army tied down in the north. But eventually he had to come to the Continent himself.

In 1339 King Philippe attempted to make the English monarch similarly look to homeland defence. His Norman subjects were eager to attack their English rivals in fishing and trade, but they lacked ships. Philippe hired an impressive Italian fleet, hoping that the threat of an invasion could force Edward to station so many knights and infantry at the port cities that his army on the Continent would be weakened. Froissart recounted the subsequent events:

> King Edward was obliged to remain at Vilvorde, where he
> maintained daily, at his own cost, full sixteen hundred men-at-arms,
> that had come there from beyond sea, and ten thousand archers,
> without counting the other followers of his army. This must have
> been a heavy expense; not including the large sums he had given to
> the German lords, who thus paid him back by fair promises; and
> the great force he was obliged to keep at sea against the Genoese,
> Bretons, Normans, Picards, and Spaniards ... to guard the straits
> and passages between England and France; and these corsairs only
> waited for information of the war being commenced, and the
> English king, having challenged the king of France as they
> supposed he would, to invade England and ravage the country.

The great naval battle at Sluys, 1340, reduced the threat considerably. The French lost so many men (perhaps 18,000) and ships, that they had to hire Spanish vessels and sailors in order to harass the long English maritime lines of communication with Gascony.

SCOTLAND

Edward had many foreign volunteers for his wars with Scotland. Sumption suggests that a principal attraction was chivalry. Certainly Edward could not offer high wages and Scotland was too poor for profitable looting. But professional warriors like Walter Manny fought in these conflicts and eventually settled down in England, basking in their high reputation and the considerable fortunes they had made in the king's service. Hainault (a French speaking region north of France, the home of Edward's queen) provided many knights, but also Holland, Brabant, Germany and even France. There was always some booty to be taken from defeated foes, and ransoms – even from Scots – could be considerable.

Edward's strategy was to move swiftly and strike hard, using his superior numbers and weaponry effectively. In practice, it was less glorious than it sounded – it meant mounting many of his infantry on cheap horses and living off the land. It was also necessary to hold the Scottish ports, so that French reinforcements could not unload their warhorses safely.

English tactics had proven effective in past encounters with Scots – who often showed more enthusiasm than good sense. In general the English sought to present a line of spearmen on a narrow front, supported by dismounted knights, with archers to the flanks. The Scots would charge, only to be cut down in rows by the hail of arrows. The English, famed for holding their ranks against the fiercest assaults, would eventually drive the demoralised Scots in wild flight from the field. The result was decisive victories at relatively low cost. Or the Scots would break through, routing their numerically superior foe.

In general the Scots preferred to avoid combat, relying on the English inability to occupy the entire country. Then, when the English armies went home, they would retake the castles and cities. It was a strategy of poverty and patience, but it worked often enough. English efforts to stifle these revolts by pre-emptive slaughters of potential enemies only made the clan coalitions stronger and more determined.

Meanwhile, Edward was running out of money. Creditors were wary of loaning him funds for war except when jewels (even the crown!) and hostages were given in pawn.

BRITTANY

Brittany, in Barbara Tuchman's words, was France's Scotland. King Philippe could not ignore the disputed inheritance there any more than Edward could his northern neighbour. Great heroism and great tragedies marked this war, and England and France poured huge sums into efforts to prevail. The cost of defeat was too high – 1066 proved that – not to do everything necessary for victory.

Froissart was more concerned with acts of courage and initiative than with money, though he understood fully that these were all connected. Froissart was also relatively gender-neutral in assessing courage and tenacity. In 1342, when Jeanne of Flanders, duchess of Brittany, was hard pressed by French forces which held her husband prisoner, he related this story:

> I wish now to return to the countess of Montfort, who possessed
> the courage of a man, and the heart of a lion. She was in the city of
> Rennes when she heard of the seizure of her lord; and, notwith-
> standing the great grief she had at heart, she did all she could to
> comfort and reanimate her friends and soldiers; showing them a
> young child, called John, after his father, she said, 'Oh, gentlemen,
> do not be cast down by what we have suffered through the loss of
> my lord; he was but one man. Look at my little child, here; if it
> please God, he shall be his restorer, and shall do you much service.
> I have plenty of wealth, which I will distribute among you, and will
> seek out for such a leader, as may give you a proper confidence.'
> When the countess had, by these means, encouraged her friends
> and soldiers at Rennes, she visited all the other towns and
> fortresses, taking her young son John with her. She addressed and
> encouraged them in the same manner as she had done at Rennes.
> She strengthened her garrisons both with men and provisions, paid
> handsomely for everything, and gave largely wherever she thought
> it would have a good effect. She then went to Hennebon, near the
> sea, where she and her son remained all that winter; frequently
> visiting her garrisons, who she encouraged, and paid liberally.

Her logical alliance was with England. Unless her fishermen could set out in their vessels and her merchants sell the catch, she could not pay anyone to fight for her. English vessels plying the seas often came across her defenceless fishermen. Only Edward could offer her seamen protection.

Froissart wrote a thrilling narration of her resistance to the French invasion:

> The countess, who had clothed herself in armor, was mounted on
> a war-horse, and galloped up and down the streets of the town, en-
> treating and encouraging the inhabitants to defend themselves
> honorably. She ordered the ladies and other women to unpave the
> streets, carry the stones to the ramparts, and throw them on their

enemies. She had pots of quicklime brought to her for the same purpose.

At critical moment, she sallied out at the head of her knights and broke up the attack.

King Philippe, discouraged by his lack of success in this border wars, authorised private armies to attack his enemies. However, he did not foresee that when a two-year truce was signed, the demobilised soldiers would spread across the embattled territories, some hiring out to the local lords, others forming bands and living from extortion, loot and ransom. As civil order collapsed, propagandists from each party blamed the other side for all the ills of the era.

THE BATTLE OF CRÉCY

As the truce came to an end in 1345, it was clear that the contrasting strategies were leading nowhere except mutual financial exhaustion. The courtiers of France, not impressed by their monarch, were especially snide in their insinuations that his reluctance to give battle to English forces was not prudence, but cowardice. As for Edward, he had not achieved anything more than frustrating Philippe's efforts at expansion. Patience was running out. More daring strategies were proposed.

In 1346 Edward transported his army across the Channel to Normandy. Though the Normans were strongly anti-English and had not been ruled by Edward's ancestors since the days of King John, he still considered them his lawful subjects. His announcement that no one in his forces should molest innocent people was, however, ignored from the beginning. Fires of burning villages lit the horizon as far the eye could stand to see; refugees clogged the roads, hurrying ahead of English marauders. Meanwhile, English ships descended on coastal towns, with orders to do as much damage as possible.

The fear that Edward's mercenary Welsh and Irish troops inspired was shown at the surrender of Caen, when the constable of France and other leading knights expected to be massacred. Seeing an acquaintance from the crusades in Prussia, they called on him for protection – which, with a ransom also in mind, he provided. These notables were lucky. 2,500 others, less well-born, were not.

As Edward's plundering expedition moved toward Rouen, the French king dithered. At length, Philippe summoned the forces then employed in attacking Gascony and ordered his Genoese mercenary crossbowmen (who had expected to be employed at sea and were unhappy at not having been paid) to join him; he then gathered his army near Paris and ordered blocking forces on the north bank of the Seine to prevent the English from crossing and making their way safely to Flanders. To be certain that he had the English trapped, Philippe ordered the bridges across the river destroyed.

When Edward was within twenty miles of Paris he realised that a gigantic French army was awaiting him there. His choices were not good. It was unlikely that the French would allow him to withdraw safely to the coast and load his men aboard ships, even if sufficient shipping was available. Most likely the French would wait until the knights were boarding, then massacre them. Moreover, it was late in the season.

It was impossible for Edward to escape south to Gascony – too far and too many rivers. His only hope was Flanders. Happily for him, his men managed to build a makeshift bridge across the meandering Seine and drive away the handful of French knights at the crossing. Meanwhile, by accepting a challenge to a formal battle, Edward lured the French army south of the river, to a camp near the proposed battlefield. It was to be something like a tournament's mêlée, only on a grander scale, and with infantry involved.

The French knights must have been thrilled. Not only were they well practised for such artificial warfare, but they were better equipped and more numerous. They celebrated their anticipated victory, probably unable to believe their good luck.

Their gullibility gave Edward a head start. He led his forces across the Seine and broke the bridge down behind him, then raced toward the Somme, which was not yet properly defended by the forces of King John of Bohemia. He was followed by the French royal army, now thoroughly enraged at the unchivalrous trickery, moving twenty-five miles a day, a killing pace, but one that closed the distance quickly. Edward feared being trapped at the Somme, caught between more numerous enemy armies, while his own men were exhausted, ill and demoralised. Turning to the coast, he found a marshy ford that his scouts managed to force; his last men crossed just as the tide rolled in to frustrate the French pursuers. The supply ships and reinforcements were not waiting, however. Edward had to make his way north overland, followed closely by the gigantic French array that was now stretching out along the narrow roads so that wagons, supplies and infantry units began lagging behind. Within a day's march of safety, Edward found the battlefield he wanted – near the village of Crécy in Picardy; there he paused to face the French van. At least now, should the day be lost, there was a good chance that he and many of his men could escape what earlier would have been certain death or capture.

Philippe's army arrived toward the end of the day, confident that they could finally crush their elusive prey. Once that was done, the war would be won – the English could be completely expelled from the Continent and their allies brought to heel. Philippe had perhaps 12,000 mounted warriors and 6,000 Genoese mercenaries; he had left his 20,000 or more infantry far behind on the road.

The French king had no need to commit his forces to battle immediately, but the criticism of his past caution were still ringing in his ears. No doubt his advisors were warning him against once again missing the opportunity for a decisive victory. Yet there were good grounds to delay other than to bring of the rest of the army and to fight when everyone was fresh: the English seemed to be in a desperate situation from which they could not retreat easily; also, Edward's position was strong, so that flanking it might be better than a head-on attack; lastly, it was beginning to rain – that gave an additional advantage to defending infantry. If Philippe had announced a plan, it might have been different, but he was apparently still undecided on his tactics until the last moment, at which time some knights, without orders, moved directly against the English. He could have sent units to Edward's rear, cut off access to food and water, and awaited his rival's surrender at leisure. But Philippe's vassals, already enjoying the forthcoming victory and reportedly discussing how to divide up the captives among themselves, remembered that Edward had already slipped out of two traps in this very campaign. Moreover, where would they camp? It was late in the day and the logistical situation was a mess. Better to attack now, eliminate the danger of an English sally against a disorganised, half-erected camp, and worry about supper later. With overwhelming numbers, better equipment, and – in spite of the forced march – more rested forces, how could the French army lose? Froissart, as usual, is an exciting guide:

> The English, who were drawn up in the three divisions, and seated
> on the ground, on seeing their enemies advance, rose undauntedly
> up, and fell into their ranks. That of the prince was the first to do
> so, whose archers were formed in the manner of a portcullis, or

harrow, and the men-at-arms in the rear...

You must know, that these kings, earls, barons and lords of France, did not advance in any regular order, but one after the other, or any way most pleasing to themselves. As soon as the king of France came in sight of the English, his blood began to boil, and he cried out to his marshals, 'Order the Genoese forward, and begin the battle, in the name of God and St Denis.' There were about fifteen thousand Genoese cross-bowmen; but they were quite fatigued, having marched on foot that day six leagues, completely armed, and with their cross-bows. They told the constable, they were not in a fit condition to do any great things that day in battle. The earl of Alençon, hearing this, said, 'This is what one gets by employing such scoundrels, who fall off when there is any need for them.' During this time a heavy rain fell, accompanied by thunder and a very terrible eclipse of the sun; and before this rain a great flight of crows hovered in the air over all those battalions, making a loud noise. Shortly afterwards it cleared up, and the sun shone very bright; but the Frenchmen had it in their faces, and the English in their backs. When the Genoese were somewhat in order, and approached the English, they set up a loud shout, in order to frighten them; but they remained quite still, and did not seem to attend to it. They then set up a second shout, and advanced a little forward; but the English never moved.

They hooted a third time, advancing with their cross-bows presented, and began to shoot. The English archers then advanced one step forward, and shot their arrows with such force and quickness, that it seemed as if it snowed. When the Genoese felt these arrows, which pierced their arms, heads, and through their armor, some of them cut the strings of their cross-bows, others flung them on the ground, and all turned about and retreated quite discomfited. The French had a large body of men-at-arms on horseback, richly dressed, to support the Genoese. The king of France, seeing them thus fall back, cried out, 'Kill me those scoundrels; for they stop up our road, without any reason.' You would then have seen the above-mentioned men-at-arms lay about them, killing all they could of these runaways.

So much for the expensive mercenary crossbowmen of Genoa, the best in all Europe. *The Chronicle of Jean de Venette* emphasised the rain. The downpour caused the Genoese crossbow strings to shrink, so that the weapons were rendered ineffective; the English archers, in contrast, had taken off their bowstrings and sheltered them under their helmets. No matter. The proud knights of France rode the Genoese down without mercy, trampling some under hooves, slashing others to death. It was the last easy killing the Frenchmen did that day. As the first line of knights approached the English lines, their horses were shot down by flights of arrows. The fallen beasts, many of which must have still been thrashing around in pain and fear, created a barrier beyond which the second line could not easily advance; other horses, perhaps panicked by the booming English cannonfire mentioned in some accounts, bolted. Knights were unhorsed, falling in heaps and unable to rise again – their mail armour was both heavy and awkward, and what might not have been a problem on the bare ground was a death sentence when a knight lay under a pile of wounded and dying men and horses. As the last attackers retreated, English bowmen and Welshmen moved agilely among the fallen, slitting throats and robbing the corpses – frustrating Edward's hope of collecting ransoms. But the king could not supervise every part of the battlefield. He ordered his knights mounted, then charged. King Philippe fought bravely, having two horses slain under him, and was wounded in the face, but at length he realised that if he did not flee, he would be captured. He abandoned the royal banner, the standard-bearer having been slain at his side, and the sacred Oriflamme of St Denis.

Such is the traditional description of the battle. However, Crécy, like all battles, was more complicated. The French had regrouped repeatedly, each time resuming the attack. This may have been random acts of courage, such as that of the blind king of Bohemia, John, who arrived late and demanded to be led into battle. Or it may have been better coordination than we have been led to believe. Nevertheless, the outcome was the same: a massacre of the French knights.

The French, needing a scapegoat, murdered many of the surviving Genoese.

Edward laid siege to Calais and eleven months later was its master. Once Calais and Rouen were in Edward's hands, he had Normandy as a base for attacks directly upon his French rival's heartland.

THE BLACK DEATH

Military activities lessened in the years to follow. The French kingdom was disorganised, first by the loss of so many important nobles, then by the death of the king from natural causes. But even more significant, some think, was the impact of the plague. This epidemic began the next year, spreading from Mediterranean ports inland, striking the urban centres ferociously and rural communities only slightly less hard.

The name 'the Black Death' was invented only in the nineteenth century, but it was quickly adopted by popular culture in every European land until today the public accepts it without question. The fearsome ring of the phrase lends itself to the images of people fleeing infected cities, of public prayers and self-flagellation designed to attract the attention and pity of the deity, and carts filled with grotesque piles of rigid corpses. *Ring Around the Rosie* dates from a later epidemic, but the principle is the same: *All Fall Down.*

In western Europe as much as a third of the population perished within a few years. Perhaps twice that number. This had a tremendous ripple effect: famine, disruption of trade, lower tax revenues, lessened willingness to put one's life at risk in hospitals and public service, and a growing callousness toward human life in general.

The immediate impact on the war was minimal, other than the obvious reduction in tax revenues and inflation. Sumption notes that most of the victims were the very young and the very old, so that recruiting was not affected until about 1360; also, it struck the nobility less often than other classes, so the number of knights and ambitious royals was hardly affected.

In the short term the kings of England and France hesitated to take their armies into a plague district; the chances were too good that all the soldiers could fall ill at the same time, with many of them sure to die and the rest unable to defend themselves or care for those who had been struck down – fighting would be out of the question. After a few years, however, it was noticed that no one ever caught the plague twice. Therefore, survivors could safely march through plague-ridden lands, and most likely, the number of disease-free men and women was now sufficiently great that it was difficult for the disease to spread to those who still lacked immunity. New outbreaks of the plague were terrible, but they neither occasioned the number of deaths nor the panic of the original epidemic.

THE FIRST BANDS OF ROBBERS

Edward III faced such financial problems that he could neither take advantage of French weakness nor consolidate his recent conquests; he could not even ward off the French armies that were again striking into Gascony and Flanders. The French king was equally unable to defend his lands. As a result, there was a breakdown of public order along the borders of Flanders, Brittany and Gascony.

Bands of robbers were holding towns and villages to ransom, and some English garrisons were doing the same. Pay was irregular and the captains of companies were more like independent contractors than royal officers. When an area's resources were exhausted, they would move to places that had not yet been looted into penury.

The most famous of these commanders was Robert Knollys, who had risen from obscurity to occupy several castles in Brittany. Feared for his ruthlessness, but admired for his military and diplomatic skills, he became one of the greatest English captains. This region would produce the most fierce warriors of the next generation, among whom was the French hero, Bertrand du Guesclin.

Similar bands arose in France, most notably the giant company of Arnaud de Cervole, known widely as 'the archpriest' because his first career had been in the Church; expelled from his parish by the archbishop of Bordeaux (an English partisan), he enlisted in the French forces and earned fame, wealth and a good marriage.

These independent military units were called *routiers*. The victims referred to most of them as *English* because their allegiance was to Edward, but in fact many were Gascons. A favourite tactic was escalade – slipping quietly up to a town's walls by night, placing tall ladders up to the battlements or simply clambering up like monkeys, and then, by setting fires and making noise, they would confuse and frighten the defenders into flight. They could then sack the town and escape before reinforcements could arrive. Sleepy and bored night watchmen often failed to see their approach – old walls had odd angles and suburban houses obscured the views. Defenders learned only slowly to correct these defects.

A French effort to take Calais by surprise failed when the Italian commander of the garrison, Aimeric of Pavia, agreed to open the gates in return for a large bribe, then informed Edward III. The king hurriedly crossed the channel and set a trap. The French, confident that all Italians were devious and untrustworthy, paid Aimeric the first instalment of the bribe, then, when the French royal banner appeared on the gate, hurried across the drawbridge. There they found themselves trapped – the drawbridge was raised and the portcullis lowered; meanwhile, Edward and his son, the Black Prince, sallied out against the waiting army, routing them into the sands and marshes where many drowned. First lesson: never trust anyone you believe is devious and untrustworthy. Second lesson: almost nobody in this era was anything else.

King John II (1350–64) of France, deciding that low morale among the French nobility was a major problem, created the Order of the Star. This expensive emulation of Edward III's Order of the Garter may have contributed somewhat to his chief vassals' willingness to engage the English in battle again.

$$\times$$

THE BATTLE OF POITIERS

By 1356 Edward III was busy in Scotland; command on the Continent was exercised by his talented sons, Edward, the Prince of Wales (*the Black Prince*, so called by the French for his livery, though the term was not used in England for another 200 years), Henry of Lancaster and John of Gaunt. Their strategy was to wear the French down by long plundering raids (*chevauchées*) through central France.

His opponent was John II, known later as John the Good – the untalented Philippe's untalented successor. Happy is the country whose peacetime ruler is called 'the Good'; alas for that same country in wartime. Sumption, looking at John's efforts to restore order to the kingdom, is highly critical of the devaluation of the currency in 1352, the simultaneous imposition of price controls and non-payment of debts, and the lavish expenditures on the ceremonies for the Order of the Star. In the short term John had enough money to raise armies, but each army went down to ignominious defeat. In the long term the economy was dislocated – and the incomes of those living from fixed rents, the Church in particular, fell dramatically. John was not a lucky monarch – Sumption summarises his policies as 'inglorious in the north and scandalous in the south'. In 1355 he devalued the coinage eight times and in 1356 he again suspended payments on his debts. Many vassals began to murmur that he was incompetent and should be replaced; rumours of plots and treason abounded.

When John heard of the Black Prince's raid into the rich lands along the Loire River, he had to act. He could not allow royal revenues to sink even farther, or what remained of his reputation to vanish. He certainly had men enough to defeat any ordinary feudal army.

Awkwardly, the Black Prince's forces were not a typical feudal army — England had what amounted to a monopoly on the longbow, and by now it was a rare French army that could defeat a force of properly led English archers. It was also a rare community that did not shudder for generations after being visited by a rapacious force of sturdy islanders. Although the English prided themselves on the accomplishments of these men, which were almost always outnumbered (causing the Duke of Wellington to quip once, late in life, that the English race had deteriorated so far that ten Frenchmen *could* beat one Englishman). Nevertheless, by no means were all the soldiers and knights born and bred in England. Many were Gascons, English subjects from the time of Eleanor of Aquitaine almost 300 years before; others were Germans and yet others French; a few were Irish and many were Welsh.

John summoned his vassals to assemble at Chartres. He sent home the infantry units — a widely criticised move — partly because he believed that only cavalry could move swiftly enough to catch the Black Prince, partly because infantry were not effective against archers. When he set off southward, the royal array was large and encumbered with many baggage carts. Consequently, it was disorganised. The hurried march to cut off the Black Prince's escape disorganised it more. Enthusiastic volunteers in search of chivalric adventure could not make up this deficiency.

The Black Prince was unaware of the king's approach until he was almost upon him. He then sent messengers to search for his brother, Henry, duke of Lancaster, who, with Robert Knollys, had earlier led the king a merry chase through Normandy and was now believed to be just to the west. If they could join forces, it would be safe to offer combat — and the prudent king, according to habit, would probably retreat. However, Henry could not be located. Reluctantly, the Black Prince started south. It soon became apparent that his booty-laden wagons were moving too slowly to leave the French behind, and, rather than be overhauled, he took his column into the woods, certain that the king would hesitate to follow. Ambush would have been all too easy.

John did not worry. By staying on the roads he could easily get in front of his adversary. He could then force the Black Prince to accept combat on French terms.

After John had taken up a blocking position on the old Roman road to Bordeaux, with his prey still struggling thorough the forest, his strategic situation was much better than his father's at Crécy. However, the king was learning how difficult it was to placate his fire-eating vassals. His men were willing to wait for the Black Prince to straggle down on to the plain, but that was all – he did not have the kind of authority that could impose an unpopular strategy on an unruly army. His vassals wanted to fight – that is, they wanted to ride the enemy down, if possible; if not, they would dismount from their horses and attack on foot – that would avoid having injured or dead mounts interfere with their advance. They obeyed the king for the moment, but they were impatient.

When the Black Prince came out of the woods and looked down the road, he saw that further movement west and then south was impossible; moving east made no sense, since that was the way back into France. Hoping for a French mistake, he took up a defensive position on a wooded slope, with vineyards and a hedge that promised to impede French horsemen in any charge; there was a steep slope and a small marsh on one flank that extended to a small river, and archers dug a deep ditch on the other. But there was no water and the food had been exhausted. The soldiers were complaining about their plight – they were tired, hungry, thirsty, and aware that they were badly outnumbered again. The Black Prince initially welcomed a cardinal sent by the pope to mediate. Hoping to escape without fighting, he offered to free all prisoners without ransom, to surrender all captured castles and towns and to sign a seven-year truce, perhaps even to surrender Calais. But he became suspicious that the prelate was attempting to drag out the negotiations until his supplies were gone. Besides, King John rejected the offer unless the prince accepted further humiliating conditions.

It was not to be. As King John conferred with his vassals, he learned that there were problems with his own supplies and that his men were losing confidence in him. The English had slipped away before. He did not want to attack head-on, but there was no way to flank the English. At least one prominent French noble spoke in favour of starving the English out. But he was hooted down. The king chose to be delighted at his men's fighting spirit – he would attack, he promised, and attack soon. He ordered his knights to be ready to advance on foot, the hill being steep and one lesson of Crécy being that horses were easy and vulnerable targets. Another prudent measure was to dress nineteen other nobles in black and the royal insignia, thus making it more difficult for the English to concentrate their fire on him. The last moment for sober reflection vanished when scouts saw English supply wagons moving away, across the river and into another forest. The king, fearing that the English forces would follow, ordered his knights forward. That command was unnecessary – some of his commanders, seeing movement in the English ranks, had already mounted and attacked. These met the usual fate of heavy French cavalry charging English archers.

The royal strategy at Poitiers was to advance on foot in three lines. As the first line struggled through gaps in the hedges and vines, they formed protective clumps behind their shields and moved on uphill. The English archers fired into the mass of slow-moving knights from the flanks, but without causing many casualties. The decisive moment came when the heavily armoured men had struggled almost to the top of the hill, only to encounter English knights charging downhill. Many French knights, knocked into piles, were unable to get back on their feet. Meanwhile, the second line had come up. After almost two hours of fighting the French line wavered, and when the dauphin was led from the field, perhaps at the king's orders, most of the surviving knights followed him. The king then led the third line into the battle, suffering few casualties because the archers had emptied their quivers. These were fresh men, and there was a moment when they might have broken the English line, but the king was unable to direct his men toward a weak point. As the archers threw themselves on to the tiring knights, a small band of English knights galloped in from the flank. The Black Prince, seeing the effect this was having, ordered the horses brought up, mounted as many knights as he could, and charged. The French king and his best knights were surrounded and soon surrendered. Froissart described the scene:

> The prince of Wales, who was as courageous as a lion, took great delight that day to combat his enemies. Sir John Chandos, who was near his person, and had never quitted it during the whole of the day, nor stopped to make prisoners, said to him toward the end of the battle; 'Sir, it will be proper for you to halt here, and plant your banner on the top of this bush, which will serve to rally your forces, that seem very much scattered; for I do not see any banners or pennons of the French, nor any considerable bodies able to rally

against us; and you must refresh yourself a little, as I perceive you are very much heated.' Upon this the banner of the prince was placed on a high bush: the minstrels began to play, and trumpets and clarions to do their duty. The prince took off his helmet, and the knights attendant on his person, and belonging to his chamber, were soon ready, and pitched a small pavilion of crimson color, which the prince entered. Liquor was then brought to him and the other knights who were with him: they increased every moment; for they were returning from the pursuit, and stopped there surrounded by their prisoners.

While the king was escorted to a very pleasant captivity in England, all hell was loosed on his kingdom. Robbers and kidnappers seemed to be everywhere. Though various assemblies attempted to pass regulations for reforms and new taxes, the nobles and clergy rejected the plans – and from captivity the king encouraged resistance to any new taxes.

The citizens of Paris slaughtered the royal officers in the very presence of the dauphin, peasants murdered their lords. The rebel leader, Étienne Marcel, took the dauphin captive and called the Estates-General into session; he was the *de facto* ruler of France until the dauphin escaped and collected followers to make war on Paris. Marcel, for his part, hired English archers and stationed them around the city, then plotted to put on the throne Charles of Navarre (Carlos the Bad, 1349–87), the husband of John's daughter Joan. Charles of Navarre, like Edward III, had a claim on the throne from his mother and he hated the Valois family, which had thrown him into prison for various excellent reasons, including murder, until his escape in the midst of the recent administrative chaos. Charles was plausibly more capable of governing than the immature dauphin; he had experienced mercenaries from his own kingdom, and if he could acquire Champaign and Burgundy, he would be powerful indeed. Meanwhile, taxes could not be collected, troops could not be paid, and mercenaries who were dismissed by their employers struck out on their own. That is, as freebooters. As the name implies, their goal was booty and they were free men, going wherever they wished and doing whatever they wanted. Froissart, the lover of chivalry and noble gestures, described this process:

> About this period, a knight, named sir Arnold de Cervole, but
> more commonly called the archpriest, collected a large body of

men-at-arms, who came from all parts, seeing that their pay would not be continued in France, and that, since the capture of the king, there was not any probability of their gaining more in that country. They marched first into Provence, where they took many strong towns and castles, and ruined the country by their robberies as far as Avignon. Pope Innocent VI. [1352–62], who resided in Avignon, was much alarmed, as not knowing what might be the intentions of the archpriest, the leader of these forces; and, for fear of personal insult, he and the cardinals kept their household armed day and night. When the archpriest and his troops had pillaged all the country, the pope and clergy entered into treaty with him. Having received with proper security, he and the greater part of his people entered Avignon, where he was received with as much respect as if he had been son to the king of France.

The Archpriest could never have risen this high if he had remained in holy orders. He dined with the pope and his cardinals, received absolution for all his sins, and enjoyed other honours until he finally promised to lead his army away. He took 40,000 crowns from the pope to pay his men, who then dispersed to various locations.

At this time, also, there was another company of men-at-arms, or robbers, collected from all parts, who stationed themselves between the rivers Loire and Seine, so that no one dared to travel between Paris and Orleans, nor between Paris and Montargis, or even to remain in the country; the inhabitants on the plains had all fled to Paris and Orleans. This company had chosen for their leader a Welshman named Ruffin, whom they had knighted, and who acquired such immense riches as could not be counted. These companies advanced one day near to Paris, another day toward Orleans, another time to Chartres; and there was no town nor fortress but what was taken and pillaged...They rode over the country in parties of twenty, thirty, or forty, meeting with none to check their pillage; while, on the sea-coast of Normandy, there were still a greater number of English and Navarrois, plunderers, and robbers. Sir Robert Knollys was their leader, who conquered every town and castle he came to, as there was no one to oppose him. Sir Robert had followed this trade for some time, and by it gained upward of

100,000 crowns. He kept a great many soldiers in his pay; and, being very liberal, he was cheerfully followed and obeyed.

France fell into chaos. Upstart bands took control of the countryside. Peasants who had been robbed and burned out could not pay taxes, and without taxes royal officials could not hire troops to restore order. It was a cycle of increasing violence and impoverishment that would last, with several short interruptions, for years.

Most of these companies, Fowler notes in *Medieval Mercenaries*, organised themselves much as they had been when in royal service, but others, such as the Gascons – who supplied a disproportionate number of warriors and brigands – were more loosely organised. Many lords from the foothills of the Pyrenees brought their volunteers north.

There were oddities, Sumption notes, such as Étienne Marcel accusing the dauphin of being ineffective in fighting the English, then hiring English bowmen to hold St Denis and other strong points around Paris against him. The heir to the absent king, who was beginning to see the connections between foreign enemies, the free companies, his uncooperative vassals, the refusals to pay taxes, the peasant uprisings, the machinations of the pope and the interests of the merchants, was powerless to do more than ride the wave of patriotism that was sweeping the country. Marcel and Charles of Navarre were on the eve of a coup, after which they would murder all their enemies and declare Charles king, but the Parisians struck first. Marcel was among their first victims.

Charles of Navarre then established a base just outside Paris and sent out a call for men-at-arms. Soon mercenaries from Brabant, Germany, Hainault and Bohemia were flocking to him. Froissart says that these warriors came willingly to serve under him because he could pay them out of the fortune he had amassed thanks to his connection with the late provost. As freebooters spread across northern France, demanding food and money, they soon had the dauphin's men confined to their castles; they were so secure that they could ride around the countryside unarmed, visiting one another, just as if France were at peace.

Eliminating these pests became a high priority for the dauphin – right after coming to some accommodation with Charles of Navarre. But he could not raise an army without money; the country had been stripped clean by the foreign locusts, and there was simply nothing left to take. The mercenaries had, without planning to do so, almost guaranteed their own safety – the lords who wanted to destroy them lacked the means to do so, and the rest wanted to hire their services.

The most common answer was to hire more mercenaries and use them to suppress the competition. This was not easily done, because the mercenaries were smart enough to see through whatever rhetoric attempted to disguise the strategy. You might use a thief to catch a thief, but it was much harder to persuade one mercenary to kill another. Still, that was the only method the royal advisors could think of. They hired mercenaries, put them under the command of the Archpriest, then gave him the task of ridding the country of freebooters. He failed miserably.

Large towns proved almost impossible for the freebooters to capture. Their armies, so formidable in the field, were too small for sieges. The technology was still ineffective, and the defenders too numerous and determined. But cities were willing to pay the companies off. Already suffering from the cost of building new walls and hiring garrisons, the ever-heavier taxes and the floods of refugees who had to be housed and fed, cities could not afford to have commerce interrupted.

This seemed to be Charles of Navarre's strategy for taking Paris. He had stationed English troops in small forts all around the great city, all living off the countryside. The defenders eventually realised that they could capture these small forts while the garrisons were away pillaging. That prevented the companies from flitting from one undefended stronghold to another, but it did little to crush them. In 1359, when Charles of Navarre abandoned his claims to the crown, saying that he wanted to prevent the destruction of France, he was unable to persuade his troops to disperse; the bands remained in their lairs and preyed on the communities round about. Only in the Champagne region were local forces able to crush the companies and execute their leaders. Elsewhere the companies prevailed and prospered until they had stripped the country bare.

One bizarre plan to rid France of the mercenaries was to hire the king of Denmark, Waldemar IV (1340–75) to invade England and free King John; Waldemar dreamed of re-establishing Danish rule over the island kingdom, to match the empire he was trying to create in the Baltic. But the French lacked the money to pay him and Waldemar had wars sufficient to keep any monarch busy. Another plan was for the king of Hungary, Louis the Great (1342–82), to hire the free companies to fight the Turks, but that war was far away, the opportunities to collect booty would be few, and the chances of being slain great; moreover, the Germans in the Rhineland resisted the archpriest's efforts to lead east the forces he had hired with papal and imperial money – Charles IV (1347–78), a close friend of Pope Urban V, had grand plans for strengthening imperial authority, reviving the crusades and restoring order in France. The problem was that nobody in Germany wanted the companies to pass through their lands, because the routiers might decide to ravage them rather than fight Turks. Fowler calls the entire venture 'misconceived and badly handled'. The pope, hiding behind his stout fortifications at Avignon on the Rhône River, then tried to send the free companies into Italy, but the mercenaries considered his treasury a better prize. He was saved by local resistance along the way – but those Frenchmen had fought to protect themselves, not to save the pope.

These freebooters were often called 'Englishmen', as many were. But it was a thoroughly international force, as Froissart informs us:

> During all this time, the king of England was making such great preparations for his expedition into France, that the like was never seen before; on which account, many barons and knights of the German Empire, who had formerly served him, exerted themselves much this year, and provided themselves handsomely in horses and equipage in the best manner they could, each according to his rank, and hastened as fast as possible, by the frontiers of Flanders, to Calais, where they remained, to wait for the king of England. It happened that the king could not come thither with his army by the time appointed, which caused such numbers to remain at Calais, that there were no lodgings for them, nor stables for their horses. In addition to this, bread, wine, hay, oats, and all sorts of provisions, were so scarce, that none could be had for money.
>
> Thus did these mercenary Germans, Bohemians, Brabanters, Flemings, Hainaulters, both poor and rich, wait from the beginning of August until St. Luke's day [18 October]; so that many were forced to sell the greater part of their jewels. If the king had arrived then, they would not have known where to have lodged him and his people, except in the castle, for the whole town was occupied. There was also some doubt if these lords who had spent their all, would have quitted Calais, for the king or any one else, if their expenses had not been allowed out of good-will to him, in hopes of grace and favor; others, with the expectation of gaining from the plunder of France.

One small community, Peronne, decided that it could defend itself if it could attract a competent commander with a disciplined force. Asking around whether a trustworthy Frenchman existed who was not yet engaged, they learned that Galahaut de Ribemmont was nearby. They sent him a letter offering him twenty livres per day, ten livres for each knight under his command, and for any 'lance' (a man-at-arms and a squire) seven livres. He set out for Peronne the next day with thirty lances, but his numbers increased along the way. Not long afterward we learn that these mercenaries had as much difficulty telling one another apart as we do. Froissart tells us:

> The same morning, sir Reginald de Boullant, a German knight belonging to the duke of Lancaster's division, had rode forth since daybreak, and, having made a large circuit without seeing any one, had halted at that spot. The two squires, being come thither, imagined they might be some persons of the country, who had placed themselves there in ambuscade, and rode so near that each party saw the other. The two Frenchmen, therefore, consulted together, and said, 'If they be Germans, we must pretend we belong to them: if they be of this part of the country, we will tell them who we are.' When they were so near each other that they could speak, the two squires soon perceived, by their uniforms, that they were Germans and their enemies. Sir Reginald de Boullant spoke to them in German, and inquired whose soldiers they were. Bridoul de Tallonne, who well understood that language, answered, 'We belong to sir Bartholomew Burghersh.' 'And where is sir Bartholomew?' 'He is,' replied he, 'in the village.' 'For what reason has he stopped here?' 'Sir, because he has sent us forward, to see if we can find anything to forage in this part of the country.' 'By my faith, there is not,' answered sir Reginald; 'for I have been all over it, and have not been able to pick up anything. Return to him, and tell him to advance and we will ride together as far as St. Quentin, and see if we cannot find out a better country, or some good adventure.'

The need to deal with these ruffian bands was obvious to everyone, but there was also a desire to have mercenaries available. This meant that serious efforts to disband the free companies was possible only at those rare moments when the kings agreed upon a general peace.

The treaty of 1360 confirmed Edward III's conquests in the south of France. While Edward sent Chandos and others to restore order there, the French king brought in Prince Henry of Castile (Enrique, 1369–79), who employed Spanish mercenaries to eliminate perhaps half of the free companies. Further plans to lure the free companies out of France, hopefully to some distant war in which most of them would die, all came to naught. Anarchy ruled over wide areas, as Froissart explained:

> While the commissioners and deputies of the king of England
> were taking seisin and possessions of the aforesaid lands, according
> to the articles of peace, other commissioners and deputies were on
> the frontiers of France with commissioners from that king, order-
> ing all men-at-arms, who were garrisoned in the different castles
> and forts of France, to evacuate and surrender them to the king of
> France, under pain of confiscation and death. There were some
> knights and squires attached to England who obeyed, and sur-
> rendered, or made their companions surrender such forts as they
> held; but there were others who would not obey, saying that they
> had made war in the name of the king of Navarre. There were also
> some from different countries, who were great captains and pil-
> lagers, that would not, on any account, leave the country; such as
> Germans, Brabanters, Flemings, Hainaulters, Gascons and bad
> Frenchmen, who had been impoverished by the war; these persons
> persevered in their wickedness, and did afterwards much mischief
> to the kingdom.
>
> When the captains of the forts had handsomely delivered them
> up, with all they contained, they marched off, and when in the
> plain, they dismissed their people; but those who had been so long
> accustomed to pillage, knowing well that their return home would
> not be advantageous for them, but that they might perhaps suffer
> for the bad actions they had committed, assembled together, and
> chose new leaders from the worst disposed among them... Their
> numbers were perpetually increasing; for those who quitted the
> castles and towns on their being surrendered, and who were
> disbanded by their captains, came into those parts; so that by Lent
> they amounted to at least sixteen thousand combatants.

The result of discharging the mercenaries from English and French service thus resulted in the creation of new armies, not peace. These armies, moreover, lacked the few restraints that their royal employers had put upon them – Froissart, in fact, suspected that Edward encouraged them to remain in France rather than return home, where they might become a nuisance. To make the matter worse, the free companies were reinforced by what Froissart called *Tard-Venus* (latecomers). The sole goal of these impromptu soldiers was to enrich themselves.

The crisis came in April of 1362, when a French army of 6,000 horsemen went in pursuit of a body of routiers at Brignais on the Rhone River. The French commander, hearing that these newcomers were undisciplined and only half-armed, led his knights toward an equal number of brigands, pennons flying, in expectations of an easy victory. His scouts located the companies on a plateau at Brignais, but reported them to be less numerous and more poorly armed than expected. The greatest difficulty was reaching the enemy atop a steep hill, but since the foe seemed more like desperate peasants than warriors, he ordered his men to clamber up to them despite the barrage of rocks and stones. Thus occupied, he did not see the freebooters' main force come through the woods until it struck his rear. The French army was quickly overwhelmed, only a handful of men escaping.

Fowler's more reliable description of the battle is more complex – the French divided their forces, part assaulting the hill, the rest fighting a 'set-piece battle on a plain'. When the companies on the hill routed their opponents and came down to strike the main army in the rear, they surrounded, then killed or captured almost the entire force.

The routiers then spread out, ravaging, collecting ransom, growing ever larger. It would be years before they were brought under control. As Froissart recounted:

> They collected their companies together, and kept advancing to-ward Avignon, at which the pope and cardinals were much alarm-ed. These companions had chosen, at the Pont du St. Esprit, a captain to command the whole of their forces, who was commonly styled the friend of God, and the enemy of all the world.
>
> There were at that time in France, besides these companies, many other pillagers, English, Gascons, and Germans, who were desirous of living there, and who maintained many garrisons in fortresses. Although the commissaries from the king of England

had ordered them to evacuate these castles, and to leave the country, they had not obeyed, which was very displeasing to the king of France, as well as to his council.

These new latecomers, spurred by the hope of looting the papal treasury, hurried to join the victors of Brignais to form what became known as the 'Great Company'. In their imagination, they were already sacking Provence, the richest part of southern France.

When the Pope Innocent VI. and the Roman college saw themselves thus threatened by these accursed people, they were exceedingly alarmed, and ordered a croisade to be published against these wicked Christians, who were doing everything in their power to destroy Christianity (like Vandals of old, without right or reason) by ruining all the countries whither they resorted; by robbing, wherever they could find anything; by violating women, both young and old, without pity; and by killing men, women, and children, without mercy, who had done no ill to them; for he was reckoned the bravest, and most honored, who could boast of the most villainous actions.

The pope and the cardinals had therefore a croisade publicly preached. They absolved from every crime and sin all those who should take the cross, and voluntarily give themselves up to destroy these wretches. The cardinals elected the lord Peter de Monstier, cardinal d'Arras, by some called cardinal d'Ostia, to be the chief of this croisade; who, upon his nomination, immediately left Avignon, and went to Carpentras, seven leagues distant, where he fixed his quarters. He retained all soldiers, and others, who were desirous of saving their souls, and of gaining the foresaid pardons; but he would not give them any pay, which caused many of them to depart and go into Lombardy; others returned into their own countries, and some divided themselves into several companies, over each of which they nominated captains, and took up their quarters in different places. Thus they harassed the pope, the cardinals, and the merchants in the neighborhood of Avignon, and did a great deal of mischief until the summer was far advanced of the year 1361.

Jean de Venette was more forthright: 'Those sons of Belial and men of iniquity, warriors from various lands who assailed other men with no right and no reason other than their own passions, iniquity, malice and hope of gain and yet were called the Great Company'. Many were Bretons, hardened by the cruelties of their own civil war.

The Great Company was the largest force of freebooters ever assembled. Thoroughly international and professionally organised, it included young English fighters like John Hawkwood, who accompanied part of the army to Italy when the pope made arrangements for it to fight on the other side of the Alps. This 'White Company' was employed by the enemies of the Visconti of Milan, among whom the pope was prominent. The remainder of the army continued to plunder southern France.

The French king, desperate to pay his ransom, agreed to marry his daughter to the Visconti upstart, Gian Galeazzo. 600,000 gold florins flowed into the royal coffers, Chaucer went to Milan with the bride, Petrarch came north to praise the wise king, and Froissart, with the queen's encouragement, began to write his chronicle. But it was not enough and it was quickly spent. King John, unable to pay his ransom, returned voluntarily to England, where he died in 1364.

Charles V (1364–80) was luckier. When civil war broke out in Spain in 1365 – Henry of Castile against his reigning half-brother, Pedro the Cruel (1350–69) – the English and French naturally took opposing sides. Sumption does his best – which is pretty good – to explain this confusing situation which must have puzzled contemporaries almost as much as it confuses us. Fowler's reconstruction of the campaign is less ambitious, and therefore clearer.

Henry was the eldest son of his father's prolific mistress; failing in his effort to displace Pedro, he had fled for his life and taken up the profession of mercenary soldier. He had the support of Aragon, which had been fighting Pedro for a decade, and France, since Pedro seemed to have murdered his queen, the sister of the French monarch. Charles of Navarre, declaring himself neutral, closed his borders; though this did not stop Chaucer and friends from touring his kingdom, it prevented Pedro from hiring Gascon and English mercenaries.

To draw the free companies out of France and into Spain, Charles V signed a peace treaty with Edward and began to hire routiers. Jean of Vedette recorded of this, 'the thieves and robbers who in time of war had heaped ill upon ill and loss upon loss ... began little by little to decrease and diminish in numbers'. The wealth they had stolen, he noted, melted away like snow in the sun. A few must have shrugged – easy come, easy go. But most dragged themselves home in disgrace or signed on to the Spanish expedition.

In 1366 du Guesclin led Breton mercenaries out of Normandy, which they had been looting from end to end, and marched south to Avignon, where Pope Urban V gave them absolution and money, then on to Aragon, where Prince Henry was waiting. In an effort to make this venture seem to be a crusade – against a tyrant surrounded by Jews and Muslims – the pope excommunicated Pedro and Henry crowned du Guesclin king of Granada. This implied that war against the Moors would follow the conquest of Castile. It was a reasonable cover story that paralysed English efforts to stop the campaign. The troops did not care. Muslim Spain was known to be fabulously wealthy. Similarly, the people of Aragon could approve of that more than expanding a wearying regional conflict.

Du Guesclin's men, whose gleaming armour greatly impressed Spanish observers, were quickly hustled across Aragon, lest they decided to tarry and enrich themselves from the local population; they were followed by packs of Germans and Frenchmen eager to loot defenceless villages and towns. So great was du Guesclin's force, perhaps 12,000 men, that King Pedro fled from place to place without fighting and at length sailed away.

Henry, imagining that the kingdom was firmly in his grip, dismissed most of his mercenaries. By allowing most du Guesclin's victorious troops to return home, Henry made a serious mistake – no king was ever securely on his throne, and certainly not Henry. The mercenaries would have liked another war, but they were already rich beyond belief.

The defeated king of Castile, now a fugitive, called on the Black Prince. This seemed the opportunity for English intervention, since there was no secret that du Guesclin would eventually move against Charles of Navarre, then cross the Pyrenees into Gascony. But the Black Prince was short of money and, moreover, at the moment needed every man he had to suppress banditry. Froissart related the principal arguments for him to act:

> Great complaints were daily made to the prince of the bad conduct
> of the free companies, who were doing all possible mischief to the
> inhabitants of the countries where they were quartered. They
> pressed the prince to hasten his march, who would willingly have
> complied, if he had not been advised to let Christmas pass over, so
> that he should have winter in his rear.

Du Guesclin's forces were, meanwhile, slowly disappearing. Some, paid off, went home. The English and Gascons, perhaps 4,500 of them, joined the Black Prince. The rest were dispersed as an army of occupation, and not all of the commanders were trustworthy – du Guesclin had to hang several for conspiring against his life.

When the Black Prince ordered an army to be raised, Chandos hurriedly sent word to the free companies: the game was afoot. There was no way the French could prevent him from leading his army into Navarre – Charles having had himself taken prisoner as an excuse for not attempting resistance. The Prince of Wales, still only thirty-six, was at the height of his power and popularity. Troops swarmed to him.

Du Guesclin, recruiting locally, may have raised an army of 66,000 men, an incredible size for that era. If true, he had six to ten times the number of the Black Prince. The army's fighting qualities, however, being questionable, du Guesclin concluded that it would be wiser to defend the passes and avoid a general engagement.

The Black Prince's army, in contrast, resembled, in Venier's words, a veterans' reunion – all the great names of the past twenty years were there. Even so, the campaign was not an easy one. He set out early in 1367, having waited for the mountain passes to be snow free, yet hoping to avoid the intense heat of a Spanish summer. There were obstacles to overcome – rivers to cross in the face of resistance, the lack of food and fodder, disease – but eventually the Black Prince brought his array to a place between Najera and Navaretta where du Guesclin had to fight or give way altogether. Then came one of those unforgettable moments that soldiers so often remember vividly, whether it is the assembling of forces at Waterloo or the vast armada at Normandy. Just before the desperate work of fighting begins, there is the spectacle of battle, or impending battle, the inspiring rituals of parade and display, and a rare glimpse of the commanding officers. Froissart described this with breathtaking prose:

> When the sun was risen it was a beautiful sight to view these batta-
> lions, with their brilliant armor glittering with its beams…The prince,
> with a few attendants, mounted a small hill, and saw very clearly the
> enemy marching straight toward them. Upon descending this hill, he
> extended his line of battle in the plain, and then halted. The Span-
> iards, seeing the English had halted, did the same order of battle; then
> each man tightened his armor, and made ready as for instant combat.

Sir John Chandos advanced in front of the battalions, with his banner uncased in his hand. He presented it to the prince, saying: 'My lord, here is my banner: I present it to you, that I may display it in whatever manner shall be most agreeable to you; for thanks to God, I have now sufficient lands to enable me so to do, and maintain the rank which it ought to hold.'

...The English and Gascons soon after dismounted on the heath, and assembled very orderly together, each lord under his banner or pennon, in the same battle array as when they passed the mountains.

It was delightful to see and examine these banners and pennons, with the noble army that was under them. The two armies began to move a little, and to approach nearer each other; but, before they met, the prince of Wales, with eyes and hands uplifted toward heaven, exclaimed: 'God of truth, the Father of Jesus Christ, who has made and fashioned me, condescend, through thy benign grace, that the success of the battle of this day may be for me and my army; for thou knowest, that in truth I have been solely emboldened to undertake it in the support of justice and reason, to reinstate this king upon his throne, who has been disinherited and driven from it, as well as from his country.' After these words, he extended his right arm, took hold of don Pedro's hand, who was by his side, and added, 'Sir king, you shall this day know whether you will have anything in the kingdom of Castille or not.' He then cried out, 'Advance, banners, in the name of God and St. George!'

It was a hard-fought battle, but more complicated than any one medieval chronicler described. Fowler's reconstruction in *Medieval Mercenaries* emphasises the English achieving tactical surprise by a flanking march, the ineffective formation thrown up by the defenders, and the low morale of Henry's men. The Black Prince overwhelmed the few warriors willing to fight for du Guesclin. The French hero was soon a prisoner again.

This made little difference in the long run. The most that can be said was that the free companies were out of France for a period, that some mercenaries did perish, the Navarre forces were quieted, and many English bowmen and cavalry became rich enough to contemplate going home and investing their earnings.

Otherwise, Najera was a disappointing victory. King Pedro made himself so unpopular that only Englishmen wept when du Guesclin ('needing a war', in Venier's phrase, to repay 100,000 gold coins to the king for his ransom and revitalise his career) promised to recover Henry's kingdom. The immensely popular *Chanson de Bertrand du Guesclin* credited him with pausing on his way back to Castile to give the duke of Anjou victory in his contest with Joanna of Naples, one of the tougher women of medieval history, and the pope excommunicated him for extorting money from communities along the way. No one doubts he was acting the mercenary soldier then. He had little difficulty in capturing the northern cities of Castile, but the process of taking the southern towns was slow. The apparent stalemate (Pedro was accused of having hired Muslims and Jews) ended when Henry confronted Pedro in du Guesclin's lodgings – lured there, perhaps, by a promise of a negotiated surrender – and, after a shouting match, murdered him. Although chroniclers' accounts differ, Pedro seems to have started the scuffle and might well have killed his half-brother if Henry had not had friends present.

England had been unable to improve its strategic position. Gascony had already suffered a severe decline in population and subsequent French invasions would make that even worse. That once rich wine land would become a drain on the English Exchequer.

In the years to come, Bertrand du Guesclin would rally the French forces and retake towns and castles from the English one by one. By the end of 1370, Fowler says, the year du Gueslin was named constable, he had eliminated the great companies from most of France. His victory at Pontvallain, a minor combat compared to great battles of the past, was the turning point – he surprised the English forces, then ran the surviving units to ground. This native of Brittany, with a name no Frenchman could pronounce, became a national hero. He would ransom Englishmen who could pay, but executed French captives as traitors. There was nothing soft or sentimental about him. He was a war machine. Naturally, he used mercenary troops in his liberation of French provinces from 'foreign' rule.

This was possible because Charles V, known as 'the Wise', persuaded his subjects to accept new taxes on salt and on each hearth. In time these taxes would produce great revenues and would remain the mainstay of the royal government until the French Revolution. Also, John II had installed Charles's brother, Philippe the Bold (1363–1404), in Burgundy – a vast territory which stretched from the south of France into the Low Countries – restoring order in those lands. Unfortunately, like all the king's nearest relatives, Philippe yearned to be an independent monarch or – yet better – to become king of

France himself in place of Charles's unhappy successor, Charles VI (1380–1422), who was periodically insane.

MORE WAR

When the conflict resumed, the French generally had the better of the fighting. England was experiencing domestic unrest, and the new young king, Richard II (1377–99) was an ineffective leader. Worse, some of those he selected to fight on his behalf were no better.

Take, for example, the 1383 'crusade' of Bishop Henry Despenser. All that demonstrated was that each of the two rival popes (Rome and Avignon) were quite willing to use whatever means were available to defeat the other. In short, not even the Church could be trusted to work for peace. Though all parties listened politely to papal representatives, no secular ruler and few ecclesiastical ones were willing to sacrifice themselves on the altar of someone else's vision of peace.

The English still had heroes such as John Chandos. But it is one thing to be a hero, another to be a heroic king. In this age, in England, it took a king to win a war. And the Black Prince, uncrowned, had gone to an early grave in 1376, a year before his father, the great Edward III. Fifty years of national triumph would be followed by decades of defeat.

THE WAR SLOWS ... AND STOPS

Local forces continued to make headway against bands of robbers and thieves, partly because, with the end of the English raids, farmers did not have to turn to plundering themselves to avoid starvation. Siege operations against frontier fortresses continued, because these could be mounted relatively quickly and perhaps even terminated before a relief army could be gathered.

Even important castles were vulnerable, because financial restraints kept the garrisons small. Without troops to sally out and drive away the forces filling the moats and digging tunnels, to destroy siege machinery and drive away besiegers' horses and cattle, the most any commander could do was to send for help.

A typical siege did not actually involve significant fighting. The two sides sized up each individual situation, then made a practical agreement, as in the case of the castle at la Roche sur Yon, a key fortress in Anjou. After the English had surrounded the stronghold, they set up the catapults and cannons, brought up provisions and sent out raiders to bring in more food. When ready to attack, they approached the enemy commander, Sir John Blondeau. Froissart described the scene:

> In the army of the earl of Cambridge, with sir John Chandos and the other barons, were some knights from Poitou well acquainted with the governor, and who in former times had been his companions in arms. These knights advanced to the barriers, and upon their faith and assurances held a conversation with him, and talked the matter over so ably (for he was not a sensible man, though a valiant knight,) that he entered into a treaty to deliver up the castle, if he were not succored, nor the siege raised, within a month; when he was to receive the sum of six thousand francs for the provisions in it. The treaty thus entered into was ratified; and the garrison remained quiet, under condition, that if the castle was not relieved within a month, it should be surrendered. This being done, the knight sent information of it to the king of France, the dukes of Anjou and of Berry, and to all the lords from whom he expected assistance, in order that he might be secure from any reproaches they might cast upon him. Notwithstanding these informations...no relief was sent; so that, when the month was expired, the English lords summoned the governor to perform his promise, for which he had given good hostages. Sir John... said to his companions, 'Since the king of France and the duke of Anjou are determined to lose this castle, I cannot defend it alone;' he therefore delivered it up to the English, who took possession with great joy. The governor received the sum of six thousand francs, as agreed upon for the provision in the castle, which was well worth it; and he and his garrison were escorted to the town of Angers.

The duke of Anjou, who was among the most effective French leaders, accused his governor of having (literally) sold out. According to one story, he threw him into prison; according to another, he sewed him into a sack and cast him into the river. The duke's contention was that the castle had supplies for a year and should have held out that long. One might wonder why the duke had appointed a dolt as commander. But quite likely the problem was not the commander, who was acknowledged to be valiant, but the garrison, which might have been grumbling at the prospect of enduring a lengthy siege by dangerous enemies.

Leadership is a complicated matter, of course. If it were only question of courage and technical knowledge, of calculating supplies and planning routes of march, almost anyone could be a leader. The most difficult aspect of leadership is to persuade or coerce one's followers to follow. The man or woman who can make troops risk their lives, either in pitched battle or lengthy campaigns, often without food, drink or rest, is usually a successful commander no matter how little he or she knows about the details of army life. Details are what officers and NCOs are for.

There is usually a dearth of truly talented leaders, those who can tell instinctively what the mood of an army is, who sense when daring becomes foolhardiness. Since feudal society insisted that only nobles be considered as military commanders, this meant that the pool of potential generals was small. When a gifted commander died, it could be a disaster, as Froissart informed his readers:

> Sir John Chandos, who was a strong and bold knight, and cool in all his undertakings, had his banner advanced before him, surrounded by his men, with the scutcheon above his arms. He himself was dressed in a large robe which fell to the ground, blazoned with his arms on white sarcenet, argent, a pile gules; one on his breast, and the other on his back; so that he appeared resolved on some adventurous undertaking; and in this state, with sword in hand, he advanced on foot toward the enemy.
>
> This morning there had been a hoar-frost, which had made the ground slippery; so that as he marched he entangled his legs with his robe, which was of the longest, and made a tumble: during which time a squire, called James de St. Martin (a strong expert man), made a thrust at him with his lance, which hit him in the face, below the eye, between the nose and forehead. Sir John Chandos did not see the aim of the stroke, for he had lost the eye on that side five years ago, on the heaths of Bordeaux, at the chase of a stag; what added to his misfortune, sir John had not put down his vizor, so that in stumbling he bore upon the lance, and helped it

to enter into him. The lance, which had been struck from a strong arm, hit him so severely that it entered as far as the brain, and then the squire drew it back to him again.

From that moment on, English warriors lost heart. How sad, everyone thought, that such a great hero should die in such an ignominious manner. But how much sadder, for the English, that Chandos had no equally capable successor.

English soldiers were good, but they were only as good as their commanders allowed them to be. Like everyone else, English soldiers and mercenaries wanted to survive the wars, to return home in honour with pockets full. If their commanders lacked talent or luck, they could do neither.

Meanwhile, the king of France had named Bertrand du Guesclin constable of France. One by one this ugly but extraordinarily courageous and talented commander began to win back cities and castles that had been lost. The public mood changed. While Englishmen saw little point to fighting across the sea, the French could envision victory, and, with victory, peace. The English had already learned national pride in the course of the conflict. Now the French were doing the same.

The importance of nationalism, even in its primitive medieval form, is that patriots are willing to risk their lives, even to die, for their nation; this gives any national army an advantage over mercenaries, who are left with mere technical superiority over their more enthusiastic foes.

Du Guesclin, man and legend, personified this feeling, and his armies were ultimately successful because French mercenaries preferred to serve him and the distant king than the English commanders and their even more distant ruler, as is apparent in this excerpt from Froissart:

> The English remained in battle-array in the plain, and the constable
> of France in his quarters, for he imagined that the English had
> placed a large ambuscade in a coppice on his rear. The English had
> brought with them a rout of pillaging Poitevins and Bretons,
> amounting to about two hundred, whom they sent forward to
> skirmish with the French. As soon as these pillagers came opposite
> to the battalion of the lord constable, they declared themselves
> loyal Frenchmen, and, if he pleased, would serve under him. The
> constable immediately assented, commanding them to wheel on

one side, when he learnt from them the arrangement of the English force, and that there was not any ambuscade. On hearing this, the constable was more easy than before; and having ordered his men to form, he advanced with his banner, marching on the wing of the two battalions. They had dismounted, and pushed toward the palisadoes, which they had allowed to remain standing, every one shouting, 'Notre Dame Guesclin!'

The English on seeing them issue out of their fort, drew up also on foot, and advanced with great alacrity. Their first onset was against the battalion of the constable, which was fierce and desperate. The English drove quite through this battalion, and overthrew many. But the Bretons had wisely drawn up their army: there were two battalions on the wing, who, being quite fresh, followed the constable, and, falling upon the English who were tired, beat them most dreadfully. They, however, like men of courage, turned about, without shrinking from their ill fortune, and combated most valiantly with the arms they had, such as battle-axes and swords of Bordeaux, with which they dealt many hard blows. Several excellent knights of each side adventured boldly, to exalt their renown. This battle was as well fought, as many gallant deeds performed, and as many captures and rescues took place as had been seen for a long time in all that country; for both armies were on foot, on a plain, without advantage to either. Each labored to perform his duty well, and many were slain outright or desperately wounded. In short, all the English who had marched thither were so completely discomfited that not one escaped death or captivity.

THE PEACE OF EXHAUSTION

Du Guesclin died of an infectious fever in the summer of 1380 during a siege of a free company stronghold. Bad water was suspected. After what remained of the body after botched jobs at preservation (in Venier's phrase, it was 'cut, boiled and parceled out like relics of the saints') was buried near the royal vaults in St Denis, the war slowly wound down. The English and French had other occupations to fill their time and ambitions. As Eric

Christensen said, 'not very much was happening between 1386 and 1414'.

But that did not last. In 1415 the Hundred Years War resumed, more fiercely than ever. By that time the spirit of chivalry was gone; there was little pleasure left in war, not even for those powerful nobles who could afford to have ideals. The second half of the war was more exclusively business. Chivalry hardly existed, even as cover for the coarse realities of international politics.

6
FORMING THE VICTORIAN IMAGINATION
CHAUCER'S KNIGHT AND TWAIN'S SAINT

T HE PHRASE 'I know what I know' will bring up many hits on any internet search engine. Moreover, almost everybody understands what it means: that you really don't have any substantial reasons for knowing what you do, but you are quite sure that whatever you know is right.

How is it that we acquire this certainty? In the case of song lyrics, where this phrase appears prominently, it is because we all think we know something about love and sex and people. Divorce statistics indicate that we are wrong about half the time (and American country music themes indicate a failure rate far higher than that).

Similarly, most of us have some ideas about what the medieval world was like. This is because of literature and movies. For the individual who reads, of course, knowing what we know comes from literature.

CHAUCER'S KNIGHT

Generations of American and British schoolchildren have read Geoffrey Chaucer's *Canterbury Tales*. In many cases the language has been modernised. The original, composed between 1387 and 1400, requires considerably more effort to understand than Shakespeare or the King James Bible. While most pupils do not move past the *Prologue* and the more socially acceptable stories, well-informed college and university students hurry on to the racier tales. In between lie numerous stories that modern readers do not fancy. Among these is a story told by a pilgrim who was long believed to be a pious crusader who has spent his youth and wealth fighting for his Lord.

Chaucer's knight was looked upon as a figure who personified the best ideals of chivalry and crusading. How else was one to read this passage?

> A Knyght ther was, and that a worthy man,
> That fro the tyme that he first bigan
> To riden out, he loved chivalrie,
> Trouthe and honour, fredom and curteisie.
> Ful worthy was he in his lordes werre,
> And therto hadde he ridden, no man ferre,
> As wel in cristendom as in hethenesse.
> And evere honoured for his worthynesse.
> At Alisaundre he was whan it was wonne.
> Ful ofte tyme he hadde the bord bigonne
> Aboven alle nacions in Pruce;
> In Lettow hadde he reysed and in Ruce,
> No Cristen man so ofte of his degree.
> . . .
> And of his port as meeke as is a mayde.
> He nevere yet no vileynye ne sayde
> In al his lyf unto no maner wight.
> He was a verray, parfit gentil knyght.
> But, for to tellen yow of his array,
> His hors were goode, but he was nat gay.
> Of fustian he wered a gypon
> Al bismotered with his habergeon,
> For he was late ycome from his viage,
> And wente for to doon his pilgrymage.

General Prologue, 43–78

The Knight's Tale has not been a twentieth-century favourite. This would probably surprise medieval readers, who were undoubtedly happy that the knight was the first of the Canterbury pilgrims to offer up a tale. His story of honour and love lacked the blood and guts of combat and tournament, but it was sufficient that he was able to describe the swiftly disappearing chivalric codes whose passing was almost universally regretted.

It was not just that the Knight represented the last of the chivalric warriors, but that he was the representative of a noble breed about to cede the battlefield to ruder and more brutal warriors – to mercenaries. Subsequent generations of readers had in mind not only the loss of an admirable type, but nobility in thought and blood was giving way to the lower standards and lower classes of modern times; hand-crafted products were vanishing in a mass-produced world; and men and women who understood literature, art and history were being elbowed aside by those with hands coarsened by trade and commerce. Foremost among those arguing this was John Aubrey (1626–97), a prominent antiquarian and scholar, a friend of the historian and political philosopher Hobbes, a founding member of the Royal Academy (1660), and a pioneer of field archaeology. Aubrey was well known for his extraordinarily wide reading and his unusual memory for details – hence his reputation as an antiquarian (who collected information) rather than as a historian (who evaluated facts and interpretations). Aubrey was an enthusiast who attracted a wide reading public even into the Victorian era. A great stylist, he knew how to tell a story and how to win converts to his views. His most lasting success was probably in persuading the public that the monuments at Avebury and Stonehenge were built by the Druids. Modern scholars know that this cannot be, but Druid societies inspired by Aubrey still celebrate the solstices on the prehistoric sites as often as the authorities will allow them.

Among Aubrey's enthusiasms was Chaucer's Knight. It would not be amiss to derive the traditional interpretation from his view that the modern era (the seventeenth century in his case, the nineteenth for many of his readers) was marked by a similar passing away of idealism. Men and women of both eras could look back with nostalgia on the fourteenth century and, with a sigh, point to Chaucer's Knight as the last great literary figure of the Hundred Years War, when commoners began shooting down horsemen before they had the opportunity to become legends. Each audience yearned for spiritual inspiration.

TERRY JONES

In 1985 Aubrey's widely accepted interpretation was challenged by a most unlikely scholar – Terry Jones, who until then had been known only as a member of the sensationally successful Monty Python troupe. True, Jones's insights into medieval attitudes had enlivened *Monty Python and the Holy Grail* (1975), but who could take seriously anyone associated with 'the holy hand grenade'? Jones, however, was a widely read polymath who knew his stuff and knew how to present it. In *Chaucer's Knight. The Portrait of a Medieval Mercenary*, he described the knight as a strange figure for 'the quintessence of chivalry' (as one scholar had put it): no family mentioned, no coat-of-arms, unhandsome, no interest in courtesy or courtly love, and definitely not well-to-do. In an era when Englishmen were fighting in desperate wars for their king, this knight had not served in a single one. More damning, the list of crusades was less a roll of honourable service than of 'appalling massacres, scenes of sadism and pillage and, on one occasion (the siege of Alexandria) notorious for the disgrace which the English knights, in particular brought upon themselves'.

Chaucer's Knight was, Jones argued, a medieval mercenary. Moreover, he asserted, any contemporary of Chaucer would have recognised him as such.

This was taking the Establishment head-on! This was a revolutionary thesis that would make every textbook instantly outdated, a thesis proposed by an outsider, to boot. Yet, surprisingly, criticism has been mild. Perhaps this was because Chaucer was so little taught in universities nowadays that it was not worth quarrelling about. Perhaps it was because Jones tapped into the prevailing anti-war attitudes of the academy at just the right moment. And perhaps it was because his arguments were persuasive.

Or were they? While undergraduates were thrilled by his challenge to their professors, as they gained experience and perspective, they generally rethought the arguments. The Old Guard, who were unused to such passion in Chaucerian studies, were not persuaded. Jones himself soon realised that he had been too passionate in his denunciations of the professional soldiery of that era and had given too little weight to the widespread approval of religious wars: 'it was precisely because Chaucer *believed* in the old values of chivalry that he portrayed in the Knight the very type who, during his lifetime, represented the destruction of those values.' But this caveat, which he put into the preface of his second edition, suffered the fate of almost all such efforts – most readers assumed that 'second edition' meant 'second printing' (as it so often does) and, therefore, did not look to see what might have been changed.*

---

* N.B. if any reader owns any of my books printed before 1990, throw them away and get the second edition! In some cases almost every paragraph has been changed.

If we move past the contest over whether Chaucer's contemporaries would have recognised the knight as a positive or negative model, we still have to deal with three questions:

1 Why this gentle story, if the teller were so rude?
2 If the Knight had been a mercenary, why had he not fought in France? Jones employs the Knight's employment record – having fought in disreputable wars, even for infidels, when his king needed the aid of every fighting man – to suggest that contemporaries would have recognised the Knight as a crude mercenary. However, every broadsword cuts both ways, and none too sharply. The Hundred Years War provided better opportunities for wealth and fame than wars against dangerous enemies in the eastern Mediterranean and the Baltic Seas. Why did the Knight choose obscure wars posturing as crusades? He was pious, but did that mean he was of necessity stupid? Did pious people have no sense of where money was to be made?

   Perhaps a great historian of an earlier generation, Huizinga, gave us an answer in his remark that the 'knight-errant, fantastic and useless, will always be poor and without ties, as the first Templars had been'.
3 Why was Chaucer so subtly critical of the knight, when he depicted the squire as a vain peacock, a youthful fashion-plate? Chaucer generally pulled no punches. Why did he disguise his criticism of the knight so carefully? Unless, as Jones suggests, contemporaries would have picked up on the subtle hints, then failed to let us in on the joke.

Those were powerful questions, almost as powerful as the inertia of tradition.

Jones has not been discouraged. After all, his book went into a second edition, with its corrections, and sold well. Money has charms that sooth many a wound.

'THE KNIGHT'S TALE'

The Knight's story took place in Athens – a city Chaucer's listeners would have known well because it was ruled by Latin lords. Theseus, the king of Athens, was with Hippolyta, the queen of the Amazons, when he met a

125

group of mourning women. Told to his horror that they were widows who were not allowed to bury their slain husbands, he vowed revenge upon the tyrant. Marching with his 'hoorde of chevalrie' upon Thebes, he slew King Creon and made it possible for the bones to be properly buried. While his men were stripping the dead – a universal post-combat activity for the lower classes – they came upon two young men, side by side, badly wounded. They were Palamon and Arctia, cousins of Creon's family and, therefore, dangerous to Theseus's control of the city. He sent them to Athens, to be held in prison without possibility of ransom. And so on.

Ransom was a subject that all Chaucer's contemporaries understood.

THE SQUIRE

Most readers are more interested in the knight's squire than in the knight. From the *Prologue* it was clear that he was familiar with the most recent fashions in popular high culture, and when he was asked to speak, he was instructed to talk of Love.

The squire's tale was about a Tatar ruler who often warred on Russia, slaying many stout heroes. Still in the prime of life, he had two fine sons and a beautiful daughter, Canacee. One summer day he held a lavish feast. Suddenly, into the hall came a strange knight. Not green, as another similar tale has it, but on a horse of brass, holding a mirror, with a ring on his thumb and an unsheathed sword on his belt. The horse, he said, could bear the ruler to even the most distant land swiftly. The mirror could reveal all matter of secrets, whether an enemy's approach or a lover's falsehood. The ring, if worn by Princess Canacee or carried in her purse, would allow her to understand the speech of birds. The sword would not only cut through any armour, but, when applied flat to a wound, would cure it instantly!

The squire did not finish the tale, a lucky accident for which the modern reader is thankful.

THE TEN WORTHIES

Maurice Keen has written at length about outlaw knights and free companies, at one point citing a conversation that Du Guesclin, *the tenth worthy* of contemporary chivalry (the first nine were heroes of antiquity), had with a mercenary captain. 'This is an excellent wine,' he noted. 'How much did you pay for it?' The response was witty but disconcerting, 'I don't know, the vendor was not alive at the time we acquired it.' Is this the way a 'worthy man' would have behaved?

There were, in short, contemporary critics of chivalry. But the remedy of the time was not to debunk chivalry or do away with it. It was to appeal again to the spirit of loyalty and service that lay at the heart of the chivalric code. Ridicule came in with Cervantes, in *Don Quixote*, but it was not widespread until modern times.

MARK TWAIN'S MIDDLE AGES

America's greatest novelist, Samuel Clemens (Mark Twain, 1835–1910 – coming in and going out with Halley's Comet, he said), wrote three 'historical romances': *The Prince and the Pauper* (1881), *A Connecticut Yankee in King Arthur's Court* (1889) and *Personal Recollections of Joan of Arc* (1895). As novels they are either marred (or made readable) by his wry sense of humour. That is, he was a smart alec and proud of it. Most of his comments on medieval society were aimed directly at contemporary counterparts; and he never lacked an opinion on any subject. It is at this cross-section of the humorous and serious that Terry Jones and Mark Twain meet.

TWAIN'S RULES OF WRITING

After reading James Fennimore Cooper's popular novel, *The Deerslayer*, Twain wrote a critique that has made it forever impossible for Twain's readers to ever enjoy Cooper again. At least, not in the way Cooper intended. At that time, in 1895, after Twain had already completed his three 'medieval romances', he wrote the essay which included his rules for writing. These first five should be kept in mind by every author:

1 A tale shall accomplish something and arrive somewhere.

2 The episodes of a tale shall be necessary parts of the tale, and shall help develop it.
3 The personages in a tale shall be alive, except in the case of corpses, and that always the reader shall be able to tell the corpses from the others.
4 The personages in a tale, both dead and alive, shall exhibit a sufficient excuse for being there.
5 When the personages of a tale deal in conversation, the talk shall sound like human talk, and be talk such as human beings would be likely to talk in the given circumstances, and have a discoverable meaning, also a discoverable purpose, and a show of relevancy, and remain in the neighborhood of the subject in hand, and be interesting to the reader, and help out the tale, and stop when the people cannot think of anything more to say.

In each 'romance' Twain introduces minor characters either as foils to the narrator or for comic relief. In *Saint Joan*, for example, he has a giant nicknamed the Dwarf and a boastful coward nicknamed the Paladin. Whether these and the other minor characters actually talk like human beings may be questionable. Twain could never resist a joke or an opportunity to express an opinion.

Twain would have enjoyed an evening with Terry Jones. Twain was famous for his collection of wise and witty friends and entertaining them in his home. Terry Jones is good at that, too.

'THE PRINCE AND THE PAUPER'

Although the Prince (Edward VI, 1547–53) and Tom Canty (the prince's common-born look-alike) lived in the sixteenth century, the social conventions and even the language are closer to the Middle Ages than to the democratic present. Twain was a master of American dialects and personalities (to read *Huckleberry Finn* silently is to miss half the fun), but his efforts to imitate those of an earlier era are only partly successful (perhaps they should be read aloud, too, preferably to a youthful audience). When young Edward takes his new acquaintance into the palace, this conversation results:

'What is thy name, lad?'

'Tom Canty, an' it please thee, sir.'

'This an odd one. Where dost live?'

'In the city, please thee, sir – Offal Court, out of Pudding Lane.'

'Offal Court! Truly 'tis another odd one. Hast parents?'

When the prince proposed an exchange of clothing, the misadventures began. Edward was thrown out of the palace as an interloping pauper, while Tom Canty found himself in the ill-fitting guise of a prince. Called to the bedside of the expiring Henry VIII, the courtiers explained that the boy had gone mad. The king was doubtful.

> He put a question to Tom in French. Tom stood silent a moment, embarrassed by having so many eyes centred upon him, then said, diffidently – 'I have no knowledge of this tongue, so please your majesty.'
> The king fell back upon his couch; the attendants flew to his assistance...

The king then advised, in a statement sure to bring joy to the heart of every poor young scholar: 'Over-study hath done this, and somewhat too much of confinement. Away with his books and teachers – see yet to it! Pleasure him with sports, beguile him in wholesome ways, so that his health my come again.'

'A CONNECTICUT YANKEE IN KING ARTHUR'S COURT'

This slim book was more fanciful, the manuscript of a stranger who claimed to have been transported somehow – he isn't quite sure how – back into the sixth century:

> ... there was a fellow on a horse, looking down at me – a fellow fresh out of a picture-book. He was in old-time iron armor from head to heel, with a helmet on his head the shape of a nail-keg with slits in it; and he had a shield, and a sword, and a prodigious spear; and his horse had armor on, too, and a steel horn projecting from

his forehead, and gorgeous red and green trappings that hung
down all around him like a bed-quilt, nearly to the ground.

'Fair sir, will ye just?' said this fellow.

'Will I which?'

'Will ye try a passage of arms of land or lady or for – '

'What are you giving me?' I said. 'Get along back to your circus,
or I'll report you.'

Informed that he was a prisoner, and faced by a very dangerous-looking
weapon, the narrator agreed to accompany his captor to Camelot. While the
knight was arranging to display him to the knights of the Round Table, he was
allowed to wander around inside the castle. There he encountered an old man:

'Friend, do me a kindness. Do you belong to the asylum, or are you
just here for a visit, or something like that?'

'Marry, fair sir, messemeth – '

'That will do,' I said. 'I reckon you are a patient.'

He soon met Arthur's famous knights, who were hardly more
sophisticated or intelligent than country boys looking for opportunities to
fight and brag. Worse, Merlin was a cheap trickster and Arthur was ready to
believe anything any of them said. As the narrator listened, bored and
unbelieving, to the exaggerated tales of Launcelot's most recent feats of
arms, he noticed:

Well, it was touching to see the queen blush and smile, and look
embarrassed and happy, and fling furtive glances at Sir Launcelot
that would have got him shot, in Arkansas, to a dead certainty.

As for the stories, they were bawdy to the extreme, and totally implausible.
Hence, like Froissart's reports, they were terribly popular:

Now Sir Kay arose and began to fire up on his history-mill, with
me for fuel. It was time for me to feel serious, and I did. Sir Kay
told how he had encountered me in a far land of barbarians who all
wore the same ridiculous garb that I did – a garb that was a work of
enchantment and intended to make the wearer secure from hurt by
human hands. However, he had nullified the force of the enchant-

ment by prayer, and had killed my thirteen knights in a three-hours' battle and taken me prisoner, sparing my life so that so strange a curiosity as I was might be exhibited to the wonder and admiration of the king and the court.

The narrator's knowledge of astronomy saved him from a burning, and soon he was in charge of everything in Arthur's realm. Known by his new title, 'the Boss', he brought in electric power, telephones and, most important, soap! He even tried to find alternative employment for the knights of the Round Table: 'Knight-errantry is a most chuckle-headed trade, and it is tedious hard work, too, but I begin to see that there is money in it, after all, if you have luck.' However, when the market goes bust, all you have left is a 'rubbish pile of battered corpses and a barrel or two of busted hardware.' This made him very unpopular.

What was worse is the unwillingness of anyone, noble or commoner, to imagine a better or even different state of affairs. Perhaps what the place needed was a guillotine and executioner, but the narrator was not the man for that. The sixth-century commoner's understanding of political economy was about equal to that of the average star of stage and screen – nil.

'SAINT JOAN'

In contrast to the slapstick comedy of *A Connecticut Yankee*, Twain's last essay into medieval history was upbeat and serious. It was, purportedly, a recollection of one of Joan's closest associates:

> When we reflect that her century was the brutalest, the wickedest, the rottenest in history since the dark ages, we are lost in wonder at the miracle of such a product from such a soil.
>
> . . . Joan of Arc, a mere child in years, ignorant, unlettered, a poor village girl unknown and without influence, found a great nation lying in chains, helpless and hopeless under an alien domination, its treasury bankrupt, its soldiers disheartened and dispersed, all spirit torpid, all courage dead in the hearts of the people through long years of foreign and domestic outrage and oppression, their King cowed, resigned to its fate, and preparing to

fly the country; and she laid her hand upon this nation, this corpse, and it rose and followed her. She led it from victory to victory, she turned back the tide of the Hundred Years' War, she finally crippled the English power, and did with the earned title of DELIVERER OF FRANCE, which she bears to this day.

And for all reward, the French king whom she had crowned stood supine and indifferent while French priests took the noble child, the most innocent, the most lovely, the most adorable the ages have produced, and burned her alive at the stake.

France in 1429 was in chaos – the English held Normandy in the west, Paris in the centre of the nation and Gascony in the south; the Burgundian duke held the north, the east and part of the south, and what little remained was dominated by independent-minded lords and rampaging gangs of unemployed mercenaries and robbers. The dauphin had no plans, no ambition and no advisors who were any better than he. Years of military disaster had taught them all to hide in their mouldering fortresses and hope that the English would go away.

Into this situation a young girl, inspired by visions, thrust herself. She was not even French, as most people understood France – she came from Lorraine. To everyone's surprise the dauphin believed her prediction that he would be crowned king in Rheims and would eventually retake all of France from the English. He gave her an army to relieve the city of Orleans, which had been besieged by the English for seven months. It was up to her, however, to persuade the army's leaders to let the troops fight.

The opportunity came sooner than expected. As Joan arrived at Orleans, a battle was in progress:

> ...when we approached the French were getting whipped and were
> falling back. But when Joan came charging through the disorder
> with her banner displayed, crying, 'Forward, men – follow me!'
> there was a change; the French turned about and surged forward
> like a solid wave of the sea, and swept the English before them,
> hacking and slashing, and being hacked and slashed, in a way that
> was terrible to see...then our forces to the rear broke through with
> a great shout and joined us, and then the English fought a
> retreating fight, but in a fine and gallant way, and we drove them to
> their fortress foot by foot, they facing us all the time, and their

reserves on the walls raining showers of arrows, cross-bow bolts, and stone cannon-balls upon us.

Not satisfied with victory in the field, Joan ordered an assault on the walls, which was ultimately successful. The French had won their first battle! It was too much of a shock for the generals – they had to find some of way reining in this impulsive maid. But, according to Twain, the courtiers had lost control of the army: 'France was going to take the offensive; that France, so used to retreating, was going to advance, that France, so long accustomed to skulking, was going to face about and strike. The joy of the people passed all bounds.'

The attack on the next fort was too daring for any of the generals, but Joan would brook no delay – that would merely give the enemy time to reinforce their endangered positions. As it was, 'The English fought like – well, they fought like the English; when that is said, there is no more to say.' Joan's army prevailed. Her next stroke was at the centre of the defensive system; and it, too, was successful.

The hot-blooded English commander, Talbot, restrained his temper long enough to accept terms for an honourable surrender, but marched away in a fury, determined to collect another army and return to take full revenge for his humiliation. However, his plans were upset by Joan's immediate offensive, the attack on his fortress at Jargeau. Although Joan's artillery blew holes in the wall, the defenders fought like furies:

> The enemy's resistance was so effective and so stubborn that our people began to show signs of doubt and dismay. Seeing this, Joan raised her inspiring battle-cry and descended into the fosse herself. …She started up a scaling-ladder, but a great stone flung from above came crashing down upon her helmet and stretched her, wounded and stunned upon the ground. But only for a moment… There was a grand rush, and a fierce roar of war-cries, and we swarmed over the ramparts like ants. The garrison fled, we pursued; Jargeau was ours!

Talbot was too late, but he could still save the situation if he could bring the French to combat in open country. Hastily collecting all the forces he could, he marched immediately upon Joan, who was by now already known as the Maid of Orleans and was widely hailed as a saint. One sharp combat could restore the world to its proper balance, he believed, one battle that could tear away Joan's grasp on French morale. But there could be no delay.

It was already too late. When Joan published her famous challenge, demanding that Talbot take his men home while they still had time, the English response was a threat to burn her alive and advice that she should go back to her proper trade of minding cows. Her inspiring response was: 'Go back and say to Lord Talbot this, from me, "Come out of your bastilles with your host, and I will come with mine; if I beat you, go in peace out of France; if you beat me, burn me, according to your desire".'

Reinforcements began to appear in Joan's camp. Knights and mercenaries who had sceptically mocked her now offered their services. Their numbers and status were sufficiently impressive to overcome the king's ministers, who were still seeking to block her every move – caution, combined with jealousy and incompetence, would have had her wait. Wait for what? The courtiers could not say, but they advised waiting.

Perhaps they were right, had Fastolfe (Twain added an optional 'e' to the name) been the English commander. He would have allowed her to wear down her army in attacks on strong fortifications, then struck. 'But that fierce Talbot would hear of no delay.' He took up a strong position toward nightfall, awaiting the customary wild French cavalry charge, then the deadly rain of English arrows, the slaughter of the wounded, and the enrichment of the soldiers from the bodies of the fallen.

But Joan told the army to make camp. The night was dark, and the rain light but steady. By morning the English army was slipping away, enticing her to follow into a trap. Joan did not pursue, but moved on the nearest English forts, persuading the garrisons one by one to surrender. Talbot had to turn again.

Joan lay in wait. She knew where the English were, but they had only the vaguest ideas as to the size of her force or its location.

The two armies came together near the village of Patay. Talbot's army was strung out on the march; the van and the artillery were well to the front, the main force following along at a distance. When the van encountered the first French resistance, it formed a line of battle; then Fastolfe urged his main force into a gallop to join them. He had no warning that Joan was watching from a height, waiting for him to get firmly into the trap.

Her generals urged her to attack, to catch Fastolfe in the flank. But she waited. 'Now', they said. 'Not yet, wait', she responded.

At last, finally ready, she ordered the charge, with the horsemen to come in on the English rear:

Fastolfe's hard-driven battle corps raged on like an avalanche toward the waiting advance guard. Suddenly these conceived the idea that it was flying in panic before Joan; and so in that instant it broke and swarmed away in a mad panic itself, with Talbot storming and cursing after it.

The battle was over quickly. The last major English army had been routed. It was not Shakespeare's *Henry VI*: 'The fraud of England, not the force of France, Hath now entrapp'd the noble minded Talbot.' No matter. In seven weeks Joan had liberated France. There was now no force able to block the triumphant procession to Rheims for the coronation of the dauphin as Charles VII. There would have been little resistance to taking Paris and much of the rest of English-held France. But the king was not yet equal to the task. He left Joan to soldier on alone, and when she was captured, fighting against overwhelming forces, he did nothing to obtain her release.

TRIAL AND MARTYRDOM

Twain was no historian, at least not a historian of twentieth-century professional standards. There is much in his text that can be questioned or discarded, but his description of the trial was based on the actual words of the testimony. Also, at this point he completely abandoned the artificial formality of the French-into-medieval-English. From now on, his Saint Joan spoke almost entirely in the clear, understandable speech of the modern American middle class. And he stood on his own soapbox to proclaim:

> With Joan of Arc love of country was more than a sentiment – it was a passion. She was the genius of Patriotism – she was Patriotism embodied, concreted, made flesh and palpable to the touch and visible to the eye.
>
> Love, Mercy, Charity, Fortitude, War, Peace, Poetry, Music – these may be symbolised as any shall prefer: by figures of either sex and of any age; but a slender girl in her first young bloom, with the martyr's crown upon her head, and in her hand the sword that severed her country's bonds – shall not this, and no other stand for *Patriotism* through all the ages until time shall end?

The life-long reader of Twain has to put this book down amazed. Is this the same sceptic who derided war, who burlesqued saints in book after book, lecture after lecture, who declared once that God made man a little lower than the angels and a little higher than the French?

Yes, it is the same Twain who remarks at one battle: 'There, hand-to-hand, we fought like wild beasts, for there was no give-up to those English – there was no way to convince one of those people but to kill him, and even then he doubted. At least so it was thought, in those days, and maintained by many.'

He put these words into the mouth of one speechifier:

> The old state of things was defeat, defeat, defeat – and by consequence we had troops with no dash, no heart, no hope. Would you assault stone walls with such? No – there was but one way, with that kind: sit down before a place and wait, wait – starve it out, if you could. The new case is the very opposite; it is this: men all on fire with pluck and dash and vim and fury and energy – a restrained conflagration! What would you do with in? Hold it down and let is smoulder and perish and go out? What would Joan of Arc do with it? Turn it *loose*, by the Lord God of heaven and earth, and let it swallow up the foe in the whirlwind of its fires.

One could not get that kind of spirit from mercenaries.

7
FORMING THE VICTORIAN IMAGINATION
THE WHITE COMPANY

T HERE IS ANOTHER important genre that informs our understanding of the medieval world: the adventure story. The typical reader is a teenage boy, but books of this nature occasionally make it briefly on to the best-seller lists. Romance novels (typically with a sexy picture on the cover) and mystery novels (with dour monks) are subspecies worthy of investigation. But not here.

THE NINETEENTH-CENTURY ADVENTURE NOVEL

Sir Walter Scott (1771–1832) practically invented the historical novel. His *Ivanhoe* (1819) was so well done that the story even survived Robert Taylor's wooden acting in the 1952 movie. Scott's Robin Hood swiftly evolved into the best-known figure from the Middle Ages, and the subject of more movies than Richard the Lionheart. Many of his themes – Saxon versus Norman, poor versus rich, Jews versus Christian, knights sworn to chastity struggling with carnal desires – were set in the world of chivalry. There was suffering, the duty to resist evil, and the lust for power; pride versus courtesy; true love sacrificing itself. In short, great stories by a master storyteller. Many writers across Europe and America imitated him, and the public rushed to buy and read their works.

Audiences also attended lectures on history, much like educated Americans watching C-Span's Booknotes on television today, but in greater numbers and with more applause. It was such a popular lecture in 1889, a talk on the Middle Ages, that inspired Arthur Conan Doyle, the inventor of Sherlock Holmes, to imagine a novel set in the Middle Ages. He had just finished *Micah Clark*, a piece of historical fiction that was selling well, and was looking for a theme with potential for action. The Hundred Years War beckoned.

Doyle had already learned that grounding a plot in current politics was an effective device. His Sherlock Holmes stories were set in the context of the Afghan War, the romantic intrigues of the high nobility, the contrasts of poverty and wealth, city and country. Knowing that readers would need more familiarity with the politics and society of the fourteenth century, he provided the necessary background bit by bit as he introduced his characters.

Doyle also picked a great title.

The White Company jumps out at us. Although educated nineteenth-century readers might be expected to recognise it as a reference to the Hundred Years War, even in the twentieth century, when few outside England and France can even tell you who fought in it or why, the title comes across as inspired. A medieval *Band of Brothers*. Not *A* White Company, but a specific one.

✕

ARTHUR CONAN DOYLE

Arthur Conan Doyle was also inspired by Scott's reputation. Scott had become a national treasure. Doyle, in contrast, was famous only for popular magazine stories far removed from the tradition of thick novels bound in leather. This irritated him so much that he sent Sherlock Holmes to his death at Reichenbach Falls, falling to doom in the clutches of the master criminal, Professor Moriarty. Doyle's ambition, like other contemporaries such as Sir Arthur Sullivan, was to be known for *serious* endeavours. It was not enough that his contemporaries praised his short stories, his star-quality play in contact sports, his sturdy patriotism (including service as a military doctor during the Boer war – without pay – and later writing a strong defence of the British policies), and his unflappable good humour. Late in life, his advocacy of spiritualism made him a laughing-stock among his peers (except those who saw contact with the dead as an attractive alternative to the quarrelling varieties of Christianity). Fame remained just out of reach, except for Sherlock Holmes, who didn't even require spiritualism to rise from the dead.

Doyle worked hard for respectability, but his Irish extraction stood in the way. His mother had pushed him into medicine, a profession that paid well for doctors with wealthy patrons; but Doyle's friends were all in the literary world, not society. He could have ridden his family's rock-solid Roman Catholic reputation straight to the top of his ethnic community, but he was too rigorously honest not to tell each and everyone that he could not accept without reservations the stern and uncompromising beliefs of the contemporary Church; this guaranteed that no true Catholic would choose him as a physician. Protestants, of course, mistrusted anyone educated by Jesuits. Almost by accident, or perhaps because he had too few patients to keep himself busy, Doyle had begun writing. Soon he was earning more scribbling serials than writing prescriptions, and, once famous, he began to abandon his medical practice. Then he sought to win a reputation as a serious author.

'THE WHITE COMPANY'

The best of Doyle's novels, in his own opinion, was loosely based on an actual free company. A major figure, Nigel Loring, is most likely drawn from Sir Neil Loring, the chamberlain of the Black Prince, who participated in the expedition into Spain:

Chapter 33 – How The Army Made The Passage Of Roncesvalles

The whole vast plain of Gascony and of Languedoc is an arid and profitless expanse in winter save where the swift-flowing Adour and her snow-fed tributaries, the Louts, the Oloron and the Pau, run down to the sea of Biscay. South of the Adour the jagged line of mountains which fringe the sky-line send out long granite claws, running down into the lowlands and dividing them into 'gaves' or stretches of valley. Hillocks grow into hills, and hills into mountains, each range overlying its neighbour, until they soar up in the giant chain which raises its spotless and untrodden peaks, white and dazzling, against the pale blue wintry sky.

   ... The keys of the mountain passes still lay in the hands of the shifty and ignoble Charles of Navarre, who had chaffered and bargained both with the English and with the Spanish, taking money from the one side to hold them open and from the other to keep them sealed. The mallet hand of Edward, however, had shattered all the schemes and wiles of the plotter. Neither entreaty nor courtly remonstrance came from the English prince; but Sir Hugh Calverley passed silently over the border with his company, and the blazing walls of the two cities of Miranda and Puenta della Reyna warned the unfaithful monarch that there were other metals besides gold, and that he was dealing with a man to whom it was unsafe to lie. His price was paid, his objections silenced, and the mountain gorges lay open to the invaders. From the Feast of the Epiphany there was mustering and massing, until, in the first week of February – three days after the White Company joined the army – the word was given for a general advance through the defile of Roncesvalles. At five in the cold winter's morning the bugles were blowing in the hamlet of St Jean Pied-du-Port, and by six Sir Nigel's Company, three hundred strong, were on their way for the defile, pushing swiftly in the dim light up the steep curving road; for it was the prince's order that they should be the first to pass through, and that they should remain on guard at the further end until the whole army had emerged from the mountains. Day was already breaking in the east, and the summits of the great peaks had turned rosy red, while the valleys still lay in the shadow, when they found themselves with the cliffs on either hand and the long, rugged pass stretching away before them.

This is much better writing than Froissart's original text. Doyle's descriptions of landscape and daily life are solid, but his dialogue is awkwardly filled with outdated words: hath, forsooth. Although the gratifying sales of *The White Company* proved that strong plot lines and vivid characters can overcome even artificial dialogue, the novel was quickly pigeon-holed as a 'boy's book'. This frustrated Doyle greatly, but the chapter titles indicate why:

Chapter 1 – How The Black Sheep Came Forth From The Fold
Chapter 2 – How Alleyne Edricson Came Out Into The World
Chapter 3 – How Hordle John Cozened The Fuller Of Lymington
Chapter 4 – How The Bailiff Of Southampton Slew The Two
    Masterless Men

And so forth

Still, Doyle had made one of the best efforts to recreate for a British audience the world in which their ancestors had first demonstrated the deadliness of English arms. Military efficiency was a widespread concern in the British Empire of Doyle's day, a fact certainly not lost on patriots who had reasons to distrust the French (the Entente – the understandings that led to the close alliance in the Great War against Germany – was still thirteen years in the future, in 1904). Moreover, *The White Company* was based on the incredible feats of real Englishmen who had lived in a transitional era – the close of the Middle Ages and the appearance of the Renaissance.

THE WHITE COMPANY IN ITALY

There were actually two White Companies. The most famous was composed of mercenaries who went from France to Italy in 1361. The count of Montferrat, desperately pressed by the duke of Milan, was willing to pay very, very well for their services; and nobody else was willing to take on the Milanese Great Company, universally held to be the best army of the era. Although not entirely English, the majority of the White Company was. After routing Milan's German mercenaries in 1363, saving central Italy from Duke Galeazzo (1355–78), the company divided, most of the soldiers entering the employ of Pisa in its war against Florence. Unlike most Italian mercenaries, they fought on foot. This spared their valuable horses from danger until needed. To protect themselves from missile fire, they wore shining plate armour that led to their nickname, the White Company. For missile power of their own, they had English archers skilled in the use of the most formidable weapon of the day, the longbow.

This weapon, so named because it was taller than the widely used short bow, could, like Odysseus' bow, only be drawn by exceptionally powerful men. Moreover, it was such a difficult instrument to use that no other people were able to master it. Accuracy may not have been important for raining down masses of arrows upon an enemy, but there were moments when the difference between a good shot and a poor one was equivalent to life and death; any archer who doubted his skill might trust his legs more than his arms. Accuracy required years of instruction and practice, years that most employers of mercenary armies did not have.

The longbow's devastating penetrating power and range had costs – the weapon was expensive and the bowstring had to be kept dry. Also no archer could station himself on a crowded battlement, watching the wiggling ladder in front of him, waiting for a face to appear, and then blow it away with an iron quarrel between the eyes. A crossbowman could also thrust his weapon over the wall and fire down without endangering himself much, while an archer had to expose himself completely. As a battlefield weapon, however, the longbow was without peer.

As a result, wherever the White Company appeared, its foes usually retreated back into fortifications, as did the Florentines in 1364. The English weakness being a love of money, when the Florentines offered a huge ransom, most of the mercenaries took it, together with an immense amount of booty, and left Tuscany. That part of the army, which now called itself the Company of the Star, followed Albert Sterz south toward Siena and the Papal States. A smaller part remained in Pisan pay under the command of John Hawkwood.

DOYLE WRITES HIS NOVEL

The White Company first appeared in 1891 as a serial in *Cornhill Magazine*, the most prestigious popular publication of the time. A fabulously talented and congenial man, Doyle loved that combination of honesty, intelligence, humour and valour that marked the Victorian gentleman. This shows clearly in *The White Company*, a story set in the age of Edward III, when soldiers seemed to be least characterised by honesty, intelligence and humour. Valour we can grant them, and a few other virtues, but most armed men in the Hundred Years War were not gentlemen. Perhaps that was what made Froissart's heroes so attractive – they were at one and the same time both representative of their age and exceptions to it. Doyle was living in the industrial revolution. Perhaps the values of the machine age contrasted so strongly with knightly honour, that Doyle was right in holding chivalry up as a standard wherever he could find it.

Doyle fended off requests for more Sherlock Holmes stories in order to find time for research into the free companies of the Hundred Years War. His reliance on Froissart led him to emphasise heroic figures, balancing their individual exploits with praise of the English yeomen who had made the longbow dominant on the battlefield. The most charismatic of these heroes was John Hawkwood, who spent most of his career in Florence; as it happened, every Englishman of Doyle's era who aspired to culture also had to make a pilgrimage to Florence, or spend summers in the lovely Tuscan countryside around that fabulous city.

THE WHITE COMPANY IN SPAIN

Hawkwood was, unfortunately, not a good subject for the novel Doyle conceived. He was employed in Italy, not in France – where English heroism shone most brightly – and he married into the aristocracy and never returned home. Moreover, as Sumption says of his men, 'They set new standards of savagery in war.'

The second White Company in France was less well known, but older and largely French-speaking. It had accompanied du Guesclin into Spain in 1366, then dispersed. Some troops returned to English employ and, when Pedro the Cruel fled to the Black Prince, became part of the army raised to return the despicable but useful monarch to power.

DOYLE'S CHARACTERS

Doyle built his story around three memorable fictional characters, fellows who could be easily identified by readers. The first was a defrocked monk, who was introduced thus:

> Charges brought upon the second Thursday after the Feast of the
> Assumption, in the year of our Lord thirteen hundred and sixty-
> six, against brother John, formerly known as Hordle John, or John

of Hordle, but now a novice in the holy monastic order of the Cistercians. Read upon the same day at the Abbey of Beaulieu in the presence of the most reverend Abbot Berghersh and of the assembled order.

The charges against the said brother John are the following, namely, to wit:

'First, that on the above-mentioned Feast of the Assumption, small beer having been served to the novices in the proportion of one quart to each four, the said brother John did drain the pot at one draught to the detriment of brother Paul, brother Porphyry and brother Ambrose, who could scarce eat their none-meat of salted stock-fish on account of their exceeding dryness,'...

'Item, that having been told by the master of the novices that he should restrict his food for two days to a single three-pound loaf of bran and beans, for the greater honoring and glorifying of St. Monica, mother of the holy Augustine, he was heard by brother Ambrose and others to say that he wished twenty thousand devils would fly away with the said Monica, mother of the holy Augustine, or any other saint who came between a man and his meat. Item, that upon brother Ambrose reproving him for this blasphemous wish, he did hold the said brother face downwards over the piscatorium or fish-pond for a space during which the said brother was able to repeat a pater and four aves for the better fortifying of his soul against impending death.'

To make matters worse, it was next revealed that Hordle John had been seen in conversation with a local wench of low reputation, then had carried her off, physically, into the woods, in the plain sight of three brother monks! The verdict was inescapable, but not so the punishment. Hordle John was not about to allow himself to be scourged from the premises. Accepting punishment without argument might be proper monkish behaviour, but Hordle John was not a proper monk.

The second figure was Alleyne Edrichson, a young man who was happy with convent life:

He was a thin-faced, yellow-haired youth, rather above the middle size, comely and well shapen, with straight, lithe figure and eager, boyish features. His clear, pensive gray eyes, and quick, delicate

expression, spoke of a nature which had unfolded far from the
boisterous joys and sorrows of the world. Yet there was a set of
the mouth and a prominence of the chin which relieved him of any
trace of effeminacy. Impulsive he might be, enthusiastic, sensitive,
with something sympathetic and adaptive in his disposition; but an
observer of nature's tokens would have confidently pledged
himself that there was native firmness and strength underlying his
gentle, monk-bred ways.

Alleyne had been ready to take up the life of a cleric, but the abbot was
sending him away. When Alleyne's father had died, twenty years before, he
had left land to the monastery on the condition that the abbot would raise
the child to manhood, then return him to the world. It was a wise choice –
Alleyne's elder brother, who would inherit the estate, had already demonstrated that he was unfit to be a guardian.

Alleyne resisted leaving the monastery, but the abbot insisted that there
was more to learning than books. He may know of France and Spain by
reading, of the pope in Avignon, of the pagans in Lithuania, and the
Muslims who hold Jerusalem and of Prester John and the Great Khan, but
there is much knowledge that can only be acquired by experience. Therefore,
Alleyne must leave. If he later decides to return to the convent, he will be
welcomed back, but now is the time to enter the world. A man by years and
stature, Alleyne was still a boy in many ways. It is his journey of discovery
that becomes the central narrative of the book.

Doyle's third character was Samkin Aylward, a mercenary soldier just back
from France. Subsequent generations of Englishmen pointed to such typical
bowmen as proof that the common man was the equal of nobles in arms
and intelligence, and thus deserved to share in the full rights of Englishmen,
meaning a prominent role in the government. Doyle, aware that democracy
was increasing in his own England, used Samkin to say that *the common man
was England.**

Many critics acclaimed *The White Company* superior to anything written
since Walter Scott, but they praised it as an adventure story. This was not
Doyle's intent. He had wanted a monument to English patriotism and

---

* Ellis Peters, a modern author of murder mysteries set in the medieval past,
introduced into her highly popular Cadfael series a young man who resembled
Alleyne in many ways. Allan, who had been away from his monastery for many years,
was contemplating returning.

military valour – a celebration of the combination of yeoman virtues and noble ideals. Alas, what the public really wanted was more Sherlock Holmes. (For a medieval detective we had to wait for Umberto Eco's William of Baskerville in *The Name of the Rose*).

One cannot help but wonder what kind of a book Doyle would have written if he had sent his characters off to join John Hawkwood in Italy. After all, when Chaucer met Hawkwood in Milan in 1378, he was impressed sufficiently to mention him in 'The Monk's Tale' of *The Canterbury Tales*.

THE PROTAGONIST IGNORED: JOHN HAWKWOOD

When Hawkwood went from France to Italy, he found a political landscape that was awaiting a person with his skills and ambitions. By 1350 Italy was a complicated peninsula divided into relatively small states ruled by kings, powerful nobles, prelates, abbots, cities and the pope. The kings were confined to the extreme south, the nobles had long since ceased to be important figures, as had most clerics. The large towns had the population and the revenues to build ships, raise armies, and hire soldiers, but the weakness of the cities was a tendency to let political disputes to get out of control, leading to intrigues, mob action and assassinations. Dominant factions often sent their enemies into exile, sometimes confiscating their properties. The exiles naturally sought foreign assistance to return home and exact revenge on their enemies. This foreign assistance could be readily found in those cities which were political or trade rivals.

The pope. Well, each pope was out to protect or increase the prestige and property of his office, which each believed was tied closely to absolute power in first the Papal States, then Italy, and finally all of Christendom. But also to further the interest of his family and friends. However, since Pope Urban V was living in Avignon, his influence on Italian politics was less than it could have been.

In practice, party alignments were complicated, usually reflecting traditional rivalries rather than ideological positions. Shakespeare knew that any audience of *Romeo and Juliet* would understand why an ancient feud could exist between Montagues and Capulets; it was not necessary for him to state which family belonged to which party.

Italians had learned to avoid bloodshed and bad blood by keeping all powerful families out of power. Rather than trust to elections or drawing lots, which would eventually give authority to one's enemies, each family represented on the city councils preferred the city hiring foreigners, usually nobles, to serve as police chief and judge rather than to risk having a rival selected. This official, the *podestá*, would serve for a fixed term – usually a year – for a reasonable salary. If the city council was satisfied with his performance, they could renew his contract; if he was too high-handed or arrogant, they could replace him. It was an arrangement that suited everyone.

Not surprisingly, the podestá almost always recruited a police force from out of town. This police force was composed of mercenaries of a sort.

But who guards the guardian? There was much concern that the podestá would make his job permanent by simply seizing power, eliminating the nobles and merchants who objected, and beginning a campaign to conquer neighbouring towns – it was easy to win local support for war against traditional commercial rivals. Cities had little choice but to hire a general with experienced mercenaries and make him podestá. City councils, aware of this, did their best to seek out men who were unlikely to become dangerous – someone honest, if possible, and, if not, at least lowly born or a foreigner.

Hawkwood, for example.

SAMKIN: AN ENGLISHMAN TOO LONG IN FRANCE

Hordle John and Alleyne Edrichson were listening to a conversation at an English inn, the Pied Merlin, which was frequented by a collection of characters suitable for *The Canterbury Tales*, when Samkin made a dramatic appearance:

> 'Ha!' he cried, blinking like an owl in the sudden glare. 'Good even to you, comrades! Holà! a woman, by my soul!' and in an instant he had clipped Dame Eliza round the waist and was kissing her violently. His eye happening to wander upon the maid, however, he instantly abandoned the mistress and danced off after the other, who scurried in confusion up one of the ladders, and dropped the heavy trap-door upon her pursuer. He then turned back and saluted the landlady once more with the utmost relish and satisfaction.
> 'La petite is frightened,' said he. 'Ah, c'est l'amour, l'amour!

Curse this trick of French, which will stick to my throat. I must wash it out with some good English ale. By my hilt! camarades, there is no drop of French blood in my body, and I am a true English bowman, Samkin Aylward by name; and I tell you, mes amis, that it warms my very heart-roots to set my feet on the dear old land once more. When I came off the galley at Hythe, this very day, I down on my bones, and I kissed the good brown earth, as I kiss thee now, ma belle, for it was eight long years since I had seen it. The very smell of it seemed life to me. But where are my six rascals? Holà, there! En avant!'

At the order, six men, dressed as common drudges, marched solemnly into the room, each bearing a huge bundle upon his head. They formed in military line, while the soldier stood in front of them with stern eyes, checking off their several packages.

'Number one – a French feather-bed with the two counter-panes of white sandell,' said he.

'Here, worthy sir,' answered the first of the bearers, laying a great package down in the corner'.

'Number two – seven ells of red Turkey cloth and nine ells of cloth of gold. Put it down by the other. Good dame, I prythee give each of these men a bottrine of wine or a jack of ale. Three – a full piece of white Genoan velvet with twelve ells of purple silk. Thou rascal, there is dirt on the hem! Thou hast brushed it against some wall, coquin!'

The conversation becomes instantly more lively. Wine, Women and Song are present in abundance, and nobody knew any of the three better than Samkin Aylward – his language was larded with French phrases, his banter with the serving women was that of a Continental gallant, and his knowledge of poetry and ballads far superior to anyone else present.

Clearly, the life of a mercenary had its lighter moments. Rape and rapine are hinted at here, but the emphasis is on getting rich, and the women obviously liked the unusually ardent and polite attention.* When the conversation eventually got around to politics, and to John Hawkwood, Samkin Aylward became serious, telling his listeners that he has been sent

---

* It is clear that gentlemen were not always 'gentlemanly'; it was assumed, even in the nineteenth century, that it was not as important what a gentleman said or did, but whether or not he did it with style.

back to England to recruit men for the much-reduced White Company:

> Know then that though there may be peace between our own
> provinces and the French, yet within the marches of France there
> is always war, for the country is much divided against itself, and is
> furthermore harried by bands of flayers, skinners, Brabaçons,
> tardvenus, and the rest of them. When every man's grip is on his
> neighbour's throat, and every five-sous-piece of a baron is
> marching with tuck of drum to fight whom he will, it would be a
> strange thing if five hundred brave English boys could not pick up
> a living. Now that Sir John Hawkwood hath gone with the East
> Anglian lads and the Nottingham woodmen into the service of the
> Marquis of Montferrat to fight against the Lord of Milan, there are
> but ten score of us left, yet I trust that I may be able to bring some
> back with me to fill the ranks of the White Company. By the tooth
> of Peter! it would be a bad thing if I could not muster many a
> Hamptonshire man who would be ready to strike in under the red
> flag of St George, and the more so if Sir Nigel Loring, of Christ-
> church, should don hauberk once more and take the lead of us.

It is at this point that Hordle John, a bear of a man, called him a liar and
challenged him to a wrestling match. Samkin accepted and almost lost the
French feather bed that he had put up as a wager – Hordle John was a
formidable wrestler, far stronger than his opponent and totally
unscrupulous, a man who despised rules and codes of moral conduct. Of
course, had Samkin lost, the novel would have been over. But better training,
better conditioning and greater self-confidence won the day. And Samkin
Aylward had won over two recruits for the White Company.

The journey through time, space and exotic encounters then began in
earnest. At one point early in their travels the pious Alleyne asked,

> 'Your Company has been, then, to bow knee before our holy
> father, the Pope Urban, the prop and centre of Christendom?'
> asked Alleyne, much interested. 'Perchance you have yourself set
> eyes upon his august face?'
>   'Twice I saw him,' said the archer. 'He was a lean little rat of a
> man, with a scab on his chin. The first time we had five thousand
> crowns out of him, though he made much ado about it. The

second time we asked ten thousand, but it was three days before we could come to terms, and I am of opinion myself that we might have done better by plundering the palace. His chamberlain and cardinals came forth, as I remember, to ask whether we would take seven thousand crowns with his blessing and a plenary absolution, or the ten thousand with his solemn ban by bell, book and candle. We were all of one mind that it was best to have the ten thousand with the curse; but in some way they prevailed upon Sir John, so that we were blest and shriven against our will. Perchance it is as well, for the Company were in need of it about that time.'

When Hordle John asks about the Scots, Samkin answered:

'For axemen and for spearmen I have not seen their match,' the archer answered. 'They can travel, too, with bag of meal and gridiron slung to their sword-belt, so that it is ill to follow them. There are scant crops and few beeves in the borderland, where a man must reap his grain with sickle in one fist and brown bill in the other. On the other hand, they are the sorriest archers that I have ever seen, and cannot so much as aim with the arbalest, to say nought of the long-bow. Again, they are mostly poor folk, even the nobles among them, so that there are few who can buy as good a brigandine of chain-mail as that which I am wearing, and it is ill for them to stand up against our own knights, who carry the price of five Scotch farms upon their chest and shoulders. Man for man, with equal weapons, they are as worthy and valiant men as could be found in the whole of Christendom.'

Alleyne then asked about the French:

'The French are also very worthy men. We have had great good fortune in France, and it hath led to much bobance and camp-fire talk, but I have ever noticed that those who know the most have the least to say about it. I have seen Frenchmen fight both in open field, in the intaking and the defending of towns or castlewicks, in escalados, camisades, night forays, bushments, sallies, outfalls, and knightly spear-runnings. Their knights and squires, lad, are every whit as good as ours, and I could pick out a score of those who ride behind Du Guesclin who would hold the lists with sharpened lances against the best men in the army of England. On the other hand, their common folk are so crushed down with gabelle, and poll-tax, and every manner of cursed tallage, that the spirit has passed right out of them. It is a fool's plan to teach a man to be a cur in peace, and think that he will be a lion in war. Fleece them like sheep and sheep they will remain.'

ALLEYNE'S ADVENTURES

When Alleyne left his new friends to visit his brother, he encountered the king, Edward III, on a hunt. The king could not even speak English, and the impression he left was highly unfavourable. Nor was Alleyne's encounter with his own brother any better – bloodshed or leaving the country were the two alternatives left open to him. He chose to continue his wanderings and eventually met his two companions again. Doyle now occasionally called Alleyne's friends Sam and John, but reverted to the longer names quickly, sometimes the first name, sometimes the last. Shortly afterward they encountered a diminutive but experienced warrior, Sir Nigel Loring, who was, as it were, less fearsome than his wife.

Alleyne's companions had doubts about their new commander but eventually John conceded, 'I must crave your pardon, comrade. . . I was a fool not to know that a little rooster may be the gamest. I believe that this man is indeed a leader whom we may follow'. Sir Nigel would become commander of the roughest group of English brigands around, the White Company. But that was later. Sir Nigel's immediate problem was where to find employment for the men he had recruited. Fortunately for him, welcome news arrived soon: WAR WITH FRANCE.

THE RAISING OF MERCENARY ARMIES

AND now there came a time of stir and bustle, of furbishing of arms and clang of hammer from all the southland counties. Fast spread the tidings from thorpe to thorpe and from castle to castle, that the old game was afoot once more, and the lions and lilies to be in the field with the early spring. Great news this for that fierce old country, whose trade for a generation had been war, her exports archers and her imports prisoners. For six years her sons had chafed under an unwonted peace. Now they flew to their arms as to their birthright. The old soldiers of Crécy, of Nogent, and of Poictiers were glad to think that they might hear the war-trumpet once more, and gladder still were the hot youth who had chafed for years under the martial tales of their sires. To pierce the great mountains of the south, to fight the tawners of the fiery Moors, to follow the greatest captain of the age, to find sunny cornfields and vineyards, when the marches of Picardy and Normandy were as rare and bleak as the Jedburgh forests – here was a golden prospect for a race of warriors. From sea to sea there was stringing of bows in the cottage and clang of steel in the castle.

Then there was the mustering of armies, leaders recruiting skilled warriors for their companies, and the march to the port cities. Clearly, Doyle felt that the Englishmen of the nineteenth century had become deficient in such matters. Not only were they less warlike, but incapable to doing anything on time. Ah, what would he have said about the twenty-first century!

Doyle gave his answer indirectly in the form of a pirate attack on his unpractised heroes' transport:

Down they swooped, one on the right, one on the left, the sides and shrouds black with men and bristling with weapons. In heavy clusters they hung upon the forecastle all ready for a spring – faces white, faces brown, faces yellow, and faces black, fair Norsemen, swarthy Italians, fierce rovers from the Levant, and fiery Moors from the Barbary States, of all hues and countries, and marked solely by the common stamp of a wild-beast ferocity. Rasping up on either side, with oars trailing to save them from snapping, they poured in a living torrent with horrid yell and shrill whoop upon the defenceless merchantman.

Defenceless? It only appeared so. The bowmen had hidden themselves in order to lure the pirate ships in closer:

...wilder yet was the cry, and shriller still the scream, when there rose up from the shadow of those silent bulwarks the long lines of the English bowmen, and the arrows whizzed in a deadly sleet among the unprepared masses upon the pirate decks. From the higher sides of the cog the bowmen could shoot straight down, at a range which was so short as to enable a cloth-yard shaft to pierce through mail-coats or to transfix a shield, though it were an inch thick of toughened wood. One moment Alleyne saw the galley's poop crowded with rushing figures, waving arms, exultant faces, the next it was a blood-smeared shambles, with bodies piled three deep upon each other, the living cowering behind the dead to shelter themselves from that sudden storm-blast of death.

The hand-to-hand fighting ended, the ships continued on to Gascony, the last English stronghold in France. Once on land, Sir Nigel leads his men to join an old friend, Sir John Chandos:

He was tall and straight as a lance, though of a great age, for his hair, which curled from under his velvet cap of maintenance, was as white as the new-fallen snow. Yet, from the swing of his stride and the spring of his step, it was clear that he had not yet lost the fire and activity of his youth. His fierce hawk-like face was clean shaven like that of a priest, save for a long thin wisp of white moustache which drooped down half way to his shoulder. That he had been handsome might be easily judged from his high aquiline nose and clear-cut chin; but his features had been so distorted by the seams and scars of old wounds, and by the loss of one eye which had been torn from the socket, that there was little left to remind one of the dashing young knight who had been fifty years ago the fairest as well as the boldest of the English chivalry. Yet what knight was there in that hall of St Andrews who would not have gladly laid down youth, beauty, and all that he possessed to win the fame of this man? For who could be named with Chandos, the stainless knight, the wise councillor, the valiant warrior, the hero of Crécy, of Winchelsea, of Poictiers, of Auray, and of as many other battles as there were years to his life?

THE REALITY OF WAR

As the company moved inland Alleyne proved himself both a warrior and a gentleman. When he rescued an Italian merchant, and his attractive daughter, from mishandling by the rough warriors of the company, the merchant had no good words for Alleyne's comrades: 'But those English! Ach! Take a Goth, a Hun, and a Vandal, mix them together and add a Barbary rover; then take this creature and make him drunk – and you have an Englishman'. The English were everywhere, he complained, even in Italy: 'Everywhere you will find them, except in heaven.'

Indeed, the English did seem to be everywhere. The three companions were able to enjoy the great tournament at Bordeaux, where the greatest champions of the era entered the lists against each other. Their first desperate combat was not against French knights, but as a companion-in-arms with Bertrand du Guesclin against French peasants whose desperate condition had driven them to attack their noble masters.

Subsequent adventures along the road to war brought the companions face to face with the horrors inflicted on the civilian population:

> From time to time as they advanced they saw strange lean figures
> scraping and scratching amid the weeds and thistles, who, on sight
> of the band of horsemen, threw up their arms and dived in among
> the brushwood, as shy and as swift as wild animals. More than
> once, however, they came on families by the wayside, who were too
> weak from hunger and disease to fly, so that they could but sit like
> hares on a tussock, with panting chests and terror in their eyes. So
> gaunt were these poor folk, so worn and spent – with bent and
> knotted frames, and sullen, hopeless, mutinous faces – that it made
> the young Englishman heart-sick to look upon them. Indeed, it
> seemed as though all hope and light had gone so far from them
> that it was not to be brought back; for when Sir Nigel threw down
> a handful of silver among them there came no softening of their
> lined faces, but they clutched greedily at the coins, peering
> questioningly at him, and champing with their animal jaws.

After helping suppress the peasant rebellion Sir Nigel heard that the Black Prince was recruiting troops for a campaign into Spain. But when he suggested marching south, he was told by a scoffing Gascon: 'These are not hired slaves, but free companions, who will do nothing save by their own good wills. In very sooth, my Lord Loring, they are ill men to trifle with, and it were easier to pluck a bone from a hungry bear than to lead a bowman out of a land of plenty and of pleasure'. Apparently, France was not altogether impoverished yet.

PATRIOTISM OVER PROFIT

The soldiers were divided. Many wished to continue the life of ease and plenty in France, and one mentioned the rewards that Hawkwood and his men were gathering in Italy. But the majority chose to go to the rescue of their prince and country. Victoria would have been proud! Gilbert and Sullivan could not have staged it better, and, in fact, *The Pirates of Penzance* had been staged in London in 1880, eleven years before Doyle wrote *The White Company*.

At length Sir Nigel and the 300 men, in the company of the duke of Lancaster, arrive at their destination:

> In front of them there lay a broad plain, watered by two winding
> streams and covered with grass, stretching away to where, in the
> furthest distance, the towers of Burgos bristled up against the light
> blue morning sky. Over all this vast meadow there lay a great city of
> tents – thousands upon thousands of them, laid out in streets and
> in squares like a well-ordered town. High silken pavilions or
> coloured marquees, shooting up from among the crowd of meaner
> dwellings, marked where the great lords and barons of Leon and
> Castile displayed their standards, while over the white roofs, as far
> as eye could reach, the waving of ancients, pavons, pensils, and
> banderoles, with flash of gold and glow of colours, proclaimed
> that all the chivalry of Iberia were mustered in the plain beneath
> them. Far off, in the centre of the camp, a huge palace of red and
> white silk, with the royal arms of Castile waiving from the summit,
> announced that the gallant Henry lay there in the midst of his
> warriors.

After many 'sooths' and 'roods' and 'by my hilts', they managed to surprise the camp and carry away a prisoner dressed in the royal colours. Only later did they discover that nine knights had dressed in the royal garb to confuse bounty-hunters. A short time later the English met the enemy in the field:

As the mist parted, and the sun broke through, it gleamed and shimmered with dazzling brightness upon the armor and headpieces of a vast body of horsemen who stretched across the barranca from one cliff to the other, and extended backwards until their rear guard were far out upon the plain beyond. Line after line, and rank after rank, they choked the neck of the valley with a long vista of tossing pennons, twinkling lances, waving plumes and streaming banderoles, while the curvets and gambades of the chargers lent a constant motion and shimmer to the glittering, many-coloured mass. A yell of exultation, and a forest of waving steel through the length and breadth of their column, announced that they could at last see their entrapped enemies, while the swelling notes of a hundred bugles and drums, mixed with the clash of Moorish cymbals, broke forth into a proud peal of martial triumph. Strange it was to these gallant and sparkling cavaliers of Spain to look upon this handful of men upon the hill, the thin lines of bowmen, the knots of knights and men-at-arms with armour rusted and discoloured from long service, and to learn that these were indeed the soldiers whose fame and prowess had been the camp-fire talk of every army in Christendom. Very still and silent they stood, leaning upon their bows, while their leaders took counsel together in front of them. No clang of bugle rose from their stern ranks, but in the centre waved the leopards of England, on the right the ensign of their Company with the roses of Loring, and on the left, over three score of Welsh bowmen, there floated the red banner of Merlin with the boars'-heads of the Buttesthorns. Gravely and sedately they stood beneath the morning sun waiting for the onslaught of their foemen.

Then came the great battle the reader has been waiting for some 350 pages. The outcome bore no resemblance to reality – no brilliant flanking movement, no capture of du Guesclin, no rout of the Spanish, no unhappy realisation that the war had been foolish. Instead, there is a medieval version of the Charge of the Light Brigade in which almost the entire White Company perished, surrounded by piles of Spanish, Moorish and French dead. Doyle's three heroes were among the few survivors. Wisely taking their wages, they returned home, to be honoured by their countrymen, to marry, and to spend evenings at the Pied Merlin remembering their days of glory. Doyle concluded:

> So they lived, these men, in their own lusty, cheery fashion – rude and rough, but honest, kindly and true. Let us thank God if we have outgrown their vices. Let us pray to God that we may ever hold their virtues. The sky may darken, and the clouds may gather, and again the day may come when Britain may have sore need of her children, on whatever shore of the sea they be found. Shall they not muster at her call?

IS 'THE WHITE COMPANY' A BOOK WORTH READING?

Doyle obviously enjoyed writing *The White Company*, and he was greatly disappointed that the public did not clamour for a sequel instead of a revived Sherlock Holmes. If it is true that 'history unread is history wasted', Doyle at least made a good try at getting people to read it. His successors, authors like Michael Crichton, Sharon Kay Penman and Ellis Peters, prove that that medieval history offers great potential for the novelist.

There was a widespread pacifist movement at the end of nineteenth century that argued that no good can come from any war. Doyle disagreed. He was a strong supporter of military training, of contact sports, and of the British government, which stubbornly protected commerce, the freedom to travel, the Christian religion, the honour of women, home and hearth, and the sanctity of treaties and unspoken obligations. Doyle believed that all British wars were justified. The government repaid the favour, subsidising reprints of his books in both world wars.

After the trauma of the Boer War, Doyle wrote *Sir Nigel* (1905), a prequel to *The White Company* that described Sir Nigel Loring's service in France under Sir John Chandos. Doyle wrote, 'The fantastic graces of Chivalry lay upon the surface of life, but beneath it was a half-savage population, fierce and animal, with little ruth or mercy. It was a raw, rude England, full of elemental passions, and redeemed only by elemental virtues.'

Although Doyle avoided Hollywood's glorification of thuggery and brutality, he described the combination of rootlessness, adventure, fighting spirit, greed, boredom and ambition that drove Englishmen into the life of a professional soldier. Some were good men, some good for nothing, and some capable of rising beyond themselves. But in the end, as Doyle says at the conclusion of *Sir Nigel*:

> So lie the dead leaves; but they and such as they nourish forever
> that great old trunk of England, which still sheds forth another
> crop and another, each as strong and as fair as the last. The body
> may lie in moldering chancel, or in crumbling vault, but the rumor
> of noble lives, the record of valour and truth, can never die, but
> lives on in the soul of the people. Our own work lies ready to our
> hands; and yet our strength may be the greater and our faith the
> firmer if we spare an hour from present toils to look back upon the
> women who were gentle and strong, or the men who loved honour
> more than life, on this green stage of England where for a few
> short years we play our little part.

8

THE CRUSADES IN THE BALTIC

F ROM 1196 TO 1561 crusaders fought on the shores of the Baltic Sea against pagan and Russian Orthodox foes and brought the coastal territories of Prussia and Livonia into the sphere of western culture and Roman Catholicism. This was achieved at a high cost to the native peoples and the Germans' relationship with the neighbouring peoples – Poles, Lithuanians and Russians – but today, now that the Baltic Germans are no longer there, Estonians, Latvians and Lithuanians remain committed to the West, not to their long-time Russian and Soviet occupiers. History has its ironies.

The crusade to Prussia began as a Polish effort to stop pagan raiders from terrorising northern villages and towns; at its inception it was directed by Polish dukes and prelates who invited the Teutonic Knights, a German religious order similar to the Knights Templar and the Knights Hospitaller, to assist them.

The crusade to Livonia actually preceded this by three decades; it had originated as an international effort of Christian merchants and knights against pagan pirates and robbers. In the early thirteenth century Bishop Albert of Riga, the driving force for expanding the crusade, founded a military order, the Swordbrothers, that soon provided significant numbers, military expertise and leadership. The Swordbrothers eventually quarrelled with the bishop over sovereignty, over-extended themselves and were defeated in battle; the survivors were absorbed into the Teutonic Knights.

Within a few years of each crusade's inception, the small area that was the immediate target became a base for the conquest of more pagan regions. Nothing less than Christianisation, it was believed, could bring peace and order to lands whose peoples lived by the laws of nature rather than those of God and civilised men.

Critics of the crusading movement (and purists as well) have often wondered whether these endeavours deserved to be called crusades. The goal of the First Crusade had been to recover from the Turks sites hallowed by the footsteps of Jesus, Peter and James – since the Turks had only recently defeated the Byzantine Empire and almost taken Constantinople, contemporaries had seen the First Crusade as a reconquest of the Holy Land, not as an aggressive war; they would have been utterly puzzled by accusations made by modern historians that this was early imperialism. At that time and later, popes made public appearances to urge believers to take the cross. The Baltic crusades were different. The motivations of the crusaders to Prussia and Livonia were multiple, and they were not always benign. Churchmen supporting missionaries were eager to expand their dioceses; nobles moved to the frontiers of Christendom to better their condition; kings were interested in acquiring the native peoples' lands; and merchants wanted to expand their markets.

Aspects of these northern holy wars can be identified with chivalry. Maurice Keen has noted how both medieval men and modern scholars have seen this connection, first in conflicts against heathens, then against Muslims, as a shift in the Christian ideal away from pacifism and retreat from the world toward a forthright defence of justice and efforts to create a more perfect society. Nothing illustrates this better than papal proclamations and crusade propaganda – that taking the cross will both in change the personal life of the crusader for the better and guarantee salvation thereafter; it would also protect Christians and converts in other lands.

Central to the Baltic crusades was the failure of peaceful missions to the pagan tribes that inhabited the Baltic coastlands and islands. To a certain extent this lack of success lay in the hostility of the pagan priests, who understandably hated competition. But the new forms of western political and economic life frightened lay people, too, who worried that one of their own nobles would follow the example of Slavic leaders in Mecklenburg and Pomerania, convert to Christianity and use the institutions of the Church to make himself a feudal ruler. There was also concern that the foreigners would just take over – with little question there was a folk memory of the Viking domination of the coastline and river valleys.

While some native peoples living along the Baltic coast welcomed the Christians, others were determined to resist. All had individual members who

Bataille de l'Ecluse

The great battle at Sluys was fought in late June 1340 between 190 French-led ships blockading Bruges and a slightly larger English relief force under Edward III and his young son, the Black Prince. The commander of the Genoese mercenary fleet, Egidio Bocanegra (Barbavera), wanted to fight on the high seas, but the French constable decided to anchor his ships in four lines across the mouth of the river. Thus, the effectiveness of the Genoese crossbowmen was limited. The result was an English victory that temporarily eliminated the French as a naval power. Barbavera, however, escaped with most of his ships.

The War of Succession (1341–64) in Brittany was an important part of the Hundred Years War. When John III *Dreux* died in 1341, his territories were claimed by equally plausible heirs. Charles of Blois, a nephew of the French king, sought to take Brittany away from its traditional pro-English policies, and his countess, the redoubtable Joanna Dreux, continued the struggle after his capture by the English in 1346. The war ended in 1364, in the victory of the rivals, the Montforts.

The battle of Crécy in August 1346 was fought between about 12,000 English under Edward III and three to four times as many Frenchmen under Philip VI. With English archers slaughtering the proud French knights, it was a turning point both in the Hundred Years War and in military tactics.

The siege and looting of the town of Caen in 1346 by King Edward III's English troops, who slew perhaps 3,000 citizens.

The Judgment of Appius Magistrate of Rome. Here in the market place we see the scaffold erected on the left, with curious citizens, merchants

The battle of Roosebeke in 1382 was a dramatic moment in the rise of the Burgundian state. Philippe the Bold, regent for young Charles VI and husband of the Flemish heiress, crushed the militia armies of Flanders. This miniature depicts well the armour, weapons and intense violence of battle. Note the Flemish war wagons.

When Charles VI returned to Paris, he found the merchants taking advantage of quarrels between the king's uncles to demand a prominent role in government, meaning a veto over taxes that paid the mercenaries. When he came of age in 1388, he suppressed this rebellion. Four years later, however, he went insane. Disorder and civil war followed.

Left: *A tower in Verona. It has been said that the distinctive swallow-tail crenellations were typical of Ghibelline fortifications. Certainly they provided effective protection for warriors using crossbows against exposed enemies. Venetians considered Verona the natural northern limit of their mainland empire, controlling, as it did, the entryways to the Alpine passes.*

Right: *The bridge in Verona, the Ponte Scaligeri, is considered one of the finest surviving examples of military architecture of this era.*

Châteaux Galliard was built by Richard the Lionheart in 1196, about twenty miles up the Seine from Rouen. The cost of it was tremendous strain on the Exchequer so soon after his citizens had ransomed him from the Holy Roman emperor, but it was wide considered the most perfect castle yet constructed.

The courtyard of the castle of Federico de Montefeltro (1422–82) in Urbino. This huge Renaissance structure with its magnificent view over the Umbrian countryside was the work of one of the most successful condottieri of the sixteenth century. Frederico was also a well-educated patron of the arts and gifted conversationalist. Among the artists and writers he collected in his court were Piero della Francesca and Castiglione, the author of The Courtier, the indispensable guide to morals and manners for aspiring ladies and gentlemen.

The ancient keep of the Visconti inside the Sforza fortress. Such a tower was practically impossible to take by assault. Or to destroy. Hence, many still dot the countryside of western Europe or stand in the 'old town' of modern cities.

Castel San Angelo, once Hadrian's Tomb, was the medieval papal refuge on the Tiber, not far the Vatican. Dan Brown's Angels and Demons has one of its climactic scenes here.

Charles the Bold, Duke of Burgundy 1467–77, was the most colourful figure of his age, and perhaps the most tragic. H[e] had no one to blame for his failures other than himself, but no one ever questioned his courage. At the battle of Montlhér[y] in 1466, though badly wounded, he turned a rout into a partial victory and almost overthrew his rival, the French king Louis XI.

Henry Despenser, the Bishop of Norwich at the head of his troops in May of 1383. This project, paid for by a special indulgence for the crusade, was among the most ill-conceived and poorly executed enterprises of the era.

Sir John Chandos, the greatest of the English commanders of the Hundred Years War, leading his last charge against the French. He would trip on his long surcoat, falling so awkwardly that a French spear penetrated his visor.

Donatello's statue, produced 1447–53, of Erasmo da Narni (1370–1443), better known as Gattamelata (the honey cat), honoured the greatest condottiere *of his generation. The statue, the first large equestrian bronze since the collapse of the ancient world, stands in Padua and was commissioned by his employer, the Republic of Venice.*

Bartolomeo Colleoni (1400–75) was the most respected mercenary general of his era, serving both Milan and Venice. Thi. bronze statue in Venice was Verrocchio's most ambitious work, taking from 1479 to his death in 1488.

The family della Scalla (Scaligeri) succeeded Ezzelino as despots of Verona. The most important member of this Ghibelline family was Gangrande della Scala (1291–1329), who was a prominent patron of Dante Aligheri. The statue over his tomb at St Maria Antica in Verona shows his dog-headed helmet. His namesake, Gangrande II (podestá 1351–59) was a terrible tyrant who used Brandenburg mercenaries to maintain his hold on power.

A splendid renaissance cannon of Duke Cosimo of Florence, typical of the desire to combine the finest of craftsmanship with the best in armaments.

Leo X (Giovanni de'Medici, pope 1513–21) and his brother Giulio (Pope Clement VII, 1523–34). Leo said famously, 'God gave us the papacy, let us enjoy it.' The two brothers, whose extravagance and good taste in art was combined with political ineptitude, failed to deal with the Protestant Reformation or protect Italy from foreign invasion.

The siege of Calais, August 1346 to August 1347, followed Edward III's victory at Crécy. Edward was so frustrated by the resistance that he had vowed to kill the entire population, but he relented when six of the wealthiest citizens presented themselves for execution. This was celebrated in a famous statuary group, *The Burghers of Calais* (Les Bourgeois de Calais) *by Auguste Rodin in 1888. The outcome was not so dire. Queen Philippa of Hainault persuaded her husband, the king, to spare them.*

The battle of Sempach, July 1386, established the independence of the Swiss Confederation from Habsburg rule. It also established the reputation of Swiss warriors as the most skilful and fierce in all Europe. This painting by Konrad Grob depicted the moment when Arnold von Winkelried of Unterwalden threw himself on the Austrian pikes, opening a gap in the enemy lines that his countrymen subsequently exploited to win a decisive victory. His action, perhaps mythological, inspired Swiss warriors in their struggle against Charles the Bold of Burgundy.

Joan of Arc is variously imagined by artists and this portrait by Zoe-Laure de Chatillon expresses the romanticism of the late nineteenth century. In fact, no picture painted during her lifetime has survived. Most show her wearing armour or leading soldiers in battle, but a few show her being burned at the stake in Rouen in 1431. Although she was canonised only in 1920, she has long been a potent symbol of French patriotism.

Charles V (the Wise) reigned over France 1364–80. By ignoring chivalric conventions he managed to recover most of his lost territories from England.

Since no portrait of Bertrand du Guesclin (1320–80) survives, we can guess at his appearance only from conventional woodcuts. In any case, he was not a handsome man, but he was a fierce warrior.

Marienburg castle was the seat of the Grand Masters of the Teutonic Order. Actually three castles in one, with an attached town, it struck awe into the numerous visitors who came from France and Britain to join in the crusades against the pagan Lithuanians.

The citadel at Pskov withstood countless assaults by crusaders, pagans and Orthodox armies, allowing the citizens to act a. middlemen in the rich trade between the West and the interior of Russia.

Since stone was scarce in the north, most structures, including city walls, were constructed of brick. Left: *The walls of Tallinn still stand surrounding both the town and the citadel, the Toompea.* Below: *The walls of Riga withstood numerous sieges.*

Wolter van Plettenberg's statue was placed on the castle of the Livonian Order in Riga next to the patron saint of Livonia, the Virgin Mary. Plettenberg was a devout Catholic who spurned the opportunity to become the Protestant Duke of Livonia. He was subsequently honoured by Catholic and Protestant alike for his honesty, integrity and nobility. And, of course, for his skills as warrior, diplomat and administrator.

Typical Dithmarschen farmhouse, at the Landesmuseum in Meldorf. Though not dating as far back as the era of independence, it reflects the life style of those independent and often wealthy farmers.

This tombstone of Peter Swyn in the Lund cemetery shows the two most important aspects of the Dithmarschers' character – piety and a tendency toward violence. Swyn, one of the most prominent citizens, was murdered in 1537, as depicted here.

Wahr Di Garr, De Bur De Kumt – *Watch Out, Guard, the Peasants Are Coming!* With this cry the militiamen of Dithmarschen threw themselves at the mercenary troops of the King of Denmark. The battle of Hemmingstedt was the proudest moment in the long history of this free republic on the shore of the North Sea.

were willing to take part in extortion, theft and the murder of merchants and priests if they thought they could get away with it. (Human beings are pretty much the same everywhere.)

If paganism had not been associated with piracy, robbery and raiding, the westerners would perhaps have had more patience. But paganism was a militant religion – not in the sense of desiring converts, but its gods rewarded warriors who sacrificed to them – and booty allowed young men to amass wealth and earn renown.

The crusaders' ways of dealing with this was first war, then occupation of the lands, and lastly the incorporation of the native peoples into western society – most of them as heavily taxed farmers. Accomplishing these tasks would have been impossible if the organisers of the holy wars had relied solely on volunteers. They needed warriors willing to serve as long as necessary, even through the long northern winters. Copying the practices of crusaders in the Holy Land, they found these men first in the military orders – knights and soldiers who had taken up a religious life, but instead of simple prayer, work and rest, put their military skills to the service of the Church. Next they hired mercenaries.

It was natural for the native peoples to respond cautiously to strangers. Their experience with Vikings had been mixed. Discoveries of Viking coin hoards show that many travellers had brought their gains from commerce and military service in Byzantium and the Muslim world across Russia to the Baltic coastlands, then buried it overnight for safekeeping and not lived to dig it up. Apparently, the Baltic tribes were not innocent, peaceful children of nature.

This illustrates one of the most important hazards of the mercenary lifestyle – getting the wages home safely. A mercenary who died in service might or might not be paid (even his employer might be dead); in theory, his earnings could be taken to his family by friends, but that would depend on his being the member of a band or being accompanied by relatives. The anonymous individual was out of luck. For those who lived, there was still a long and dangerous journey home.

RUSSIA

When Scandinavia converted to Christianity, the new monarchs discouraged raids into other Christian lands. The was partly to hamper the rise of rivals, partly pious practicality, but these motives combined with better organised defences to dry up the supply of human merchandise for sale in Byzantium and the Muslim worlds. Then Byzantium lost its eastern lands to the Turks. Russia, no longer able to profit from the transit trade, began to develop new traditions and customs.

Whenever Russian rulers and churchmen looked beyond their city walls, they saw a countryside still either populated by pagans or only recently converted. They understood that they could buy furs and other forest products from these peoples for sale to westerners, and they could collect a modest tribute from them, but they were realistic enough to know that there was a practical limit to how closely they could govern them. Their policy toward these tribes, therefore, was often little more than warning them to abstain from robbing merchants and to pay their annual tribute. Here and there the churchmen founded a monastery, but on the whole the clergy worried that contact between True Believers and pagans would result in a mutual exchange of cultural practices and values, an exchange that would lead Christians away from the Orthodox Church and into perdition.

Thus it was that the Russian states of Novgorod, Pskov and Polotsk collected tribute from tribes on the Baltic coast (today's Estonia and Latvia), but did not rule them directly. Hence they had little ability to prevent Roman Catholic missionaries from entering those regions from the west; nor did they have much desire to do so – the hard feelings that followed the Byzantine massacre of Latins in 1184 and the crusaders' capture of Constantinople in 1204–5 still lay in the future. Although it would be incorrect to suggest that the two religious communities viewed each other unhesitatingly as worthy and valued representatives of a common belief – the Schism of 1054 would last over 900 years – there was still an occasional willingness to recognise one another as *Christians* rather than *Schismatics* who would lead to hell anyone they could persuade to perform the sign of the cross backwards.

LIVONIA

When the first Roman Catholic merchants appeared in Livonia in the late twelfth century, most came from the international merchant community at

Visby on the island of Gotland. This town is today a popular tourist site, famous for its ancient walls and the museum displaying the bodies and weapons of warriors buried in a mass grave after the sack of the city in 1361. Gotland was centrally located in the Baltic Sea, easily accessible from all directions, and Visby's market was open to merchants from Sweden, Denmark, Germany and Russia.

At first most of the merchants were descendants of Vikings, but as the Holy Roman Empire became wealthier and more prosperous, its Saxon inhabitants pushed east into the Slavic regions of Holstein and Mecklenburg. When these Saxons established a trading centre at Lübeck in 1141, all that prevented them from sending ships into the Baltic Sea was fear of competitors from Denmark and pagan pirates from the southern shores of the sea – the land of the Wends, Slavs who had been death enemies of the Saxon Germans for several centuries. Both Danes and Wends had the distressing habit of capturing ships and throwing Saxon crews overboard. They also did the same to one another whenever possible. The Danes long tended to have the better of the exchange, but all states experience declines, and when Denmark went through a period of difficulty in the eleventh century, the Wends became the dominant power in the western Baltic. This made it easy for St Bernard in 1147 to bring Christian Scandinavians and Christian Germans together to crush the pride of the Wendish pagans and bring them to the baptismal font.

After crusaders from Germany, Bohemia and Denmark defeated the Wends, Danish and Lübeck merchants were joined by adventurous commercial travellers from Hamburg and Bremen in sailing to Gotland. From Visby they made their way to Livonia in their commodious merchant ships, many of which were round-bellied vessels with high sterns and forecastles, with a large sails billowing from sturdy masts. The *cog*, as this new ship was called, relied upon wind power rather than rowers and hence was much more economical to operate. Moreover, under full sail a cog could crush the smaller Viking-style warships of the native Kurs and Estonians, who had become the masters of the eastern Baltic waters and now raided Scandinavian coasts with impunity. When becalmed or at anchor in the wide, shallow rivers of the Baltic coastland, the cog's high sides made boarding difficult. Archers stationed in the forecastle and on the after deck could shoot down on their enemies with crossbows, picking them off one by one.

Any young man with a crossbow and the lust for adventure could easily find employment as a mercenary, protecting merchants from pirates, thieves and unhappy customers.

The merchants were also accompanied by missionaries, usually German monks. Whenever a merchant set up a shop in a settlement, the missionaries asked permission to take up residence as well; they often stayed through the winter, presumably paying well for their lodgings and food, and earning goodwill by assisting the natives deal with western merchants who came each spring and remained until fall. They dispensed medical advice and told stories from the Bible and recounted the miracles of the saints. The missionaries were, in all likelihood, the best free show in town. That made the local shamans very unhappy – not only were the competitors depriving them of income and prestige, but they derided the practitioners of magic and dispensers of herbs as misguided fools who were as useless in dealing with disease as they were dangerous to one's prospects of earning eternal life.

Modern readers, knowing how primitive the westerners' own medical practices were and how deeply their beliefs were coloured by superstition and ignorance, can smile that this conceit. But the western visitors were more advanced in technology, education and social organisation. There were also many more of them and they were very good warriors. But it was the ability of the western leaders to demand money and military service from their subjects that was decisive. Feudalism, as Marx noted, was a more advanced and effective social and political system than its predecessors.

While any western lord – secular or cleric – could mobilise his resources more effectively than clan leaders and give orders more quickly than clan councils could deliberate, we must not forget the religious zeal that inspired everyone. This was especially true of the missionaries.

When foreign priests began planting their own crops and doing better than the Livonian and Estonian farmers, jealous shamans began to spread stories about their using witchcraft. The missionaries must have been amused, but also comforted by knowing the successful outcome of similar contests in the Bible and in the lives of the saints. Missionaries lacked almost every necessity of life except self-confidence and a firm belief that God was with them. Nevertheless, they did not make many converts at first – peoples who attribute good harvests to fertility gods are reluctant to abandon their ancient beliefs. There were also the troubling changes that accompanied the commercial contacts. Money changes everything, not just hands. How, the village elders must have worried, can we protect our ancient culture and customs?

THE CRUSADE TO LIVONIA

The Chronicle of Henry of Livonia, a thirteenth-century composition universally praised for its style, its drama and the importance of the events described, opens with the story of the most successful missionary to the Daugava River (Düna, Dvina) in what is today Latvia. Meinhard, a priest from Segeberg in north Germany, arrived with merchants from Visby in the spring of 1180, with a very small retinue of priests and servants. Meeting with some success among the Livs (hence the name Livonia), he asked for permission to spend the winter. The Livs were a weak tribe dwelling on the islands in the Daugava River, along the coast and in scattered settlements that extended north up the Aa River valley; Meinhard established his mission on an island in the Daugava regularly visited by merchants. One day that winter a warning came that Lithuanian raiders were on their way. The tribesmen, far from offering resistance – as Meinhard had expected – scattered and hid in the forests. Given that whenever the ground was not covered with snow, it was muddy, this seemed a poor strategy. The raiders could easily track the fugitives to their hideouts. Of course, the Livs had experience in this matter and obviously found hiding more successful than fighting – the Lithuanians were tall, strong, incomparably more numerous, and accustomed to victory.

When the danger had passed, Meinhard asked his hosts why they did not build proper fortifications. The response was that they did not know how. This was only partly true – almost every hilltop in the region had once been topped by a fort. More important than this was the refusal to empower leaders who could persuade, inspire or force the warriors to fight. The tribesmen liked their primitive clan democracy, and they understood that once they gave any leader authority, he would expand it, whether he intended to or not, until he became king. This was the organisational weakness of the region – while western Slavic tribes had become feudal states, with castles, cities, vassals, abbeys and churches, the tribes in the eastern Baltic had not.

Meinhard reflected on this, then offered to build a brick castle and provide mercenaries to defend it. The natives were excited to hear his proposal, despite the accompanying conditions – that they undergo baptism and pay taxes and tithes to support his church. His was a reasonable request, everyone agreed, since Meinhard would have to hire artisans to make the bricks and lay them; and while merchants who were present in the summer would assist in guarding the castle, none of them would remain through the winter, much less do so for free. The initial capital outlay was comparatively great, but Meinhard collected funds for the construction from merchants on Gotland and his brother monks in north Germany, and proceeded to build two brick forts on islands at Holm and Uexküll. He then recruited mercenaries in Gotland as garrisons.

When the Lithuanians arrived the following winter, they laughed at the Christians' folly. In the summer they might have collected dry wood to fill the moat and then asphyxiated the garrison with smoke, but this was winter – and the snow would have buried firewood beneath feet of cover. Hurriedly they attached ropes to the corners of one of the forts and tried to pull it apart; this had always worked against log fortifications. But the brick walls remained firm, and crossbowmen shot down many of the attackers. After the Lithuanians withdrew, the Liv populace emerged from their hiding places and congratulated the priest and his men. But the Livs were less happy when Meinhard reminded them that now it was time to pay the first taxes. A few were baptised and began to pay their tenth to the Church, and about the same amount in taxes. Most of the natives, however, treated Meinhard's demand as a huge joke – they had tricked him into building forts, and he had believed that they would willingly become his subjects and pay him taxes! A mere priest! And a foreign priest at that.

Far away, however, the pope saw Meinhard as more than a mere priest. He saw him as a gifted personality who could build a great church among a people living in darkness. If asked whether he meant that literally, the pope would probably have been puzzled until reminded that there was little daylight in winter. But the darkness he meant was metaphorical. The native peoples did not lack for talent and ability – the ones the pope had met were intelligent enough – but they did not even have a form of government that permitted them to defend themselves. Unless the Church stepped in soon, the entire region would remain under the domination of Orthodox Russians and pagan Lithuanians.

The pope was worrying unduly. The Russian princes of Polotsk, Novgorod and Pskov had indeed been collecting tribute from the nearest Estonian and Lettish tribes, but the revenue was not great enough to justify making the bonds tighter. Moreover, although the princes had converted a handful of the leading *seniors*, the heads of the clans whose council meetings constituted the main lawmaking and judicial body of each tribe, this had not led to the others accepting Orthodox Christianity. It was the same issue that had made the Livs reluctant to entrust any one noble with authority. While it was important to have a chief who could speak on the tribe's behalf as a co-religionist of the distant sovereign, they feared more demands for taxes and for military service. The councils insisted on retaining control of all aspects of government except religion, which was the realm of the shamans, and if a prominent noble became a Christian – Catholic or Orthodox – the remaining elders and the priests might have advised that everyone else remain pagan in order to limit that individual's ambitions.

Nor were the Lithuanians interested in expansion. That would come later. What this relatively numerous and warlike people needed at this time were items for trade. Their own country produced marvellous horses, but it was so covered with hills, swamps and nearly impenetrable forests that there were no commercial products worth speaking of. Worldly goods were acquired through warfare – attacking Christian settlements in Russia and Poland, and carrying away prisoners and cattle from the tribes in Livonia and Estonia. They would divide up the captives – the kings and nobles taking the largest share, of course – then sell them to the slave traders in Poland and Russia, taking care to make sure that Poles saw only Livonians and Russians saw only Poles; if they could transport the booty all the way to the nomadic pagan tribes on the steppe, the profits would be all the better.

With Lithuanians coming at the Livs from the south, and Estonians raiding from the north, it was relatively easy for Meinhard's successor, Bishop Albert, to establish a fortified commercial centre at Riga and to make allies of more tribes. What Bishop Albert could not do was give fiefs to a sufficient number of German knights to defend his new subjects. First, he could not make the natives into serfs without driving them into the arms of their common enemies. Second, he wanted to keep as much of the tax revenues as possible for himself. And last, he understood that knights would eventually challenge his authority. He gave a few large fiefs to relatives, but his handful of knights had to support themselves by collecting taxes and supervising justice – just like ministeriales in Germany.

On the bishop's travels to Germany and Italy – to meet with the Hohenstaufen emperor-elect and Innocent III – he spoke to the public about the needs of his mission. The money poured in, and so did volunteers for the holy war. But the expenses were always greater than revenues. The money was quickly spent, and the crusaders went home at the end of a summer or a year. Albert wanted to hire mercenaries to garrison his castles, but he could not afford to do so. He simply lacked the funds.

Albert's solution was to found the new military order, which would provide a body of knights – well-trained volunteers who had taken vows of poverty, chastity and obedience. With enough prayer, cabbage and beer, they could take on any foe.

Most importantly, these Swordbrothers cost almost nothing. For a promise of one-third of the lands to be conquered, they were willing to serve even in the most isolated and unpleasant locations on the frontier. The bishop could have called on an existing military order, but he wanted knights who would be utterly dependent on him and, therefore, obedient. How little he understood the psychology of such men. Or perhaps he knew the risks, but thought that this was the best chance he had.

This passed the bishop's problem of regional defence to other hands, but the Swordbrothers were never able to persuade enough pious knights to forsake the world and join them. Salvation was a worthy end, but fasting, prayer and celibacy did not attract many warriors even in those days. As the crusader state grew, the Swordbrothers had to add mercenaries to their numbers. Awkwardly, the taxes of each newly conquered region were insufficient to the military order's growing needs. Only constant expansion offered any hope of resolving the financial crisis – in theory, expansion would provide larger number of native warriors and more taxes, but in practice tribes that had once been dominant were much less willing to accept foreign rule than those which had been traditional victims. Eventually, following a 1223 native uprising in Estonia that slew a third of the order's members and slaughtered hundreds of other Germans in the Danish provinces – including many knights and gentry – the Swordbrothers annexed the Danish lands and invaded the lowland regions of Lithuania.

The vicious cycle of hiring mercenaries to expand, then expanding in order to pay the mercenaries, led the Swordbrothers straight to disaster. It was not a matter of evading disaster, but only of *when* it would take place. This happened first on the swampy banks of the Saule River in 1236, with hundreds of crusaders slaughtered by Samogitian Lithuanians and their highland allies. Lastly, a papal legate ordered the return of Estonia to Denmark. The Swordbrothers, who had earlier agreed to submerge their membership and lands into the Teutonic Knights, rebelled. In 1240–42 they joined in a coordinated attack on Novgorod, which ended in disaster at the battle on the ice of Lake Peipus. Their last surviving knights were dispersed – some sent to the Holy Land, replaced by knights recruited from north Germany who shared the language spoken by the German merchants and clergy of Livonia. The Teutonic Order had resources throughout Germany which could be used to hire as many mercenaries as were necessary, but it was also sufficiently popular as to require relatively few of them.

For practical reasons – mainly the distance from Germany and Prussia, but also the complicated relationship with the bishop of Riga – the knights in Livonia were given considerable autonomy from the rest of the Teutonic Order. They became known as the Livonian Order.

ALEXANDER NEVSKY

The one connection that modern movie fans have to the Swordbrothers is through Sergei Eisenstein's 1938 movie *Alexander Nevsky*. Although there are other films set in the era of the northern crusades, *Alexander Nevsky* is the only one that western audiences see. The dramatic story of the Novgorod prince's rout of the Teutonic Knights on the ice of Lake Peipus became all the more authentic through the director's skilful use of black-and-white film and silent movie techniques (there was dialogue, but the film was less a 'talkie' than a spectacle), then overlaying the whole with Prokofiev's stirring score. The film was deliberately anachronistic and spectacularly successful.

Eisenstein used considerable artistic license, but, having grown up in Riga, he was well acquainted with the costumes and iconography of the Middle Ages, and with the narrative sources of the crusading era as well. Unfortunately for those who rely on his film for historical information, Eisenstein's understanding of the actual events was minimal or they did not apply well to the uplifting patriotic and socialist story he wanted to tell. The grand master of the Teutonic Knights was not at the battle, nor the Livonian master, nor even the acting Livonian master. Having the crusade organised by a papal legate was somewhat accurate, and the twenty-year-old Alexander had smashed the Swedish prong of the western aggression in 1240 on the banks of the Neva River, giving him the title Nevsky. But the crusader army came from Danish Estonia, the bishopric of Dorpat and former Swordbrothers now in rebellion. If there were any Teutonic Knights present at the battle on 5 April 1242, they were few in number.

Eisenstein also had to cope with contemporary politics. In 1938 Stalin held absolute power in the Soviet Union – and no movie was released without his *personal* approval. No viewer should miss the references to internal enemies, capitalists, the impending war with Nazi Germany, the threats from sneaky

orientals and evil Catholic prelates, and the importance of giving unconditional support to the national leader. *Alexander Nevsky* is a superb example of
how a movie made for propaganda can live on as exciting entertainment.

In reality, Prince Alexander later collaborated with the Great Khan,
ultimately being entrusted with the governance of the entire northern part of
Russia so that he could collect taxes and provide soldiers to the Mongol
Horde more effectively. He was murdered in 1263 while visiting the khan.
Novgorod remained independent until 1471–89, when it was subjected by
the grand duke of Moscow, Ivan III (1462–1505). The Orthodox Church
declared Alexander Nevsky a saint in 1547.

One could argue that Alexander had few choices and that he did his best
under the circumstances. In helping fasten 'the Mongol Yoke' around the
necks of the Russian people, he protected his subjects for a while from the
worst effects of foreign rule. However, one should not argue that Alexander
was an early communist who relied on the peasant masses doing their
patriotic duty against foreign aggressors. His army was largely composed of
professional archers, and Novgorod provided a well-trained citizen militia
and much money.

THE TEUTONIC ORDER

The Teutonic Knights had been established during the Third Crusade as a
hospital order to care for German knights who were being ignored by the
established English–French orders. In 1198 crusaders who saw the order's
knights emptying bedpans persuaded the pope to transform the organisation
into a military order. Though the 'German Order' (a more exact translation
of its name) grew rich quickly under the leadership of Hermann von Salza,
who was a major figure in the Fifth and Sixth Crusades and was a friend of
Friedrich II, there was too little room in the Holy Land to deploy its forces
effectively. Though the grand masters and the members continued to see the
Holy Land as their primary field of operation, they sent knights first to
Hungary (where they succeeded so well that jealous nobles and prelates had
them expelled), then to Prussia and later to Livonia.

The military order consisted of knights, men-at-arms and priests, all
represented in the assemblies that passed laws, debated policies and elected
officers. The grand master and his council conducted diplomacy and led the

armies in battle, while *castellans* governed regions and *advocates* oversaw the governance of converted native peoples who were allowed to retain many ancient customs, including the councils of elders.

Bishops oversaw religious life, including the education and spiritual care of the native peoples; abbots were important in the countryside, and friars in the towns. But no one was allowed to challenge the authority of the grand master in Prussia or the regional master in Livonia. Immigrants were settled in swamp and forest lands, or areas which had been depopulated by war; and towns sprang up along the Baltic coastline and the Vistula River. The revenues from taxes, estates and gifts gave the grand master a reputation for incredible wealth.

This wealth could be used to hire mercenaries.

THE CRUSADE TO PRUSSIA

In the fourteenth century the crusade to Prussia began to attract ever larger numbers of volunteers, and from an ever greater distance. Some made the journey out of piety, some for adventure, and some for money. Jean Froissart recorded examples of nobles taking advantage of truces in the Hundred Years War to make the journey (*Reise*) to Prussia. Sometimes the vow to take the cross was not easily fulfilled, as the adventures of the duke of Geldern demonstrated – he was taken prisoner in Pomerania, but after the grand master stormed the castle in which he held prisoner, he would not leave until his captor (who had prudently fled) released him from his vow not to attempt escape until ransomed. Such extravagant devotion to the cult of chivalry may have been unusual, but many young squires saw this crusade as an opportunity to have a memorable adventure and to earn knighthood as well.

In 1377 the duke of Austria went on crusade in Prussia, accompanied by 2,000 men and one of the better poets of the era, Peter Suchenwirt:

Dâ sach man wûchsten, prennen	There was destruction, burning,
Slahen, schiezzen und rennen	slaying, shooting and charging
haid ein, pusch ein, unverzagt,	through meadows and tickets,
rechts als der fûchs und hasen jagt	just like chasing foxes and rabbits.

The poem made it clear that the duke was seeking an opportunity to 'win his spurs', the symbol of knighthood. Many squires had come, too, in hopes of being dubbed as well – not only would the crusade be something to boast about through a lifetime, but the expensive ceremony of knighthood would be practically free! Suchenwirt quoted a prominent lord as he pulled his sword from his scabbard to do the duke his honour, 'better knight than squire!' (*Pezzer ritter wenne chnecht!*).

While on crusade, the poet implies, the duke of Austria and his friends paid most of the costs of obtaining equipment, travel and the lavish entertainment. This suggests that the line between impoverished volunteer and mercenary is blurred at best, and evidence further indicates that some who received expense money were actually taking thinly disguised wages. This practice was sufficiently distasteful as to be seldom mentioned, but it was more satisfactory than cancelling the expedition or being embarrassed by having too small a force to claim a seat at the famed Table Round that Suchenwirt described.

✕

THE CONVERSION OF LITHUANIA

After the conversion of Lithuania to Roman Catholicism in 1386/87, the Teutonic Knights found it increasingly difficult to persuade knights and clerics that their holy war was in defence of the Church against pagan and Orthodox enemies. They were able to continue the crusade only because the cousins who ruled Lithuania and Poland, Vytautas (baptised as Alexander) and Jagiełło (Jogaila in Lithuanian, baptised as Ladislas), had a long history of changing their religion, or seeming to promise to do so, to suit their political ends. Vytautas was first baptised as a Roman Catholic in Poland after he escaped from Jagiełło's prison in disguise, then again for the grand master of the Teutonic Knights in Prussia. After achieving a cautious reconciliation with Jagiełło, he underwent a baptism in the Russian Orthodox Church. When Jagiełło married the heiress to the Polish crown, Vytautas demonstrated his loyalty anew by undergoing another baptism, non-German and non-Russian, in Cracow.

The great siege of Vilnius in 1394 with the aid of English knights and archers and the flower of French chivalry was the greatest expedition of its kind. (See my book, *The Teutonic Knights, a Military History* for more details) Five years later Vytautas and Jagiełło led their forces to assist the grand master in subduing the last pagans in the Baltic, the fierce Samogitians north of the Nemunas River.

Although the Teutonic Knights obtained sovereignty of this region, they found it difficult to govern. First of all, the knights of the order had decided not to force Christianity on the people immediately (despite the outcry of churchmen who were concerned about the souls of the newly subject peoples and who may have wanted the order's lands for themselves), but first to make them comfortable with Christian habits such as commerce and feudal rank. This offended those warriors who considered themselves above the peasant class, but were not freed from taxes like the nobles selected to provide military service. The exemption meant little until 1409. The tax levied that year provoked a rebellion that widened into war with Vytautas and Jagiełło.

There was no good reason for this war to have occurred. The rulers of the three states had cooperated in military operations in Russia against the grand duke of Moscow, in Russia against Novgorod, on the steppe against the Tatars, and in the Baltic against pirates. Together they could have changed the political and religious situation in Eastern Europe significantly.

It is worth pausing in this story to look at the pirates, partly because eliminating piracy was one of the original goals of the crusade to Livonia, but also because pirates often begin their careers as components of a regional navy or as privateers hired by a local ruler to attack the commerce of his rivals. Privateers were a sea-borne form of mercenary warfare.

PIRATES AS SEAFARING MERCENARIES

The line between pirate and privateer is clear: a pirate was a free-enterprise thief; the privateer was licensed by a government to attack the vessels and towns of an enemy on whom war has been declared. In practical terms, of course, the distinction was harder to maintain. Enemy ships attempted to disguise their identity, ships of neutral states carried contraband, and crews wanted their share of the loot, no matter what the niceties of legal status were. Privateers tended to become pirates when peace returned, and pirates signed on as privateers whenever war was declared.

The most famous privateers in the Baltic were the Victuals Brethren (in German, *Vitalienbrüder*). These arose during a three-sided war – the claimant to the Swedish throne, Queen Margaret of Denmark, and the duke of

Pomerania – for control of the rich province of Scania, today southern Sweden, and the trade routes across the Baltic. Also involved was the Hanseatic League, a loose collection of German commercial cities led by Lübeck, Hamburg and Bremen; and the Prussian and Livonian cities. The war had brought the first privateers out as allies of one or the other of the challengers, but they became a formidable force only after the Danes began a long siege of Stockholm in 1390. The privateers allied with the Swedish king began delivering food through the many waterways leading to the city. The king, pleased at the discipline and loyalty of his new allies, gave them letters of marques authorising them to make war on his behalf and granting them possession of the strategic island of Gotland.

The Danish queen hated the Victuals Brethren not only for their having saved the king from certain defeat, but also because they had been collecting much of their foodstuffs from her subjects; that is, as she saw it, they were stealing it from her. However, there was little that she could to do drive them from their strongly fortified base in Visby.

The pirates might have been able to eke out an existence for many years if they had been able to restrain their members more. But when the war slowed down, one group advocated continuing the war, raiding Pomerania and looking for Danish fishing and commercial vessels; another advocated picking on the rich ships of the Hanseatic League that were sailing to Riga and Reval, to Polotsk, to Pskov and to Novgorod. Yet another group advocated taking service in the employ of the bishop of Dorpat; war seemed likely there, and rich merchants could be found on the rivers in summer and on overland trails in the winter.

The bishop of Dorpat, Dietrich Damerow, was an ambitious prelate whose plans dovetailed nicely with the traditional policies of the city's mercantile elite and the numerous hereditary nobles. All were of German descent, and though a few could boast of ancestry that included Russian nobles and native princesses, their ties were to nobles and merchants elsewhere in Livonia and in the Holy Roman Empire.

The policies of Dorpat were simple and straightforward – first, freedom to act independently from both the Livonian Order and the archbishop of Riga, who were otherwise usually bitter rivals; and from the other prelates and cities of Livonia; second, to call on these rivals in trade and politics for help whenever war with one of the nearest Russian states (Novgorod or Pskov) or with Lithuania threatened. Damerow brought to these ancient practices his irritating personality and a desire to make a great reputation for himself – his likely goal was to advance his career in the Church, perhaps being first archbishop of Riga, then reaching even higher office.

The Livonian master saw Dorpat's traditional policies as a perennial nuisance, but Damerow's as an immediate threat. Whenever the master would want to use a trade embargo to put pressure on Russians or Lithuanians, Dorpat's merchants would ignore his requests to cooperate. Whenever Riga merchants had difficulty with their Russian counterparts in Polotsk, Dorpaters would tell the Russians that they had nothing to do with it; similarly, whenever Reval complained about robbers to Pskov or Novgorod, Dorpat merchants would disclaim any part in the quarrel. Still, Dorpat was a passive nuisance; its merchants and nobles had no territorial ambitions. Damerow, in contrast, was aggressive; he created difficulties rather than merely taking advantage of them. His immediate goal was to undermine the Livonian Order, even to destroy it.

This situation had already become a crisis before the master heard that some of the Victuals Brethren were sailing to Dorpat. He asked why this was happening. No response. In 1398 Grand Master Conrad (III) von Jungingen had had enough. He called his knights together and explained the situation. The provocations were nothing new – the Teutonic Knights had discussed the Dorpat situation often. But this proposal was unprecedented – to put the order's knights on ships and transport them across the sea to Gotland, to destroy the pirate base. The knights having voted favourably, the grand master then contacted Vytautas of Lithuania, whose plans for annexing Russian lands could be disrupted by disorder on his Dorpat front. Vytautas not only liked the plan, but he sent warriors to join the expedition. (These may have been the equivalent of hostages, but their presence was welcome.)

Prussian cities belonging to the Hanseatic League provided ships, which set sail despite the lateness of the season. Within weeks the pirate base existed no more, and the bishop of Dorpat capitulated to the Livonian master.

THE BATTLE OF TANNENBERG

The great war that began in 1409 between the Teutonic Knights and the rulers of Poland and Lithuania was a significant turning point in the history of the Baltic region. There was no need for the conflict, except that perhaps the three powers ultimately had to determine which would be supreme in the region, the well-established Teutonic Order or the rising powers of Lithuania and Poland.

The three states had cooperated effectively through much of the decade 1399–1409, but when an uprising began in Samogitia, Grand Master Ulrich von Jungingen suspected that Vytautas and Jagiełło had encouraged the rebels. Most of his castles had fallen quickly, and he would probably not be able to recover them if he had to guard his other frontiers against Lithuanian and Polish attack. He decided to try an economic blockade first, then, if necessary, war.

Jungingen's decision to prevent Polish grain from reaching famine-stricken regions of Lithuania brought on war. Polish and Lithuanian nobles, and patriotic churchmen demanded action. Vytautas and Jagiełło acted cautiously, well-aware that the army of the Teutonic Knights had not suffered a major defeat in living memory; moreover, that it was at the height of its powers, with many experienced, well-trained knights, with formidable castles stocked with supplies, and with what many believed to be an inexhaustible reservoir of revenues.

In addition, the grand master had excellent intelligence services. Merchants passed on information about every ruler whose lands they crossed; in return they were given favours that were good for business; churchmen wrote letters or whispered gossip into the right ears; and factions opposing the Lithuanian and Polish rulers sought aid and comfort from him. Learning that Vytautas and Jagiełło were discussing a joint military campaign, Ulrich von Jungingen decided to strike first.

Lithuania and Samogitia could not be attacked as long as Jagiełło represented a danger to the southern frontier. Therefore, it seemed logical to strike at the Polish threat first. This was most easily done on the eastern bank of the Vistula, where the grand master sent units in August of 1409 to destroy the fortress at Dobrin. A second army swept up the other side of the river, capturing the strategic fortress of Bydgoszcz. A third force struck from the Neumark into Great Poland, but turned back after burning some border districts.

A second offensive followed in September, directed at Krone – the commander reported killing 500 Poles in a one-sided battle, but did not capture the Polish strongpoint. A report noted that only one knight from the order's army died, killed 'at the head' of the charging cavalry. This suggests a massive wedge-shaped formation designed to burst a defensive line apart.

Another force struck east of Dobrin at the communication route to Lithuania, territories belonging to Johan of Masovia.

In October it was the Polish turn. Jagiełło ordered an assault on the fortifications of Bydgoszcz, but after 200 of his men died, he called the attack off. The Teutonic Knights might have been able to hold the place until the grand master's relief army arrived, but the order's commander had been killed in action, struck by an arrow, and the mercenaries in the castle surrendered when they were promised they could take with them all their possessions. A complicating factor was a large quantity of salt that had been stored there since spring, apparently deposited by two ships originally hired to transport it down the river, across the Baltic Sea, and up the Nemunas River to Lithuania. The mercenaries had demanded a share of this booty earlier, but the order's late commander had refused – the castle had been surrendered to him, not to the mercenaries.

Soon afterward the grand master's army marched down to face the royal array, but neither commander was willing to hazard battle. After emissaries sent by King Wenceslas of Bohemia arranged a truce, both sides withdrew into winter quarters.

This was not an important campaign except in one respect – the grand master kept detailed records of expenses. This *Soldbuch* (payment book) has been used by the Swedish scholar Sven Ekdahl to describe in detail the process of recruiting and employing mercenaries, and he has done this imposing task, one that has daunted many an ambitious doctoral student, better than anyone else to date. Teutonic thoroughness has its virtues, and no Germans of the fifteenth century were more thorough than the grand masters of the Teutonic Order.

Recruiting mercenaries for these armies had a particular difficulty – the grand master had wanted his attack to come as a surprise. Therefore, the two recruiting officers who were sent to Silesia and the nearest German states (Pomerania, Meissen, Thuringia, and Brunswick and Lüneburg) were authorised to raise quietly 200 *lances* (a *Spieß* or *Gleve*) for six months' employment. The instructions to the recruiters emphasised that each *lance* was to consist of a man with armour, a man with a crossbow and a youth, each with a horse, and that they be honest, capable of fighting and well mounted. The pay was to be twenty-four Hungarian ducats, equivalent to eleven marks, and while no promises were made to replace horses and equipment lost in combat or on campaign, everyone knew that there was a custom to make 'gifts' which covered such eventualities.

Most 'guests', as both mercenaries and volunteers were called, qualified for spiritual benefits as well. However, because crusading expeditions had been suspended after the subjection of Samogitia, the habit of taking the cross to fight the pagans had fallen into disuse. Now and in the future, though 'crusaders' would be welcomed, everyone understood that most came for the money. Even Heinrich the Rich of Bavaria, who was in Prussia two years later, had not become famed for his wealth by spending his own money on someone else's war.

Ekdahl demonstrated that most of the mercenary leaders were knights or nobles. In addition to these short-term mercenaries, there were long-term arrangements with prominent rulers. The most important was with the dukes of Pomerania, who were paid to remain friendly or neutral and to allow recruiters to spread out through their lands. A special arrangement with the lords of Sagan and Oels was evolving so that they became future recruiters and leaders of mercenary armies in Prussia.

A number of musicians (pipers, trumpeters, drummers) were hired as well, and two cannonmasters from Brunswick. Lastly, there were a 'large number' of squires with two horses which could be risked anywhere. (The grand master had reservations about his hired men demanding repayment for *good* horses lost on the campaign.)

The grand master's mercenaries did not participate in the early campaigns east of the Vistula in any significant numbers, though undoubtedly there were sergeants (men-at-arms) in the garrisons who did, men who were serving on multiyear contracts. This was a result of time pressure – it was simply not possible to get recruits from Germany, Pomerania or Silesia to that front quickly enough. Instead, they gathered in West Prussia and the Neumark.

There was an initial disruption of the 1409 invasion from the Neumark because Duke Wartislaw of Pomerania failed to appear as promised. The governor of the Neumark hurried to see what the problem was, but the damage to the campaign had already been already done. The next problem was providing sufficient food and hay for the new arrivals until they could cross the Polish border again and sustain themselves from plunder. The assembly point was in Schlochau, in West Prussia, whence they were dispersed to other castles where provisions were more plentiful.

Among these mercenaries were probably five members of the same family, Borsnicz – Kunze, Hannus, Jon, Nickel, Paczko. The financial records for 1410 did not survive, but they are recorded as having left the grand master's employment the following year.* The mercenaries were soon

---

* Other mercenaries with the same name, thus very likely having some relationship, included Czenke von Borsnicz, who together with Nickel von Logau brought 120

brought together to repel a raid by the Polish commander of Bydgoszcz on the Vistula fortress at Schwetz. They ambushed the raiders, recapturing all the cattle and horses that had rounded up. Meanwhile, the commander of Schwetz, Heinrich von Plauen, captured the Polish commander, then hurried south to Bydgoszcz and captured the castle.

Forty mercenaries led by Heinz von Borsnitz formed the new garrison. These were the men who later quarrelled over the salt; moreover, when Jungingen sent reinforcements, workers and war machines to their assistance, they turned them away, saying that they were solely under the commander of the castellan of Schlochau.

Complaints began coming in. The mercenaries were given to theft, were undisciplined and untruthful, and were unreliable. The grand master indicated that he was ready to release them from his service as soon as he could replace them. However, the only action Ulrich von Jungingen took was to assign an officer from the Teutonic Order to share command. As we have seen, this officer was killed by an arrow during the Polish assault.

In contrast to the negative comments about Borsnitz's men, Heinrich von Plauen wrote to praise Borsnitz as an energetic and capable leader. As a result, Jungingen gave him a responsible position in leading the mercenaries who later fought at Tannenberg.

In all, there may have been as many as 800 lances, with a total outlay of at least 46,000 marks. The costs were probably significantly higher once the payments to prominent noble allies were reckoned in.

The mercenaries played no significant role in this short war. Nevertheless, the net of alliances was important for recruiting an even larger force the next year. Unfortunately, the *Soldbuch* for 1410 is missing. Therefore, we can only guess how many mercenaries the grand master hired to face the 40,000 Poles,

---

lances to Prussia in June of 1410, thus arriving too late to see action until sent to Marienburg in mid-July. At the end of January Czenke was paid 300 gulden for his services. By that time he had risen high, serving in the grand master's council and being entrusted with important financial duties requiring courage, honesty and efficiency. Among his men was Gunzel von Borsnitz, who was paid for having brought one lance and an archer; two presumed brothers from Silesia, Hermann von Borsnicz, who brought two lances, and Pritzlaw von Borsnitz, who brought four lances and two archers; and Conrad von Borsnicz (perhaps identical with Kunze above), who had four lances. The most famous member of this extended family was Heinz von Borsnitz, a vassal of the duke of Oels. The paybook indicated that Heinz was a *Ritter*, that is, a knight. Most well-born mercenaries were referred to politely as *Her* (Sir), a more ambiguous title.

Lithuanians, Russians, Tatars, Moldavians, and the Czech mercenaries that Jagiełło led into east Prussia. Jungingen had arrayed his main force north of Bydgoszcz, anticipating a repetition of the 1409 campaign. But the Polish king had arranged to meet Vytautas in Masovia, with a plan to strike north into Culm. Jungingen, alerted by papal and imperial peace commissioners that the king had built a bridge across the Vistula, shifted his force to the east bank of the river to block the invaders. But Jagiełło moved east and north through the wilderness toward the bishopric of Ermland; the grand master followed, moving ever farther from his bases. As Vytautas's Tatar scouts spread terror through villages and towns, Jungingen realised that his strategy of defending fords and forest paths was not working. He attempted an overnight march on the royal camp, but failed to achieve surprise. Deciding neither to attack nor to retreat sufficiently to allow his men to rest and to eat, he put his 20,000 men into a defensive position, then pulled back in order to allow the Poles and Lithuanians to align their forces opposite his. He thus abandoned the traps his exhausted men had dug or built to frustrate the opposing cavalry, removed his artillery from its most advantageous position, and left his knights standing in the heat in heavy armour, their horses suffering from the lack of food and water, until Jagiełło had finished hearing several masses.

The battle on 15 July, 1410, nevertheless seemed to go well for the grand master at first. A critical moment was reached when the Lithuanians and their Russian and Tatar units launched a terrific assault on the 'crusaders' stationed opposite them. When the Lithuanian attack failed, the mercenaries followed the retreating formations. This was standard practice – to turn a retreat into a rout. However, this was not a general retreat – the other formations stood fast, and the mercenary cavalry made no attempt to strike into their now exposed flank, but rode off into the distance. Vytautas, seeing the gap in the line, gathered every man he could and charged. What remained of the crusader left flank collapsed. The grand master's units in the centre, now attacked from the front and the flank alike, begin to flee. Ulrich understood that an orderly retreat was impossible, since the roads leading to the rear were too narrow to accommodate his forces; already they were clogged with frightened fugitives. His only chance to lead his last units in a charge directly at the Polish king. When that failed and he fell in combat, panic set in among the few units remaining intact.

The subsequent episodes of combat resembled a slaughter. Poles and Lithuanians pressed upon the unprotected backs of the fleeing soldiers, chased down individuals who tried to escape through the woods, ambushed the mercenaries as they came back with exhausted horses, and then murdered all the captives except those who could be expected to pay high ransom. About 8,000 men had fallen on each side.

Given that at the end the German forces were slaughtered almost without resistance, they must have given good account of themselves early on, before thirst and exhaustion overcame men and beasts. They had been better armed and better trained, so much so that outside experts had expected them to win easily despite the disadvantage in numbers. Previous grand masters had been able to keep their armies in check. But Ulrich had not. His mercenaries' wild pursuit of a seemingly beaten foe, without assuring that the foe was indeed beaten, had led straight to disaster.

Few of the lower-born mercenaries would have been spared. They were generally not the kind of men who could pay ransom, and the Poles would not have wanted to see them in arms again. A gigantic burial pit barely sufficed to hold the bodies of the executed captives. Those with money, among whom was Heinz von Bursnitz, were ransomed. In fact, he was released so quickly that he appeared in the order's service with forty lances in Marienburg on 20 July! This while officers of the order faced long imprisonment yet.

Jagiełło, having wounded to tend and dead to bury, was unable to follow up his victory instantly, but there seemed no reason to hurry. If Heinrich von Plauen had not hurried from Schwetz to Marienburg with his men, then rounded up every man and mercenary in the region, the Polish king would have found this key fortress, one of the largest in Europe, unprotected. Later it was clear that, had the king pushed his men harder, he could have rolled up the entire network of castles quickly.

Mercenary soldiers and the 'ships' children', that is sailors, saved Marienburg from capture. Heinz von Bursnitz was apparently soon dismissed. But only briefly. The grand master needed mercenaries, even poor ones; and it is not clear whether Heinz was considered good or bad. At least he was alive – he seemed to have a knack for staying alive, or was it simply an extraordinary skill in knowing when and how to surrender?

Plauen ordered the commander of the Neumark to raise another mercenary army. By the time the Poles abandoned their unenthusiastic siege of Marienburg, this army was ready to move. Plauen moved on the Polish castle at Stuhm, a fortress the king had built just south of Marienburg to threaten the heart of the order's domains. It is presumed that Jagiełło filled it with mercenaries, since his vassals' terms of service had expired. Not surprisingly, the garrison surrendered and was allowed to leave with all their possessions.

Plauen's fortunes varied. On the whole, he was successful in recovering the order's cities and castles, but there were setbacks. Heinz von Bursnitz reappeared, only to be captured in battle in October of 1410. The next we hear of him is after his death, in a 1431 document issued by the duke of Oels that mentions his son, Kunze.

The Teutonic Order never recovered from the disaster. The grand master could be replaced easily, but not so his officers and knights. More importantly, mercenaries who formerly served for relatively affordable wages were now sceptical that their employer would be victorious against Polish and Lithuanian arms. They now expected more pay, and to be paid promptly. This was not a promise that the grand masters of the future could fulfil.

9
THE HUNDRED YEARS WAR
PART TWO

JEAN FROISSART OFTEN MENTIONED Aymerigot Marcel, an important commander of free companies. His familiar name came from his common oath, 'Yes, may God help me'. But Marcel's fame comes from a moment when God did not help. In 1390 Marcel's castle was under siege. Froissart reported that he had written for help, but:

> ...the letters from the king of England and the duke of Lancaster had failed in the effect he looked to from them. He therefore thought of another expedient, which was to leave his castle and ride night and day unto the garrisons in Perigord and other places, to call upon...Gascon and Bearnois men-at-arms of the English party, and entice them by fair speeches to enter Auvergne for the sake of plunder, and then to advance to La Roche de Vendais, some morning or evening, and capture the knights and squires before it, which would bring them more than one hundred thousand francs for their ransoms, without counting smaller articles of pillage.

Marcel should have ridden straight to an English garrison, but he felt safe in stopping at a cousin's castle. The cousin was wanted by both the duke of Berry and Charles VI, who were otherwise less than friendly to one another – one reason that Auvergne was in chaos. Marcel arrived unannounced, accompanied by only a page. He was shown to a private chamber where he could bathe and change his clothes, then, when he was ready, he went down to his cousin without putting his sword or armour back on. To his surprise, he was overpowered by the servants, loaded with chains and thrown into the most secure dungeon. The cousin, who had watched this with satisfaction, then wrote a letter to the duke of Berry, offering to exchange Marcel for a full pardon of past sins.

The duke of Berry smiled when he read the letter and said to his courtiers, 'Would you like to hear news? Aymerigot Marcel is caught; his cousin, Tournemine, holds him in prison.' There were universal murmurs of approval, muted by questions of what would happen next. Marcel deserved to hang – the punishment of a low-born criminal – but everyone was realistic enough to know that the king was a pragmatist who might well let him go free. Marcel might be more useful to the crown alive than dead. Besides, the king was mentally unbalanced.

'I don't know,' the duke said, as he ordered his boat readied to cross the Seine to the Louvre, where the king and royal council were staying. As it happened, the mood at court was to make an example of the prisoner. A pardon for all crimes was written out for Tournemine and a great reward authorised, then Berry was put in charge of bringing Marcel to Paris – that is, the duke sent a lesser official onto the dangerous roads where a rescue attempt might be made – and deliver him to the Bastille, thence to the provost of the Chatelet.

Marcel could not believe what was happening. He should be punished for nothing more than rape, rapine, murder and treason? He was not kept long in the Bastille, but was soon delivered to the Chatelet. The procession through the streets must have been spectacular, passing as it did through the marketplace to the royal compound that sprawled across the island and the right bank of the river. Marcel offered 60,000 francs for his pardon, but no one was willing to accept it. He was told that the king was rich enough now and did not need money. Moreover, he was not even given the usual delay before trial, so that he could not seek out help from powerful friends. He was condemned to death on the grounds of treason.

In accordance with the contemporary practice of humiliating criminals, he was first carried in a cart to the market place, where the cart was turned around several times so that everyone could see that it was actually Marcel and not, as rumour might later have it, someone else; this also allowed the common citizenry to mock him. Taken to the gibbet, he was expected to listen to a list of his crimes read aloud and the justification for his death sentence. Marcel paid no attention to this. Instead he talked at length with one of the officers, discussing the political situation in Auvergne; apparently, the officer had been instructed to learn what he could about Marcel's associates, and whether or not they might be willing to surrender. His information was insufficient to save him. The executor came forward with his axe – the sentence of hanging had been commuted to a more honourable end. His head was cut off, his body was quartered, and the four parts were displayed over the principal gates of the city.

Such were the perils of the mercenary life. Those who were astute enough to recognise that the situation was changing made their peace with the king, often obtaining titles and offices, and in some cases, continuing to command armies. Those who were too slow (or too proud, or lacked connections) were hunted down one by one and eliminated. This surely came as a surprise to them (and the public at large), because such efforts to eliminate the free companies and private warfare had almost always failed before.

There was probably no good reason for the Hundred Years War to resume. The French held most of the disputed lands, and the English had a strong memory of the civil strife that had made it impossible to defend them. Henry IV (1399–1413) was too wise to leave a divided kingdom for an uncertain war across the Channel. His son, Henry V (1413–22), saw the situation differently.

SHAKESPEARE'S AGINCOURT

By 1415 it was France which was in turmoil. The royal family was divided. The king, Charles VI, being periodically insane, was supervised by relatives who quarrelled over the lucrative post of regent. Unfortunately for everyone, the king would recover his sanity, undo all measures taken by the regents, and then relapse into insanity.

One uncle, Philippe the Bold, Duke of Burgundy, had slowly made himself independent of royal control; his son, John the Fearless (1404–19), even allied himself with England against the king. It appeared quite likely that this alliance of England and Burgundy would succeed in tearing the French kingdom apart, with the Burgundian duke to have the northern and interior provinces, the English the southern and western.

To the allies' astonishment, however, Henry V's invasion of Normandy did not have the success he had imagined. The citizens of Calais held out longer than anyone anticipated, disrupting his plans to occupy the rich farmlands of the Vexin that lay just up the Seine River. Since Normandy could not raise enough grain to feed itself, without the Vexin the Normans would have to surrender to the first French army that appeared, no matter how thankful the citizens of Calais might feel for not having been massacred to the last man.

Henry's army did not have many knights. He could not afford them. Instead, he had filled out his ranks with English bowmen and Welsh irregulars. This was a gamble. Such troops had been successful against French armies in the distant past, but not as often now that French knights were wearing plate armour.

The disadvantages of plate armour were cost and weight. But France was rich and the nobles were willing to spend large sums to protect themselves against arrows and simultaneously impress their peers – plate armour, when properly polished, gleamed in the sunlight, almost dazzling the eyes, and French nobles had an endless supply of servants to polish their gear.

The only open question was leadership. Henry was still inexperienced, and the French king was only periodically in command of his senses. It could be a contest of incompetence, comparable perhaps only to the earlier summit meeting of the French king with the Holy Roman emperor, Wenceslas of Bohemia – the king was insane at the time and the emperor drunk. Surprisingly, the results were no worse than obtained by the usual meetings of heads of state.

If military experts could have been interviewed, they would probably have given the English king poor marks. He had captured one major town, but his army was about to disintegrate from exhaustion, cold and disease. The French, in contrast, were rested and healthy; moreover, there were many, many more knights in the royal array.

When reports arrived in Calais that a huge French army was gathering near Paris, Henry realised that it was time to go. There was no point in attempting to defend his newly captured towns – the fortifications were in disrepair and food was in short supply. There was no sense in fighting, either – the odds were too great. Henry's men were suffering from diseases brought on by bad diet and polluted water, excessive labours and poor hygiene. Escape was possible only to the north, in Flanders. In a situation reminiscent of Crécy, Henry had almost reached safety when he chose to stand and fight. This made for one of the great battle scenes in theatre history, the battle of Agincourt in Shakespeare's *Henry V*, a combat immortalised in two movie presentations – the idealised patriotic version of Laurence Oliver filmed during World War II (1945), which moved from the stage of the Globe Theatre to the battlefield, and the relentlessly realistic post-Vietnam film (1989) by Kenneth Branagh. Which is better depends on your taste. Both are worth watching.

Shakespeare understood the realities of medieval warfare. There were indeed moments of pomp, moments of glory, but there was also hardship, suffering and waiting. The worst was waiting for the anticipated defeat, with no alternatives to battle available, not even desertion. We see this best in Act IV, as the king's men attempt to sleep, knowing that in the morning they must face an overwhelming number of French knights, the best their enemy had to offer. Westmoreland sighed, 'O, that we now had here but one ten thousand of those men in England that do no work to-day!'

Henry responded, 'No, my fair cousin; If we are mark'd to die, we are enough to do our country loss; and if to live, the fewer men, the greater share of honour'. He then ordered him to allow anyone who so wished, to depart – with pay in his purse! Then he gave one of the greatest speeches of all time:

> We would not live in that man's company
> That fears his fellowship to die with us.
> This day is call'd the feast of Crispian:
> He that outlives this day, and comes safe home,
> Will stand a-tip-toe when this day is named,
> And rouse him at the name of Crispian.
> He that shall live this day, and see old age,
> Will yearly on the vigil feast his neighbours,
> And say *To-morrow is Saint Crispian*:
> Then will he strip his sleeve and show his scars,
> And say *These wounds I had on Crispian's day*.
> Old men forget; yet all shall be forgot,
> But he'll remember, with advantages,
> What feats he did that day: then shall our names,
> Familiar in his mouth as household words, –
> Harry the King, Bedford and Exeter,
> Warwick and Talbot, Salisbury and Gloucester –
> Be in their flowing cups freshly remember'd.
> This story shall the good man teach his son;
> And Crispin Crispian shall ne'er go by,
> From this day to the ending of the world,

But we in it shall be remembered,
We few, we happy few, we band of brothers;
For he to-day that sheds his blood with me
Shall be my brother; be he ne'er so vile,
This day shall gentle his condition;
And gentlemen in England now-a-bed
Shall think themselves accursed they were not here;
And hold their manhoods cheap whiles any speaks
That fought with us upon Saint Crispin's day.

Shakespeare was a playwright, so we do not have to worry about whether Westmoreland's assessment of the men was more realistic than Harry's, or whether Harry answered as he did because he did not have the money to pay a larger army. And we certainly do not have to quibble as to whether he quoted the protagonists correctly. The main points of the exchange are valid, above all the implication that kings raised the best army they could afford, not the best available. (As Donald Rumsfeld said in 2005, 'You go to war with the army you have…')

Each movie accurately shows the English army standing in a strong position at the top of a long slopping hill, with forests protecting the flanks and the camp in the rear. The French had to come at the English straight on – or risk having Henry slip away. Though Charles VI authorised a flanking movement around the woods, the rest of the army was unwilling to wait for the English lines to be disrupted by the need to protect the camp.

One part of the battle of Agincourt that interests modern historians is hardly mentioned at all – the muddy conditions that caused the French horses to slip as their riders tried to turn them away from the sharpened stakes that suddenly became visible when the English bowmen retired a few paces to take protection behind the barrier. After the first unit of horsemen had retreated, the following formation came to a halt as it reached the low pile of slain horses and knights, remaining there under a shower of arrows. The horses, sensing a connection between oncoming volleys and the cries from stricken steeds around them, bolted for safety, disrupting the main force coming on next. Dying horses blocked the way, injured animals struggled to get to their feet, enthusiastic knights urged their mounts forward toward the bowmen on the other side of the confused mass, devastating flights of arrows knocking down the closest Frenchmen – it was a nightmare for the attacking knights, who looked in vain for some command.

But King Charles was as much at a loss for ideas as anyone else. Worse, even had he known what to do – retreat, most likely – how could a mentally unstable monarch communicate that to his army? Command and control had completely broken down. Perhaps he knew better than to order further attacks, but since the attack had begun almost spontaneously, without alternative plans being discussed by the leaders, all he could do was to lead the way to the rear.

Many of the French knights, seeing the attack totally disrupted, had withdrawn from the field before the king. At that the English had charged into the writhing mass of knights and horses. Foot soldiers moved nimbly over the bodies, slitting throats and robbing corpses, while the mounted warriors did their best to take prisoners of everyone who appeared likely to offer a substantial ransom. If these prisoners were temporarily in the hands of commoners, the English knights could always offer a share of the gains. For common soldier, there was little alternative but to agree – only nobles stood a reasonable chance of protecting a prisoner, and only nobles were likely to collect a ransom; commoners attempting to collect a debt were like tailors of a later generation – lucky to get anything. After all, there were honourable debts – gambling, for example – and the rest one could postpone indefinitely. Ransom would be paid only to one's peers.

When the French knights who had been sent around the woods fell on the English camp, Henry had no troops to spare for guarding the captives – there were still many French knights who could yet become involved in the fighting. Not knowing that the French king was intent only on getting back to Paris as quickly as possible, Henry ordered the captives slain. Many a ransom was lost in that massacre.

WAR FOR PROFIT

Profit was one of the great motivating factors of the era – to make a fortune by capturing prominent men and selling them back to their relatives. This was, some commentators were already noting, only one step from kidnapping. Why, after all, confine one's activities to the battlefield? Why not just stop travelers on the road and demand their money? Or, if one suspected that there was more money at home, hold them prisoner until relatives paid for their safe return?

While this was often done crudely, the kidnappers relying on the breakdown of law and order, it could also be done as a clever act of statecraft, as the new king of Poland, Jagiełło, demonstrated in 1388. Seeking ways to hinder the enemies of his Lithuanian homeland, the Teutonic Knights, he sought to interrupt the passage of crusaders across Brandenburg and Pomerania to Prussia by acquiring strategic territories then up for sale, thus forcing the crusaders to take the more expense sea route, then disrupting that by an alliance with the king of Denmark.

Jagiełło's plan to purchase the territories failed when the grand master of the Teutonic Order, Conrad II, was able outbid him; also because the grand master's political allies raised a cry about German territories going to a foreigner, demanding that the emperor, Wenceslas of Bohemia, forbid any sale to the Polish king.

Jagiełło saw another opportunity for mischief in Stolp, a province of Pomerania. There were two parties in Stolp, just as there were two dukes in Pomerania, one of whom supported the Teutonic Knights, the other the king of Poland. Jagiełło suggested to the dukes that if they cooperated, he might arrange for them to inherit Masovia, an important Polish province bordering Prussia on the south.

The grand master, aware of this intrigue, countered with a reminder that Jagiełło was known for forgetting promises. If, on the other hand, he said, the dukes worked with the Teutonic Knights, they might get Dobrin, the part of Masovia currently held by the military order; moreover, they would have an ally who would defend them against Jagiełło. In any case, they would have to seek the order's help when the king inevitably changed his mind. Conrad II also offered to pay the dukes and their nobles for a promise to serve in his army when war with Poland came. This kind of 'money-fief' was common, honourable and profitable.

Jagiełło was determined to disrupt this arrangement. In December of 1388 the young duke of Geldern, Wilhelm, was making his way across Pomerania. Wilhelm had taken the cross twice before, in 1383 and 1386, but had found reasons to delay going to Prussia. The third vow had been made in the midst of a battle – promising to go on crusade if he survived, he had charged at the head of three hundred knights screaming 'Geldern' and routed his enemies. It would be tempting God to fail to join this year's winter expedition. Jagiełło, eager to demonstrate that the roads were not safe even for the most prominent crusaders, bribed Count Eckhart von dem Walde and more than forty local nobles to kidnap the duke as he passed through the bishopric of Cammin, a small territory on the coast. The count obliged, unfortunately slaying two of Wilhelm's knights during the capture, and took his prisoner to Falkenburg.

As soon as Conrad II heard of the outrage, he sent a message to the dukes of Pomerania, asking them to rescue Wilhelm. However, one duke was in Denmark and the other did not want to get involved. Angry, the grand master cancelled the winter expedition and sent the army against Falkenburg, which he took in three days of heavy fighting. Then complications set in – Wilhelm refused to acknowledge his having been rescued. He had given his word of honour that he would remain a prisoner, and the flight of the count of Walde to Poland made no difference! The duke was an honourable knight and he was determined to remain in Falkenburg until released from his oath by his captor.

Conrad II asked the emperor, Wenceslas, to intervene, but the emperor – in one of his moods, perhaps in an alcoholic stupor and momentarily friendly toward Poland – refused to act. Neither the dukes nor their vassals cooperated in any way. Conrad wrote letters, then waited, wrote more letters, then waited. Months passed. In April of 1389 the grand master sent another army to Falkenburg, captured the castle again, and had Wilhelm brought in chains into him. This should have allowed the duke to say that he had not violated his word to his captor, but it was insufficient. Eventually, the grand master had to send the duke back to Falkenburg and resume negotiations.

In time Conrad had another idea. Many decades earlier a pope had given a minor Prussian bishop the authority to protect crusaders en route to and from Prussia. The bishop now warned the count of Walde and thirty-eight other nobles that they had violated the rights of the Church and that, unless they released their prisoner immediately, he would excommunicate them. The count absolved the duke of Geldern of his oath, the Teutonic Knights freed their hostages, and on 15 August, 1389, the duke proceeded on to Prussia to fulfil his vow. The Pomeranian dukes and their nobles received cash payments; the count of Walde was never punished.

In short, profit from war came in various forms – booty, pay, ransom and even honour. Robbery was important, too. Every soldier, however base or noble, must have dreamed of slipping away from the battlefield and reaching the enemy camp before anyone else. Stealing the pay of the enemies' mercenaries would be better than being paid by an employer, because lucky men might get the wages of an entire army at once. And, while the employer might complain, a shrewd man could be off and away before the bodies had been counted and his disappearance noted.

REALITY AND LITERATURE

By 1390 employers of armies in France and England were more in control of their warriors than before. Bell's careful study of English recruitment and pay practices in *War and the Soldier in the Fourteenth Century* informs us who the commanders were, what they were paid, how contracts were drawn up, and what impact the wars of this era had on the tragic events of Richard II's reign.

Bennett's short volume of biographies, *Six Medieval Men and Women*, shows how Shakespeare had taken Sir John Fastolf, one of the more capable and admirable figures of the second half of the war, and transmogrified him into a comic figure, half coward and half fool – Falstaff. The real Fastolf served in Normandy and Gascony 1412–13, where his talents earned him posts of responsibility. In 1415 he agreed to procure a force of ten knights and thirty archers to serve Henry V for a year; the contract stipulated that each knight had to bring four horses, which implied the presence of a groom. His men-at-arms and archers received one Schilling a day or one-half Schilling respectively – about half of the going rate of two decades earlier. The contract provided that he would be able to keep the ransom of important captives and one-third the ransom of lesser men. Also that booty would be divided, while pillaging would be forbidden. How this was to be accomplished was unclear. Perhaps it was left deliberately vague.

In 1415 Fastolf was at the siege of Harfleur and the battle of Agincourt. Although no document mentions him, he was given a promotion in 1416 and performed so expertly in Normandy that the next year he was knighted. By 1423 he was governor of Anjou and Maine, in 1424 he agreed to raise a force of 80 knights and 240 archers – an extraordinarily large number of fighting men for that era. In 1425 he was awarded the Order of the Garter – a great honour. In 1429 he was on his way to Orleans, escorting a supply column, when an overwhelming French army ambushed him. There was no reason that he should have prevailed at what became known as the battle of the Herrings (with which the wagons were loaded), but his archers took refuge under the wagons and routed their mounted enemies. Fastolf's reputation soared.

The future was less kind. From that moment on, Fastolf's career followed the fortunes of England downward. Joan of Arc relieved Orleans, then defeated a small English army led by Talbot and Fastolf – for which the king stripped Fastolf of the Garter. Nevertheless, Fastolf retained his command for another decade. He retired in 1440 to his estates – some of which were the inheritance of his wife. He lived in style, surrounded by luxury, books, churchmen and the managers of his numerous economic interests. His magnificent country house was finished only in 1454, years after the death of his wife. With twenty-six bedchambers, public rooms, a chapel, dining hall and other chambers, it covered six acres and was filled with the finest objects of the age. He had assumed that he could cover much of the cost by collecting the sums owed to him from his past military service. This he did not succeed in doing – the royal debts were still outstanding when Fastolf died in 1459.

In short, he was not at all like the Fastolfe of *Henry VI*, Part 1:

> CAPTAIN: Whither away, Sir John Fastolfe, in such haste?
> FASTOLFE: Whither away! To save myself by flight:
>   We're like to have the overthrow again.
> CAPTAIN: What! Will you fly, and leave Lord Talbot?
> FASTOLFE: Ay. All the Talbots in the world, to save my life.

Nor did he resemble the coward, thief and braggart of *Henry IV*, Part 1, who raises a force of mercenaries for young Harry of Monmouth, the Prince of Wales:

> FALSTAFF: If I be not ashamed of my soldiers, I am a soused
> gurnet. I have misused the king's press damnably. I have got, in
> exchange of a hundred and fifty soldiers, three hundred and odd
> pounds. I press me none but good house-holders, yeoman's sons;
> inquired me out contracted bachelors, such as had been ask'd twice
> on the banns; such a commodity of warm slaves, as had as lief hear
> the Devil as a drum; such as fear the report of a caliver worse than
> a struck fowl or a hurt wild-duck. I press'd me none but such
> toasts-and-butter, with hearts in their bellies no bigger than pins'-
> heads, and they have bought out their services; and now my whole
> charge consists of ancients, corporals, lieutenants, gentlemen of
> companies, slaves as ragged as Lazarus in the painted cloth, where
> the glutton's dogs lick his sores; and such as, indeed, were never
> soldiers, but discarded unjust serving-men, younger sons to
> younger brothers, revolted tapsters and ostlers trade-fallen, the

cankers of a calm world and a long peace, ten times more dishonourable ragged than an old faced ancient: and such have I, to fill up the rooms of them that have bought out their services, that you would think that I had a hundred and fifty tattered prodigals lately come from swine-keeping, from eating draff and husks. A mad fellow met me on the way, and told me I had unloaded all the gibbets, and press'd the dead bodies. No eye hath seen such scarecrows. I'll not march through Coventry with them, that's flat: nay, and the villains march wide betwixt the legs, as if they had gyves on; for, indeed, I had the most of them out of prison. There's but a shirt and a half in all my company; and the half shirt is two napkins tack'd together and thrown over the shoulders like an herald's coat without sleeves; and the shirt, to say the truth, stolen from my host at Saint Alban's, or the red-nose innkeeper of Daventry. But that's all one; they'll find linen enough on every hedge.

This suggests, unfortunately, that we all tend to follow the wisdom of John Ford in *The Man Who Shot Liberty Valence* (1962), 'When the legend becomes fact, print the legend.' Have we, in moving from knight to gunfighter, come so very far?

THE RISE OF BURGUNDY

From England to Burgundy was not a great distance in those days, since the rich commercial centres of the Low Countries were the heart of the immensely wealthy Burgundian state. The tax revenues had allowed the dukes of Burgundy – Philippe the Bold (†1404), John the Fearless (†1419), Philippe the Good (†1467) and Charles the Bold (†1477) – to create a powerful state on the basis of bureaucrats and mercenaries. But it would be a mistake to think of these rulers as dispassionate modern despots. They were thoroughly medieval in their ways of thinking about power, their rights over their subjects, and their *amour propre*.

Huizinga warns the modern student not to attempt to understand the psychology of medieval people by today's standards – our ancestors were much more excitable. Hatred and envy were more significant; honour, too;

and, in the case of Burgundy, revenge. The assassination of John the Fearless in 1419 drove politics for two generations.

The dukes of Burgundy possessed the richest domains of northern Europe – lands stretching from the Channel to the Holy Roman Empire and south almost to the Mediterranean Sea – regions rich in agriculture and industry. Their immense incomes allowed them to hire mercenaries in numbers and quality superior to their opponents, and to win friends and allies by generous gifts.

Opposed to them was a characteristic of the modern world – nationalism. This threatened to tear their multilingual state apart.

There had always been an awareness of ethnic identity, but that is not quite the same as seeing strangers as fellow Englishmen or Frenchmen, and it is worlds away from being willing to die for an abstract notion of England or France. It was especially far from the minds of those who still identified with their region of birth. Normans and Gascons swore allegiance to an English king because he was their established lord, a descendant of their proud rulers of times long past. Now, however, men and women began to wonder if this was right. Should their ruler not be a Frenchman? After all, weren't all the inhabitants of the war-torn regions between the Atlantic and the Rhine French?

Not if you asked the Germans, who were the majority population in some of these lands. But in the Holy Roman Empire, too, people were beginning to suspect that something was amiss. But like most contemporaries, whenever Germans contemplated the likely consequences of having one supreme ruler, they had to wonder what traditional rights and privileges would be lost, and how many new taxes would be demanded. What would be the gains? What would be the losses?

For France, torn between the ambitions of Burgundy and England, the advantages of having a strong king seemed ever more obvious.

JOAN OF ARC AND THE MERCENARIES

By 1429 French soldiers had lost all hope of victory, being unable to defeat even small English forces of bowmen and knights. Their incompetent king, Charles VI, was dead, but his heir, the dauphin, seemed little better – he had murdered John the Fearless, provoking an endless war, but did nothing thereafter; he could not even manage to be crowned, because to do so, he would have to cross Burgundian territory. So desperate were the soldiers for an inspirational leader that they agreed to follow a simple farm-girl whose military advice was to get rid of the camp women, stop cursing, pray continually, and sing hymns while marching. To almost universal surprise, the troops agreed.

In those days camp women were essential to the army's survival – who else would keep track of a soldier's gear, set up camp, cook his meals and wash his clothes? If the men chose to protect the camp from attack rather than stay in the line of battle, that was only understandable. But Joan would not hear these arguments. The women had to go. And go they did.

No cursing. That must have practically silenced the army.

Hymns. Probably they had to learn them first.

Prayer. At least that could be left to the priests. 'Amen' at the proper moments would be enough for the troops.

It worked. Joan transformed a demoralised French army into a fighting machine. No wonder the English later accused her of witchcraft.

In 1923 George Bernard Shaw saw the potential for a clever theatrical dissection of traditional religion and the religion of patriotism. His *Saint Joan* was an instant hit. Shaw struck at the notion of nationhood by allowing Joan's accusers to argue that giving free rein to nationalism would divide Christendom and lead to horrible wars (as 1914–18); but his Joan was also an early feminist. The dauphin (later Charles VII) does not come across well. In fact, nowhere in literature or historical scholarship does he appear in a good light – his contemporaries referred to him as 'Charles the well-served'. Even his portraits show us a man we wouldn't trust to manage our stock portfolio.

This picture was unfortunately true. Once the king was crowned, he lost interest in the war. Money was short, of course, but he was also a realist – battles can be lost, and his hold on the crown might not survive a major setback. In addition, he was ungrateful, cowardly, and satisfied with having finally become the anointed monarch of France. But perhaps he saw that the English could not hold onto the French provinces forever – after all, Henry V had married his sister, and their feeble offspring had inherited her genes. Henry VI's reign (1422–61) began at nine months of age, passed through imbecility, palace intrigue, coups, and would end in the War of the Roses. Charles VII would wait until the time was right. Then strike.

Meanwhile, in 1431, Joan was burned at the stake in Rouen, the English capital of Normandy. The newly crowned Charles VII made no effort to save her.

A quarter of a century later, after the French state had recovered its strength and self-confidence, French armies easily retook Normandy. All that remained to the English was the fortress at Calais. Later, when poor Queen Mary lost Calais, her reputation was damaged beyond repair.

CHARLES THE BOLD AND THE SPIDER KING

The Burgundian duke Charles the Bold (1467–77) had revived the ambition of his grandfather, John the Fearless, to be the most powerful man in all Europe. It was the ambition of a young man (he was thirty-two in 1465, the year he had begun to govern in his father's name), the ambition of a genius reared on hatred of the French monarchs.

The French king, Louis XI (1461–83), was easy to hate. The unlovely son of an unsavoury father, Louis was a genius of a type, perhaps good, more likely evil – patriotism is more important than logic in forming an opinion here. At the very least, Louis was strange man, best remembered from Charles the Bold's description of him as 'the universal spider,' spinning his web over all of France. The spider king, immortalised by Walter Scott's novel, *Quentin Durward* (1823) sat unobtrusively in the centre of his web, every now and then pulling on a string:

> He was by nature vindictive and cruel, even to the extent of finding pleasure in the frequent executions which he commanded. But, as no touch of mercy ever induced him to spare, when he could with safety condemn, so no sentiment of vengeance ever stimulated him to a premature violence. He seldom sprung on his prey till it was fairly within his grasp, and till all hope of rescue was vain; and his movements were so studiously disguised, that his success was generally what first announced to the world the object he had been manoeuvring to attain.

Historians credit Louis with creating the first standing army, an idea that eventually weaned the mercenaries away from the habit of scouting out alternative employment, but this innovation seems to have been partly a continuation of his father's policies and partly copying from Charles the Bold. He preferred diplomacy to war, and he insisted on the absolute loyalty of the men who served. Anyone who worked for this king, worked for him and for no one else. It was a clear break with feudalism.

Such a servant was Philippe de Commynes, whose memoirs are invaluable for historians of this era. He wrote vividly about the War of Public Weal, a supposed protest against Louis's policies, mainly fiscal reform, that would strengthen his position against all enemies internal and foreign, but the rebels also feared that he would punish those who had plotted against him earlier. A more important origin of the civil war lay in the king's relatives who were unhappy for his refusing to support their extravagant political follies and expensive hobbies.

The royal relatives owed their quasi-independent status to earlier kings who had parcelled out important regions – Berry, Anjou, Burgundy and Orleans. In their youth Orleans and Anjou had thrown themselves into Italian politics, but now they were old men more interested in art and poetry, except when, as now, they believed themselves threatened. The duke of Brittany, though not closely related, saw profit for himself whenever France was in trouble.

These enemies of royal authority worked on the paranoia of Charles the Bold. Indeed, the superstitious Burgundian prince was persuaded that Louis, whose reputation for shady, even underworld connections, had murdered Charles VII by a combination of poison and magic, and if he would do that to his own father, what wouldn't he do to relatives who stood in his way? It would be best, Charles reasoned, to eliminate Louis immediately.

In 1465 Charles hired several German princes and their armies, and some Italian mercenaries. It was understood that many of the great French lords would revolt, or at least remain neutral; the Church was of the same mind. Victory in the War of the Common Weal seemed almost guaranteed.

Burgundy was incredibly wealthy at that time, and the duke's court was more lavish than any in Europe, and the beautiful women in it were lavish with their favours, too. But it was Charles's army that caught the public's attention, not the well-known luxuries of the court. Commynes's description of Charles's evolving concepts began with the battle of Montlhéry. Charles had been advised to use the tactics of the English, who had been so successful in the Hundred Years War – to put English archers in a good defensive position, strengthened by dismounted knights. Prior to the start of combat, however, Charles realised that this was not practical. First, his father had dismissed most of his mercenaries during the long period of peace, so that now he had to rely on urban militias and poorly armed and undisciplined allies; second, since the sole uniting principle of the alliance was a dislike of Louis XI, the members of the coalition mistrusted one another. Moreover, as Commynes remarked, although English archers were the best in the world, they were useless in the small numbers Charles had. Commynes was also of the opinion that the less experience archers had, the better! If that had been true, Charles would have been in good shape! Lastly, it was not practical for the Burgundian duke to stand on the defensive – he had to drive the king's forces from the field.

Charles improvised an attack. When his men routed the royalists from the field on one flank, Charles charged after them. On the other flank, however, the rapid advance exhausted his archers, who began to lose cohesion; when royal forces emerged from hiding places in the hedges and attacked, the archers were unprepared to respond. Then the Burgundian cavalry charged right through the bowmen, riding many down. The cavalry attack was subsequently repelled by the French, then routed. The rest of the army fled the field.

Charles found himself in a perilous position. He was, in effect, trapped behind enemy lines – royalists were everywhere, with only a few of his own men visible here and there, and the horses tiring quickly. Though struck hard in the stomach by a pike and cut on the neck by a sword, Charles gathered up small pockets of knights and archers and formed them into a fighting force. Then he turned on the royal army and saved the day. Thus he earned the nickname, Charles the Bold. His enemies called him Charles the Rash.

Louis XI came out of this engagement the better, though most contemporaries called it a draw. His outnumbered army should have been beaten easily, and even at the end of the day it would have broken if Charles had been able to rally more men. Only Louis's personal presence had persuaded his men to stand firm against the last cavalry charge. His subsequent defence of Paris was exemplary – he hired archers to assist his 2,000 men-at-arms. Also he employed 500 Italian cavalry and 3,000 foot led by Galeazzo Maria Sforza of Milan to harass the duke of Bourbon's lands, thus making it difficult for him to contribute to the rebel coalition; he took these troops home, however, when his father, Francesco Sforza, died in 1466 – there might be some trouble over the inheritance.

Charles had Italian troops, too, 200 men-at-arms brought by John, duke of Calabria. He had no wish to assault Paris, however – city streets were death traps for armies. He met with Louis almost privately – Charles's courtiers were appalled that he put himself temporarily in Louis's control (John the Fearless's fatal mistake in 1419 was to trust the dauphin). Commynes summarised the peace agreement by saying that some got what they wanted and others did not. No matter. The peace did not last.

Charles had learned from this war to avoid relying on feudal armies, allies or poorly trained mercenaries. He retained his vassals' levies and his small household units; and used militias for campaigns in the Low Countries, but knew that he could not rely on any of them to operate far from home – and his ambitions were not limited to the immediate neighbourhood.

Thanks to the taxpayers of the Low Countries, Charles had the means to hire the soldiers for a new army, then expand. Expansion was essential, he thought. Faced by the potential power of a unified and pacified France on one side and a reviving Holy Roman Empire on the other, he would either have to take lands from them to create a more equal balance of power or he could move through the Swiss Confederation to Italy, thus recreating the ancient Middle Kingdom of Lothair; in fact, he would attempt to do both, to seize land from France and Germany, then taking on the Swiss. But before he could do either, he had to instill discipline in his own unruly lands.

Charles's problem in the Low Countries was with burghers who were well known both for their stubborn courage in battle and their opposition to taxes and interference in local government. He was ultimately successful there – the burghers and artisans valued their lives sufficiently to surrender after the siege at Liège, where he managed to seize Louis XI and hold him hostage until he had finished massacring the rebels – but he knew that he could not rely on their soldiery soon.

Charles had begun his military career with the usual regional rag-tag assortment of feudal levies, Flemish pikemen and English archers. Learning from experience that this kind of army was not effective for distant operations, by 1471 he had begun to create a permanent army of mercenaries. Word soon spread of its deadly efficiency.

Charles's plans were carefully laid. Though he was unable to persuade Edward IV of England (1461–83) to renew the Hundred Years War, and efforts to lure the Spanish into the conflict failed as well, he expected to dismantle the clumsy French monarchy easily. He might have done this if he had concentrated on that task. But Charles was too proud and too self-confident. He listened to advice only rarely, and he took on more enemies than was wise. For years he contested with the Holy Roman emperor, Friedrich

III (1440–93), for control of the Rhineland; then, after achieving considerable success, he turned his eyes upstream, to the Swiss Confederation.

The Swiss Confederation (it was not sufficiently unified to be called Switzerland yet) was so poor that its principal export was soldiers – we tend to think of sturdy men with muscles bulging from walking up and down mountains, but in fact most soldiers came from the cities of Bern (a German-speaking canton) and Geneva (French-speaking). These soldiers had the confidence that comes from having fought the best cavalry in Germany – that of the Habsburgs – and won; so important was booty to the national economy that the *landsknechts* (as the men wielding the pikes and halberds were known) were eventually forbidden to keep anything for themselves, but were required to gather it for sharing out later – this also discouraged individuals from falling out of line to search bodies for valuables, a practice that had brought disaster to many an army and saved many a routed force. The Swiss van consisted of units of three men – a pikeman, a crossbowman and a musketeer; the main body was composed of men bearing long pikes supported by comrades wielding that odd-looking combination of short pike and axe known as a halberd. The pike, though an ancient weapon, was an unwieldy weapon compared to the spear and it was effective only when employed in a phalanx – usually in a static defensive position. The Swiss innovation was to practise marching so that the phalanx became an attacking formation. The tradition of shooting crossbows was reflected in the story of William Tell, but it was the mass formation of pikemen and halberdiers that was so formidable. The Swiss, marching to the beat of drum and fife, moved with a speed that no one else could match – clock-working marching, one could say – and they rarely retreated. To defeat a Swiss unit meant killing them all.

Observers had expected that the decisive battles between France and Burgundy would be fought in the Low Countries, today's Netherlands and Belgium, where the conflict had centred in 1471. But Louis had seen that Alsace-Lorraine was Charles's weak point. Charles had to cross those lands to reach the Swiss Confederation and his southern possessions, his subjects had to cross them to trade with Italy and Germany, and Alsace-Lorraine was Charles's base for expansion into the Holy Roman Empire. Moreover, it would be easy to persuade Germans and Swiss that their interests were the same as France's – stopping Burgundian expansion. Louis striking at the duke's access to Italian and German mercenaries and to the trade that financed his armies was a stroke of genius.

More forward-thinking than many contemporaries, Charles believed that cannon did not have to be limited in battle to sieges, but could be employed by field armies. Experts considered this questionable. Though Bohemian Hussites had used small guns mounted on wagons to halt charging cavalry until the moment for a devastating counter-attack by Czech cavalry, nobody else had ever mastered the intricate tactics of manoeuvring the wagons into line or could hold their own cavalry in check until the attackers were exhausted. The proper means of dealing with a wagon fort, it seemed, was to blast it with superior artillery, inflicting heavy losses and creating panic among the packed horsemen inside the perimeter. Infantry were believed to be helpless once cavalry forced them into a defensive box, because then, as the English had demonstrated in Scotland, archers could cut them to pieces easily.

Charles wanted more flexible formations that would allow him to get his guns in place to blast the enemy units, then launch his elite infantry and cavalry toward those that seemed ready to break and flee. Getting the guns forward was not an easy task, and ammunition could not be supplied quickly. But Charles persisted. If money was no object, none of his commanders would object. Charles hired the best cannonmasters to manage his guns, and he employed landsknechts and men-at-arms as the backbone of his army. He also hired thousands of English archers and supplied them with horses so that they could operate in conjunction with his cavalry. Charles's combination of the three arms promised to make his army deadly.

His plan was to seek out and destroy the enemy army, to win the war in one great battle. Napoleon and Clausewitz would have understood.

Charles had reason to believe that he could easily beat the French king at some future date. First, it was likely that the king's powerful relatives would eventually revolt again; when they did, Charles could intervene, this time more effectively. Second, some royal lands had not yet recovered from the depredations of the Hundred Years War; although the English armies had been driven from French soil, evidence of the recent carnage and destruction were everywhere. Third, Charles's alliance with England was strong, thanks to his 1468 marriage to Margaret of York, King Edward's sister – an event so spectacular that it is celebrated to this day with a great holiday in Brugge. Lastly, Louis XI was not well – epileptic, nervous, ill (probably malaria and certainly a noxious skin disease that even he believed was leprosy), and so prone to changing his mind that no one could predict what he would do in any circumstance. Suspicious of everyone, fearful of assassination, sly in his indirect approach to problems, enthusiastic only about diplomacy and most happy when he could deceive an opponent, he was also cruel and vengeful.

The French king, however, was more resourceful than Charles imagined – even without his presumed magical power. He was able persuade enemies of mediocre talents to despise him, and thus take excessive risks. Not for nothing was his chief enemy called Charles the Rash.

The story is well told by Commynes, who entered the service of Louis XI in 1472. The occasion was the royal reconciliation with several of his enemies, part of Louis's diplomacy aimed at stripping away Charles's allies and firming up royal alliances. Commynes came to realise that his new master had virtues hidden by his simple clothing, his humble demeanour and his paranoia.

Charles, meanwhile, had gone in the opposite direction – mad with ambition and an exaggerated belief in his destiny. He recruited several thousand Italian cavalry led by two Neapolitans, Niccolò di Monteforte, the count of Campobasso (about whom Commynes has nothing good to say), and Giacomo Galeotto. Also 3,000 English archers. He purchased a powerful train of artillery and hired masters capable of employing it effectively. When he issued his *ordinance* of 1473, with its strict system of uniforms and numbering units, it was, according to Malcolm Vale in *War and Chivalry*, the first time since the fall of the Roman Empire that insignia had no connection with social status.

Richard Vaughan, in *Charles the Bold*, praises the use of uniforms to increase morale, and the opportunities that 'spit and polish' gave officers for improving discipline; but he is more enthusiastic about the duke's many other military reforms, especially the organisation of recruiting and supply. Charles had his faults, many of them, but failing to make plans was not one of them. Carrying out plans, alas for him, was another matter. Improvisation in a crisis is usually effective when it is based on a study of alternatives; this was surprisingly not one of the duke's strengths. Even more significant for his military fortunes, Charles was not good at taking advice – he regarded his commanders as too cautious, too timid. Perhaps too Italian, preferring positional warfare over battle.

The prejudice against Italian condottieri was widespread, but it was balanced by a realisation that the Italians were the best soldiers and Italian generals like Colleoni were unrivalled. Still, there was a great distance between Charles's desire for a decisive battle and the Italian preference for winning wars by manoeuvre and diplomacy. Ironically, his most famous campaigns were determined by sieges of important fortresses and cities.

In 1474 Charles besieged the rich city of Neuss, not far from Cologne, expecting that the king of England would bring a vast army to assist in its capture. When Edward IV failed to appear with the 1500 men-at-arms and 14,000 bowmen he had raised with Burgundian money, Charles was unable to capture the city before Holy Roman emperor, Friedrich III, brought an immense army to its relief. Charles was furious about the fact that the feckless Edward had not returned any of the money so he could not hire more men himself, but he also suspected that the king taken a bribe from Louis XI!

Charles should have withdrawn from the Rhineland, but he stayed – an expensive stalemate – until 1475. Almost a year! Tellingly, he could have avoided the war by accepting the emperor's offer of a marriage alliance that would have given him significant concessions. Charles, however, wanted total victory.

Louis IX responded by improving and adding to the small permanent army that had existed since 1445, and recruiting heavily among the Swiss cantons for mercenaries. He tried to raise a force of archers in France, but had little luck – the longbow remained an exclusively English weapon. Once his forces matched the size of the new Burgundian armies, he faced problems of command and control, not to mention supply, that none of his ancestors had ever faced. But then, none of his ancestors had ever faced a challenge similar to Charles the Bold's famed army of Italian, English and German mercenaries.

Louis's attack began in the spring of 1475, when the truce expired. He struck on three fronts – too widely dispersed to have achieved much – and his mercenaries were not yet equal to Charles's. But the show of force impressed Edward IV of England, who opened negotiations and later met with the king to discuss peace. Charles bowed to the inevitable – a truce with Louis in September that was to last for nine years. Thus, the latter stages of their contest would be fought, not directly, but by proxy.

CHARLES THE BOLD'S MERCENARY ARMIES

Charles was obsessed with details. No matter was too small for him. Whenever he saw a problem, he sat down with pen and paper and wrote out detailed instructions. Nothing would be done without his permission. This was his strength and his undoing.

He loved parades and ceremonies. Often he would assemble his men, salute the officers collectively and individually, have them give their oaths of allegiance, and distribute the batons, the symbol of authority, personally. Then he would have the entire army swear allegiance. This was designed to offset the besetting sins of mercenary armies – the independence of the commanders and the lack of discipline.

His forces were not large. He mistrusted numbers. It was better, he believed, to rely on quality and good equipment. Discipline on the march was strictly enforced, right to the death penalty; discipline in camp – no swearing, no gambling, and no more than thirty female cooks and washerwomen. Each unit drilled and drilled, not just cavalry and infantry in their special manoeuvres, but together, so that they could perform effectively on the day of battle.

His best troops were his household units – mostly cavalry (counting the mounted archers), but also eight 100-man infantry companies. Their principal duty was to protect the duke and his courtiers at all times.

Charles's artillery was famous, but of limited effectiveness. The cannon were difficult to transport and fired so slowly that they were not much danger on the battlefield. Still, they were useful in sieges and for attracting tourists to Swiss museums today.

THE BATTLE OF MORAT

By 1476 Charles was widely considered unbeatable. He had occupied most of Lorraine and he was pushing toward the Alpine passes. Richard Vaughan has doubts about Charles's plans for Italy, but none about his ambition and stubbornness; as he wrote about the Neuss campaign, 'The war between Burgundy and the Empire was not only fought with armies. Manifestos, declarations of war, letters, bribes, rumours and falsifications of all kinds played their part, as they have done in every war.'

Louis XI, meanwhile, was encouraging alliances among Burgundy's many enemies. His diplomacy brought the Swiss together, though the urban cantons who wanted his money most were not supported strongly by the rural cantons. It was not for nothing that France was a rich country, and what were its riches for, if not to protect the nation by the appropriate use of gifts and bribes?

The Swiss were, on the whole, quite willing to listen to French denunciations of Burgundian ambitions. But the Swiss were not innocent of ambitions themselves, certainly not Bern, which was both expansionist and ready to make preventive war – every burgher understood that Charles was opposed to civic rights everywhere. All Bern needed was a pretext. This was quickly invented – the seizure of two cartloads of skins that were evading taxes.

According to Commynes, Charles brought his army to Granson, a fortress near Neuchâtel held by 800 Swiss; if he could take that city, he would secure access to Savoy, then to the rest of Italy. While he entertained his guests in great luxury, comfortably out of the miserable weather, his guns battered the fortress into unconditional submission. He then ordered the survivors slaughtered – hanging hundreds from trees, drowning others in the lake. It was a warning to all those who opposed him.

The effect was not that which he had intended. Volunteers flowed into the Swiss army, ready to fight in case the Burgundian duke should be so foolish as to advance further south. Still, the Swiss were not so angry as to attack him in his present position, which they could approach only on a narrow front commanded by his artillery.

Charles ran out of patience. Against the advice of his captains, who suggested that the Swiss could not supply the needs of their army long, he ordered his men to march to a new base, one better suited for offensive operations. Advancing out of Granson into the foothills on 2 March, he was attacked by swiftly moving Swiss pikemen before he could get his men into a proper formation. The leading Burgundian units fled in panic, followed by most of the rest of the army; a few cavalry units managed an attack on the Swiss phalanx but were soon driven off – no horsemen wanted to charge on to the pikes. More Swiss then arrived on the flank, making such noise that the last Burgundian units believed they were about to be surrounded; panic set in, followed by the flight of the entire army. Charles had no choice but to flee, abandoning his camp, his tent, his jewels and his reputation for invincibility.

Commynes, who was in Lyon in charge of the French scouts and spies, reported that only seven men-at-arms perished. No massive loss of blood on either side. Even so, the Burgundian alliance system began to crumble. Each ambassador who came to Louis XI received lavish gifts of money; the Swiss, benefiting from his largesse handsomely, promised to continue their war.

Charles had meanwhile rallied his men, re-equipped those who had lost their weapons and possessions, enlisted a large number of English bowmen, marched toward Bern and began a siege of the city's western outpost, Morat (Murten). Camped nearby, he was awaiting the town's surrender when his scouts reported the approach of a large force. His commanders wanted to withdraw to the plain, where their cavalry would be more effective, but Charles was reluctant to abandon the siege. He divided his forces, ordering the troops besieging Morat to dig a ditch and build a wall that they could defend easily against the oncoming army. Charles could not supervise the work personally, having been prostrated by illness and melancholy, but he was not worried by estimates that his 12,000 men were facing up to 25,000 Swiss.

Charles had good reasons for optimism. He could feed his troops, while his enemies could not – they had to attack soon or disperse. The heavy rain spoke against the Swiss conducting offensive operations, even against keeping the troops in the field. With luck the Swiss would give up and go home. But Charles was not a lucky man.

On 22 June, after holding his men almost two days in readiness for an assault, he ordered them to return to camp so that he could feed and pay them. Soon afterward the Swiss slipped through the forest undetected and attacked the wall in overwhelming numbers; this may have been an accident in timing, perhaps caused by the sudden appearance of the sun rather than Swiss military judgment or even a Swiss awareness that Charles had taken troops away from the wall. No matter. Soon the Swiss were past the wall and advancing swiftly. There was a desperate struggle in the camp, but Charles brought his units into the fray only one by one, and these were overwhelmed singly by the numerically superior Swiss units. His English archers emptied their quivers, then, when their commander fell, fled. Eventually, all Charles's force still in arms joined them, only to find the Swiss blocking the camp exits; and this time the fugitives were pursued by German cavalry.

The effect on the political situation was immediate and staggering. Charles's allies in Italy changed sides, and so many local rulers went over to the enemy that there was no hope of his recovering his bases on the borders of the Swiss Confederation. From this point on, he was on the defensive. Even so, his position was far from hopeless.

THE BATTLE OF NANCY

Charles's army was very efficient, even in defeat – perhaps two-thirds of his soldiers had escaped. Therefore, he was not afraid of the odds against him; this fearlessness was enhanced by his abandoning rose-hip tea for strong wine. Alcohol did not help his judgement.

Perhaps he was misled by the gross incompetence of some of his opponents; perhaps he counted on the efforts of the emperor and pope to persuade the Swiss to make peace; perhaps he had secret reasons for assuming that he could easily recover Nancy, the capital of Lorraine that had enthusiastically surrendered to the duke of Lorraine in the days following Morat. After demanding increased payments from his vassals, he marched on Nancy despite the oncoming winter; when the citizens did not surrender, he warned that he would capture the city by siege and take his usual vengeance upon all who resisted.

As winter set in, Charles withdrew, hermit-like, and let his beard grow; he was querulous, insulting his friends so outrageously that several left his service without giving notice. At Morat, he had been outnumbered two to one. Now, in 1477, the odds were even greater, 20,000 to 5,000, but he did not heed the advice of his counsellors to abandon the siege. Charles and everyone else understood that whoever held Nancy would exercise regional hegemony. Charles's army was not in good shape, but many observers were nevertheless still expecting a Burgundian victory. It was a contest of endurance between the citizens' suffering from cold and hunger and Charles's army wearing down from bad food, freezing weather, disease and desertion. As many as 400 of Charles's men succumbed on Christmas Eve alone.

The Swiss were spoiling for a fight, but their progress into Lorraine was slowed by the troops' stopping to rob and murder Jews along the way. As they approached Nancy, Charles took his troops out of the siege lines and stationed them in a fortified position across the road. With a river on one side and a forest on the other, he blocked the Swiss advance, apparently planning to let the cold wind wear them down before any battle could take place. He must also have been comforted by news that there was no single commander of the enemy force, but a collection of allied leaders.

Weather was undoubtedly a factor in the desertion of some of Charles's best Italian troops, but probably injured pride was more significant. Niccolò di Monteforte left, and the count of Campobasso actually went over to the enemy with 820 men, but was sent away because the duke of Lorraine, the commander of the German–French coalition, did not want any traitors in his ranks. It would be too easy to change sides in the middle of the battle and sow panic among his troops. Campobasso found a comfortable place to watch, so that he could later share in the looting.

Charles had placed his men in a strong position on a wooded slope, with a stream presenting an additional, though minor, obstacle. His guns commanded the field, while the Swiss would be advancing directly into blowing snow. The Swiss, however, were not such convenient enemies as to march into a trap. They divided their forces, with one phalanx approaching the Burgundian left along the road; this served as a diversion. The main force circled left through the woods and emerged without warning in the Burgundian rear, then attacked downhill. Its movements had been hidden by snow and wind, and by moving through wooded valleys – even though that meant wading through some icy streams.

Charles was unable to turn his artillery around, and soon the units guarding his rear were overwhelmed by the Swiss pikemen; then everyone still alive fled. Charles fought bravely, but he was eventually surrounded and cut down. Lying wounded on a frozen lake, he was murdered by plunderers who did not recognise him. Otherwise, they could have held him for an immense ransom.

It was the end of an era – both the end of Burgundian greatness and of the invincible archer. Until now the foremost lesson of the Hundred Years War seemed to be that a defensive force of archers and dismounted knights holding a strong hillside position had every advantage. From now on, the experts praised speed and mobility. Not of cavalry, but infantry.

The serried ranks of the pikemen dominated the battlefield. No immobile bands of burgher militia, but well-trained units that could manoeuvre quickly and decisively.

SUMMARY

Charles's most important legacy – the modern army – went to French kings who knew better how to employ it. Richard Vaughan was right to comment that Charles 'contrived to be defeated, often disastrously, in almost all his major battles'. But the modern army, with its flow-charts, rules, strict discipline, organisation into companies and squadrons, its insistence on drilling to perfection and centralising authority into one commander's hands, can be traced back to his ideas.

His richest lands, however, went not to France, but to the Habsburgs, who would eventually see their future south of the Alps, not in the commercial heartland of northern Europe. The money for their mercenaries would come from trade, then later from their possessions in the New World – silver from Mexico and South America.

Malcolm Vale notes that the French king eventually replaced short-time mercenaries with a standing army. That army would be French, its commanders selected by the king. Already it wore uniforms, marched to the beat of drums, responded to trumpet and flag signals and was subjected to more rigorous discipline. It did not hide behind fortress walls unnecessarily, but took to the offensive when appropriate. It would take another two centuries before this army – professional in every sense – became the best in all Europe. But the start had been made. The age of the mercenary was coming to an end.

MARRIAGES ARE CHEAPER AND MORE PERMANENT THAN WAR

It was said of the Habsburgs that 'others have to fight wars, but you, oh Happy Austria, only marry'. (*Bella gerant alii, tu felix Austria nube!*) The French king, through the Swiss, may have defeated Charles the Bold, but it was Holy Roman emperor Friedrich III who emerged the winner. Charles's daughter Mary, seeing her inheritance being swallowed up by Louis XI and not wanting to marry the six-toed dauphin (the future Charles VIII of France, 1483–98), agreed almost immediately to marry the emperor's son Maximilian.

Maximilian had originally wanted to marry Anne of Brittany, not for her famous beauty or pleasant personality, but because her lands were strategically placed – he would surround France more completely. In addition, her Breton subjects, proud of their culture and language, preferred the German connection to the French, and would likely have fought loyally for him. But Maximilian would have had to wait and negotiate, and there was no certainty that he would succeed. Mary of Burgundy was a sure thing, she was immensely wealthy, and her lands abutted Germany.

Anne, seeing no alternative to a French connection, gave her hand to the misshapen Charles VIII in 1491. This brought peace to her lands, a welcome relief from the almost constant wars of the previous century and a half. Anne's somewhat rustic habits were commemorated in this French children's verse about her wooden shoes:

C'était Anne de Bretagne	There's Anne of Brittany
Avec ses sabots.	in her wooden shoes.
C'était Anne de Bretagne	There's Anne of Brittany
Avec ses sabots.	in her wooden shoes.
Revenant de ses domains	Coming from her lands
En sabots, mirli tontaine.	in wooden shoes.
Ah, Ah, Ah	ah, ah, ah
Vivent les sabots de bois!	Hooray for the wooden shoes!

This did not stop the wars between the Valois kings of France and the Habsburg emperors of Austria (who soon ruled the Low Countries, Spain and much of Italy). The Habsburgs took the motto of Friedrich III seriously: AEIOU (*Alles Erdreich Ist Österreich Untertan*, meaning: the whole world is subject to Austria; or in Latin *Austria est imperare in omni universo.*) When one ruler, especially one who holds the title emperor, believes that he should rule all of Christendom and perhaps more, what is there to stop him? The answer was National Identity, expressed through a national army.

With the rise of national armies, the profession of mercenary soldier began to flow in new and more orderly channels. Waves of freebooters and thugs ceased to flood embattled regions.

There would be other places for the mercenary companies to attack, defend and plunder. But no longer were they to have the free run of France. The Hundred Years War was now over.

10
THE RENAISSANCE

THE MERCENARY SOLDIER was more common in Italy than north of the Alps because there were more potential employers, and each employer had more money. Also, thanks to some *condottieri* (as the leaders of Italian mercenary companies were called) making the transition from hireling to lord, they are better known to modern readers.

In fact, however, the most significant change in military strategy and tactics was probably not due to the presence of such mercenaries, but earlier, when the development of city militia companies in the twelfth century tipped the balance of battle in favour of local cavalrymen against foreign knights. Florence, Milan and other cities rose in political importance, and as their obligations increased, they hired mercenaries to relieve their citizens from onerous military service. Most mercenaries did little beyond guarding city walls and acting as local police. Hence, the increasing reliance on mercenaries was not quickly recognised as a mistake; even when some questioned the wisdom of hiring outsiders, most citizens preferred to worry about the cost rather than about subversion of the political system. Moreover, there was another reason not to rely on an armed citizenry: each state was divided along party lines, Guelphs and Ghibellines, who were quite ready to slaughter each other. Mercenaries were at least neutral.

There were many more knights in Italy than we commonly imagine, but most lived in cities, not in the countryside. Maurice Keen reminds us in *Nobles, Knights and Men-at-Arms in the Middle Ages* that each city skyline was punctuated by towers, often unbelievably tall and narrow, belonging to local aristocrats. Moreover, the death toll in some of the supposedly bloodless battles was actually fairly high. At Anghiari, Keen notes, there were 900 fatalities, not Machiavelli's famous single death.

Nor were these condottieri foreigners. Michael Mallett, in *Mercenaries and their Masters*, shows that little separated important condottieri from contemporary nobles, right down to their aristocratic habits and pretensions. Moreover, of the 350 known infantry commanders, most came from central Italy (and not just from the poorer parts), most others from Bologna and Rome. Of the foreigners, there were thirteen Slavs and Albanians, thirteen Spaniards, nineteen Corsicans, a handful of Germans and French, and one Englishman. Most of the infantrymen were born locally. For all of them war was a profession, not merely an opportunity for fighting and looting. In short, Italians were (as Italians will still tell you) more civilised than their neighbours.

Nor was this confined to the Renaissance. For most of the thirteenth century Italian armies had been composed of local nobles, local militia and mercenaries. The complications of party politics infected every city, so that policies were rarely backed by a unanimous public. Naturally, the dominant faction preferred to disarm its opponents as much as possible, and this could only be done if their numbers were replaced by mercenaries. This became practical only in later years of the Middle Ages, a period known as the Renaissance.

A generation ago the Renaissance began at 1300, with Giotto and Dante introducing new forms into art and literature. Today it has moved to the 1400s or even the 1500s, that is, to Michelangelo and Shakespeare – a reminder of how flexible our views of the past are. But the early date works very well when we begin to read the new histories that were being produced in Italy in the 1300s, most importantly the Florentine chronicle by Giovanni Villani.

Villani's career began in 1300. He was exiled from Florence about the same time as Dante, which gave him an unwelcome opportunity to travel, but he was later allowed to return. He died in his native city during the outbreak of the plague that killed 50,000 people in 1348. Villani's chronicle for the year 1302 contained two interconnected stories about mercenaries. Both revolved around Pope Boniface's quarrel with King Philippe IV of France (1285–1314), a quarrel that reflected French interests in Sicily and Spain, the pope's desire to assert his authority more widely, and the feuding factions in Italian politics. When Pope Boniface excommunicated the king, Philippe summoned a council of all the clerics of his realm to denounce the Holy Father for heresy, simony and other assorted crimes.

This might have remained a shouting match at long distance if King Philippe (the fat or the fair depending on your politics) had not contacted the pope's enemies in Rome and then sent one of his minions with drafts of money on a prominent Florentine bank to hire local ruffians. The king's men arrested the pope at his summer home in Anagni and humiliated him. Although the aged pontiff was freed by a local insurrection after three days, his mind was fatally affected – he reputedly gnawed at himself, totally mad, until he died a year later.

Boniface, whose life was less exemplary than his office deserved, had been proud, cruel and courageous. Also very warlike. He had kept 300 Catalan horsemen at his own expense, employing them so successfully that he had almost reduced Rome and the surrounding lands to order again. This, in fact, seems to be the reason that local nobles, especially the Colonna family, were willing to join in the French conspiracy – fear for their immediate secular future was greater than the danger to their immortal souls.

The Catalan horsemen had come via the struggle for possession of Sicily, with the French king assisting his relatives in Naples, the pope supporting the Aragonese (i.e., the Catalans, who had a hereditary claim on the island from Friedrich II of Hohenstaufen). With Boniface's fall, the mercenaries apparently left papal employment. The next pope, Benedict, returned to the traditional, ineffective policies of playing one party against another (White Guelphs in Florence against Black Guelphs, Guelphs elsewhere against Ghibellines, Milan against everyone), and his successors chose to take refuge in Avignon. Philippe had won the immediate contest, hands down. But long term, the mercenaries won. They were the only military force to remain effective.

Quite fittingly, the Renaissance would become identified with the mercenary soldier. Other occupations were becoming professional, too – art and music, for example. But professional warriors had a more immediate impact on politics, and politics had an impact on everything.

CONDOTTIERI

Foreign mercenaries remained a minority of Italian fighting forces until the fourteenth century. Then, when foreigners came to Italy, they came not as individuals, but in organised companies. Still, because these companies required leaders who understood the complex political alliances of the country, Italians had a considerable advantage over foreigners. Although only a few Italian states could afford foreign armies, the advantages justified the expense – Englishmen were rightly feared for their awesome archery, and they were willing to fight right through the winter; Germans and Hungarians were cheaper, but still pricey.

The states that could best afford mercenaries were Florence and Venice, but even they found it difficult to persuade voters to spend money on defence; the Papal States had already been drained dry by the popes' international political ambitions; Milan, dominated by the ruthless Visconti family, was populous, centrally located, and rich – one Visconti had even become Pope Gregory X in 1271. Consequently, Italian politics revolved around Milan's efforts to annex the other northern and central Italian states.

The plots and counter-plots of that era are difficult to follow. Renaissance politics in general were complicated, and the machinations of the Visconti family especially so. But the details are not of much importance, anyway, since nothing decisive came out of the conspiracies, bribes, treason and aggression. Each contestant made gains from time to time, but most were lost fairly soon afterward. The status quo was too comfortable for everyone – cities, nobles, despots and churchmen – so whenever one threatened to become too powerful, the others banded together against him.

THE VISCONTI

In his age, 1354–85, Duke Bernabò Visconti of Milan was everyone's foe. He had seen the weakness of the Papal States earlier than his competitors, so that even though parts of that rag-tag collection of territories (states *is* plural) were far from Milan, he sent armies to seize what he could.

Pope Innocent VI lacked the resources to resist the attack. For safety's sake, he lived in Avignon, but he still had to fear the free companies. He needed money – the Church of that time was so fabulously wealthy and corrupt that even many of its intellectuals were outraged, but there was never enough. His predecessors had committed the Church to spend huge sums so that anyone could appeal to them for justice, and even more money in efforts to dominate the politics of Italy and Germany. Moreover, revenues were drastically down – effects of the plague and the Hundred Years War. The financial crisis was met by inventing ever more creative ways of raising money.

Innocent VI's plan was first to declare a crusade against the freebooters, then to play his two enemies against one another – to send the free companies into Italy against Bernabò. Froissart described this effort:

> The pope and the cardinals had therefore a croisade publicly preached. They absolved from every crime and sin all those who should take the cross, and voluntarily give themselves up to destroy these wretches. The cardinals elected the lord Peter de Monstier, cardinal d'Arras, by some called cardinal d'Ostia, to be the chief of this croisade; who, upon his nomination, immediately left Avignon, and went to Carpentras, seven leagues distant, where he fixed his quarters. He retained all soldiers, and others, who were desirous or saving their souls, and of gaining the foresaid pardons: but he would not give them any pay, which caused many of them to depart and go into Lombardy; others returned into their own countries, and some joined these wicked companies, which were daily increasing. They divided themselves into several companies, over each of which they nominated captains, and took up their quarters in different places. Thus they harassed the pope, the cardinals, and the merchants in the neighborhood of Avignon, and did a great deal of mischief until the summer was far advanced of the year 1361.
>
> It happened that the pope and cardinals cast their eyes upon a very accomplished knight and a good warrior; that is to say, upon the marquis de Montferrat, who for a long time had been engaged in war against the lords of Milan, and was at this time so employed. They sent to him to come to Avignon, where he was received with much honor by the pope and cardinals.

Montferrat then led these forces into Italy and forced Bernabò Visconti to make peace. Next among the princes to raise a mercenary army was the Sire de Coucy, in 1369. This French lord refused a higher title because, according to the prevailing chivalric values, titles were a petty vanity; and, because he was so powerful, he could afford to rise above vanities. Again, Froissart, our incomparable guide to this era:

> Having considered there were numbers of men-at-arms in France then idle, on the account of the truce between the French and

English, he entreated the king to assist him in obtaining the free companies of Bretons, who were overrunning and harassing the kingdom for him, and lead them into Austria. The king, who wished these companies anywhere but in his kingdom, readily assented to his request. He lent, or gave, I know not which, sixty thousand francs, in order to get rid of these companions. They began their march toward Austria about Michaelmas, committing many ravages wherever they passed. Many barons, knights, and squires of France, Artois, Vermandois, Hainault, and Picardy, such as the viscounts de Meaux and d'Aunay, sir Raoul de Coucy, the baron de Roye, Pierre de Bar, and several others, offered their services to the lord de Coucy. His army was increased by all those who wished to advance themselves in honor.

Meanwhile, Bernabò attacked the Papal States again. Pope Gregory XI (1370–78), still living in distant Avignon, could do little except throw a thundering excommunication at the Visconti duke. For the legates who had to deliver this bull, however, this became something of a gigantic belch. Bernabò, after subjecting them to a flurry of furious insults, compelled them to eat the parchment.

In 1372 Gregory XI went to war with Bernabò, persuading Enguerrand de Coucy to lead his army. There is much more to say about this fascinating nobleman, the central figure of Barbara Tuchman's *A Distant Mirror: the calamitous fourteenth century*. Coucy's opponents were the English captain John Hawkwood and Galeazzo Visconti's son, the 'count of Virtue'. Hawkwood – unhappy because the bodyguards of the young count, Gian Galeazzo, did not want him exposed to danger – changed sides, joining Coucy in papal employ. The papal alliance then expanded to include the Holy Roman emperor, the queen of Naples and the king of Hungary.

Bernabò sued for peace in 1374, but he bribed the papal diplomats so successfully that he could be considered the victor. Then the Church experienced the Great Schism, an embarrassing scandal – two popes, each with plausible claims to be the properly elected Supreme Pontiff. When Pope Gregory visited to Rome in 1378, his clumsy effort to persuade the Milanese duke to change sides antagonised members of his alliance, then he died unexpectedly. The citizens of Rome rioted, threatening to lynch the cardinals if they did not elect an Italian pope. The cardinals did what the mob wanted, electing the oldest and most unsuitable Italian churchman they could think of – the crotchety old archbishop of Naples who took the name Urban VI (1378–89). The French cardinals, finding their new pontiff even worse than expected, fled to Avignon, declared Urban's election invalid, and elected as pope a Frenchman who took the name Clement VII (1378–94). In 1382 Clement proposed a plan that would end the Schism and win Naples for Louis of Anjou, the brother of Charles V. Duke Louis had arranged a marriage for his seven-year-old son to Bernabò Visconti's daughter, thus gaining him an immense dowry. Froissart described the duke's arrival in Avignon.

> The gallant earl of Savoy [Amadeus VI, the Green Count, a heroic figure by any standard], his cousin, came to meet him, attended by barons and knights, who were also well received by the pope and cardinals. During his stay at Avignon, he arranged and settled the pay and stores for the Savoyards, who were in considerable numbers, and delivered the money to the earl of Savoy. This being done, the duke of Anjou and the earl of Savoy took their leave of the pope, and set off from Avignon, following the road to Savoy and Piedmont... When they began to approach Rome, they marched in a more compact body than they had hitherto done; for the Romans, being informed of the duke's march, had thrown up strong fortifications to oppose him. They had for commander a valiant English knight called sir John Hawkwood, who had resided a long time in that part of Italy: he was well acquainted with the frontiers, and had under him a large body of men-at-arms, of Germans, English, and other nations in the pay of the Romans, for the defence of Urban at that time called pope, and who resided at Rome. This pope was not alarmed at the arrival of the duke of Anjou. When they told him he was on his march, attended by the earl of Savoy and count of Geneva [the brother of the Avignon pope, Clement VI], with full nine thousand lances of good men-at-arms, and it was uncertain if he would not come to Rome to dethrone him, for the were all Clementines, he replied by saying, 'CHRISTUS protegat nos'. That was all the alarm they gave him, and the only answer he made to those who spoke to him on the subject.
>
> The duke of Anjou, who styled himself king of Naples, Sicily and Jerusalem, duke of Calabria and la Puglia, accompanied by the

earl of Savoy, continued the march of his army through Tuscany, the territory of Ancona, and the patrimony of St. Peter, but did not enter Rome; for the duke wished not to make war on Rome, nor on the Romans, but solely aimed to accomplish his enterprise on the terms according to which he had left France. He kept up kingly state wherever he passed, and all men-at-arms praised him for the punctuality of his payments.

All these expeditions helped to empty France of unemployed mercenaries. No doubt some hoped to emulate the career of the oft-mentioned John Hawkwood.

JOHN HAWKWOOD

Hawkwood was an unusual figure. The next-to-youngest son of a man of modest wealth, he did not envision himself happy with the hunting and petty entertainments that were the high points of the lives of country gentry. Hardly more than a boy when his father died, he invested his small inheritance in weapons and a voyage overseas. He fought at Crécy (1346) and Poitiers (1356), his exploits in the latter battle bringing him to the attention of the Black Prince himself and earning him a knighthood. Peace, four years later, left him unemployed. He then enrolled in the famous White Company that made its way into Italy under Montferrat's command. Well that he did so, since his limited education had prepared him for no profession other than arms or being a gentleman. He did not even know how to read or write, much less make sense of a sentence in Latin.

Unusual also in his physical strength and mental acuity, he quickly rose to posts of responsibility, where those early gifts seemed small compared to his common sense and his awareness of the desires and fears of both his men and his employers. As Froissart wrote of him in mid-career:

Sir John Hawkwood and his companions remained in Italy, and were employed by pope Urban as long as he lived...Pope Gregory, successor to Urban, engaged him in the same manner. Sir John had also a profitable employment, under the lord de Coucy, against the count de Vertus [Gian Galeazzo] and his barons; in which, some say, the lord de Coucy would have been slain, if sir John Hawkwood had not come to his assistance with five hundred combatants, which he was solely induced to do because the lord de Coucy had married one of the king of England's daughters. This sir John Hawkwood was a knight much inured to war, which he had long followed, and had gained great renown in Italy from his gallantry.

The Romans, therefore, and Urban, who called himself pope, resolved, on Clement [the anti-pope] leaving Italy, to send for Hawkwood, and appoint him commander-in-chief of all their forces: they made him large offers of retaining him and his whole troop at a handsome subsidy, which he accepted, and acquitted himself loyally for it. In company with the Romans, he defeated a large body of Bretons under the command of Silvester Budes; the greater part of whom were either slain or taken: Silvester Budes was carried prisoner to Rome, where he was in great danger of being beheaded.

Froissart, though always readable, was not well informed about these events; certainly he had little understanding of the intricacies of Italian politics in the 1360s that made Hawkwood's rise possible. Hawkwood had gone to Italy with the White Company to fight the Visconti, then went into Visconti employ, then switched sides again, only, in 1363, to fight for Pisa against Florence. Pisa's chances seemed slim, especially after some of its mercenaries accepted bribes to go home. (This caused the German component of the White Company to become much smaller.)

Only Hawkwood and 800 of his men honoured their bargain. Even reinforced by the Pisan militia, it was a pitifully small force to face the 15,000 Florentines who marched down the river in the summer of 1364. Hawkwood's only hope was a mistake on the part of his enemies, which they carefully avoided, or some daring action they did not expect. He chose a surprise assault on the Florentine camp, striking suddenly at midday, when the enemy were lying down for a nap. A Tuscan summer is always hot, Tuscan food is always delicious and, for the midday meal, plentiful.

Hawkwood caught the Florentines unready, but they rallied quickly. They showered the Pisans with crossbow quarrels, then moved around the flanks of the attacking force and came in from the rear. Hawkwood saw the danger quickly enough to extricate his men, but the Pisans could not escape –

thousands were captured, making the victors so confident that the Pisa city council would now surrender that they went home to await the inevitable success of their diplomats.

To the Florentines' surprise, Pisa did not capitulate. Instead, a prominent merchant seized power, hired Hawkwood and his men, and continued the war. The Florentines, hoping to avoid a costly siege, tried to buy Hawkwood's services. But to their further surprise, he made it clear that he was not available for bribes. What was the world coming to, they wondered, when a mercenary would not take higher wages to work for an employer who was clearly winning.

Winning was Hawkwood's business, however, and he quickly demonstrated his mastery of it. He led his men on raids throughout Tuscany until Florence was ready for a truce. He assured his foes that it was nothing personal, purely business. His Pisan employer was naturally very pleased with his judgement of the situation and of the man.

With peace Hawkwood was unemployed. That was the inevitable fate of the successful mercenary, one of the downsides of the business that most forward-looking warriors anticipated by earning or stealing as much as they could while hostilities lasted. Hawkwood, however, did not have the reputation of gouging either his employers or his enemies. This was a disadvantage in the short run, during which he still had to pay his men, but it helped in the long run, assuring employers that he could be trusted to lead their armies even when not long before he was in command of the enemy forces.

Italy had a fragile balance of power among the major states – Venice (the wealthiest of the sea powers, which was defending its overland trade routes to the north and west), Florence (mistress of Tuscany), Pisa (its once rich trade to the east diminishing, while Florentines practically knocked at the city gates), the Papal States (currently broken into enclaves dominated by local families, while the pope lived far away in Avignon), Genoa (trapped between the mountains and the sea), Naples (ruled by a family determined to exterminate itself in murderous feuds), and Milan, which stood in the middle of one of the most prosperous regions of all Europe, the well-watered Lombard plain. Milan, everyone believed, would eventually come to dominate all of Italy. The Milanese welcomed this, even if this had to come through the efforts of one of the cruellest families in all of Italy, the Visconti. Not for nothing was the Visconti coat of arms a baby being swallowed by a snake. Everyone knew who the snake was. The rest of Italy saw itself as the baby.

The next victim was expected to be Florence. The Tuscan Republic had grown too fast, become too rich and behaved too arrogantly. It could not expect other states to come to its assistance out of good will alone. Florentines had demonstrated a weakness in failing to finish off Pisa, and now again in making a humiliating peace with Hawkwood.

Bernabò Visconti dominated the central Po River valley and the Alpine passes used by traders; he ruled industrious subjects, and his policies furthered economic prosperity. He hired the best mercenaries. All he needed was a competent general – a general who could be trusted. Naturally, he approached Hawkwood.

In 1368 Bernabò offered the Englishman a profitable commission. One of his daughters was marrying the duke of Clarence (Edward III's second son), and he suggested that it would be appropriate to have an English force at the wedding to assure that nothing amiss occurred. Hawkwood concurred. He could be a patriot and well paid at the same time. Also present were the Sire de Coucy and Chaucer, who (according to Barbara Tuchman) may have used Coucy as a model for his Canterbury squire; certainly Froissart was impressed. The wedding was a brilliant affair; Milan could well afford it.

Almost immediately a crisis arose. Charles IV, king of Bohemia and Holy Roman emperor, was crossing the Alps with 20,000 men to reassert imperial authority. Hawkwood stymied Charles' forces by breaking the dikes of the Po, flooding the broad fields that would otherwise have provided a perfect battleground for the German and Bohemian knights.

This success was followed almost immediately by an abject failure – an advance on Florence. However, Hawkwood was defeated and captured at Arezzo; he spent a year in prison before his employer managed to ransom him. Revenge was quick, and sweet: Hawkwood led his forces into papal territories, causing such devastation that the pope's already precarious finances were threatened; at one time English arrows fell close enough to the Holy Father himself to make him fear for his life. The pope arranged for peace, then fled back to Avignon.

This time, when Hawkwood advanced on Florence, he approached from the mouth of the Arno River. Not far from Pisa he encountered a small but highly prized army of Florentine mercenaries. The two armies camped in the same locations chosen in his earlier campaign, and the tactics were the same, too, except that it was the Florentines who tried to surprise his camp during mealtime. Feigning flight, Hawkwood led the enemy cavalry into a trap, then struck back to take almost the entire force prisoner. He failed to capture Pisa, which would have cut the Florentine access to the sea, but over the next two years he was able to harass the Florentines in numerous ways.

Hawkwood's successes were minor, which was not surprising, considering the strength that Florence and her allies, most importantly the pope, had raised to oppose him. Bernabò Visconti, however, was so displeased that he cut Hawkwood's pay. The Englishman's response was totally unexpected: he went over to the pope!

Hawkwood's new command was not fully satisfactory, however, because he was not given the authority to ensure that commands were followed. The foolishness of this was proven when the opposing armies stood watching one another, neither willing to make the first attack (because once a charge was repulsed, a counterstroke by cavalry was usually decisive). Suddenly, without warning, the Sire de Coucy charged. Hawkwood had to follow or see the only chance for victory vanish. When the attack failed, Coucy's men fled, while Hawkwood took refuge on a hilltop with the infantry. As Bernabò's Germans broke off the pursuit and turned their attention to looting the corpses and camp, Hawkwood saw his chance and took it – he attacked, routing the enemy.

Hawkwood received little of his back pay, but he was now allowed to recruit a large force, the so-called Holy Company composed of 1,500 cavalry and 500 archers. Using this army effectively was another matter; the pope, living far away in Avignon, was governing through French churchmen whose competence was minimal. The Florentines, knowing how desperate Hawkwood was for money, tried to bribe him to come over to their employ. Hawkwood refused, but he allowed himself to take money in return for not attacking Florence for three months.

The Florentines must have been pleased by this arrangement, because the city council subsequently voted to award Hawkwood an annual subsidy of 1,200 florins. It is almost unheard of for any government to pay a salary to the enemy commander; at least, to pay so much for so little given in return. But the Florentines were desperate: the pope had excommunicated their city council, then placed their territory under ecclesiastical censure, forbidding masses, weddings, baptisms and even funerals; the city was almost bankrupt, and commerce was almost non-existent; moreover, the pope had invited all true Christians to seize Florentine property wherever they could find it (it was amazing how many converts to his cause he made in this manner). Unable to think of anything else, the Florentines made an alliance with their ancestral enemy, Bernabò Visconti. All the Florentines had going for them was their sense of humour: they called the eight members of the city council the Eight Saints, a name that was subsequently attached to this wearisome war.

If Hawkwood had attacked in this moment, Florence would never have survived and the history of European arts and letters would have been vastly different. But it is unlikely that anyone thought this out, not even Giovanni Acuto – the name the Florentines gave Hawkwood translates as 'sharp Johnny'. He was much too busy suppressing rebellions throughout the papal domains: many subjects, realising that this might be their last opportunity to throw off their tyrannical rulers, were rising in arms or plotting to do so. Moreover, Hawkwood's debts were now enormous, and the pope would only pay in land – a small territory that he could perhaps live on some distant day, but could not convert into cash.

The grant also tied him more tightly to the papal reins, since it could be revoked as easily as it was given; and that would leave Hawkwood's two sons and three daughters without a means of support should anything happen to him. Nobody knows who the mother or mothers of the children were.

Events were not moving in his favour. Whenever he allowed his unpaid men to loot a town, news of the pillage and rape increased anti-clerical sentiments. Then the pope hired a company of Bretons, who had fought for and against the English in the Hundred Years War, but whose politics currently favoured France (and hence the pope). The behaviour of the Bretons made the English look like saints. Two of Hawkwood's subordinates defected to Florence, while Florence informed him that the city would cease to pay him the usual subsidy – unless he left Italy, which would cause the payments to resume. Then came the sack of Cesena. On the orders of the papal legate, the well connected but austere and unforgiving Cardinal of Geneva, the Bretons and Englishmen slaughtered most of the adult population, looted the homes and held the children for ransom; after three days of rampage, the city was left smouldering, devoid of people and animals.

Hawkwood may have been sickened by the excessive bloodshed – he is known to have rescued many refugees. Most likely he was also worried about his employer, who called for blood and more blood. Catherine of Siena, no stranger to blood herself, is said to have remarked about the cardinal that his justice was so extreme that it was unjust.

Not long afterward Hawkwood entered Florentine employment, then Milanese. Among the attractions of Milan was the handsome illegitimate daughter of Bernabò Visconti and her 10,000-florin dowry. (It was not much of a sacrifice, Tuchman says, for an immensely wealthy ruler with thirty-six living children.) In 1377 at age sixty Hawkwood was ready to settle down. Italian politics, however, were just heating up.

The Great Schism that began in 1378 threw every calculation into confusion. Urban VI not only outraged his enemies, but even antagonised those who should have been his friends. He tried to force his ascetic tastes on the French cardinals, then showered them with vituperation. They could perhaps have endured that for a short while – he was an aged man. But, appalled by his political bungling, the cardinals declared the election null and void, then elected as Pope Clement VII the papal legate, Cardinal Robert of Geneva, who had been Hawkwood's least favourite employer. The two popes excommunicated one another. One by one the European states chose to recognise one or the other pope, England supporting Urban, France Clement; Florence made peace with Urban and recognised his authority, though the ties were not yet close. Honest men admitted that both men had valid arguments for claiming to be properly elected, but Hawkwood, as an Englishman, a Florentine mercenary, and as a man who knew Clement all too well, had no difficulty in making up his mind – Urban, for all his faults, was his pope.

Florentine families associated with the Guelph party had traditionally dominated the government; they were not pleased by their city's new alliance with the Ghibellines and they were outraged at the Great Schism. They plotted to overthrow the government, kill their enemies, and return to the former policies. However, the very nature of a conspiracy is that to be successful, it must have sufficient members to overwhelm those who hold power; but the more people who are brought into the plot, the more likely it is to be detected. Hawkwood learned of the treason and reported it to the city government, which promptly organised riots, driving the ringleaders out of the city.

Almost immediately afterward the woollen workers in the poorest section of town, over by Santa Croce, demanded a union of their own, a voice in the city government, and higher wages. The city council, after suppressing the *Ciompi* rioters, named Hawkwood captain-general of the republic. He accepted this government's pay for four years, then supported the aristocrats in a bloodless coup. He accepted their token of gratitude: a large house, bodyguards, and an increase in pay.

With peace having been achieved at last, the city fathers agreed to allow him to serve Urban VI; in return he promised to remove all ecclesiastical penalties from the city and its leaders (a promise difficult to keep). Also, since the pope had but little money, Florence continued to pay Hawkwood's salary, with the sums to be deducted from claims that pope held against the city's treasury.

Hawkwood's expedition to Naples ended in his once more being paid by both sides in the confused conflict, each employer being fully aware of the other's payments. He acquired titles to new properties, including an imposing castle near Florence. He refused to mix into the complicated politics of Milan after Gian Galeazzo Visconti lured his uncle Bernabò into a public meeting without sufficient bodyguards and took him prisoner. Hawkwood's wife pressed him to hurry to her father's rescue, but the ageing mercenary only looked at the situation rationally: what chance was there of capturing Milan and rescuing the ugly old man? None. And who in Milan would support him? No one. And as might have been predicted, Bernabò died soon afterward. Suspicion fell on a meal of poisoned beans. Moreover, as might also have been predicted, the coup came as no surprise to Hawkwood, who had been secretly paid off by Gian Galeazzo.

Hawkwood kept his men in fighting trim by hiring them out for local wars of little significance; consequently, he had a formidable force in arms when the inevitable war between Gian Galeazzo and Florence came. Hawkwood was now seventy, but he conducted a strenuous winter campaign with the vigour of a young man. There was much hope for success the next spring, because France had become a Florentine ally. If the two armies could join, they would be invincible. Hawkwood moved quickly to the rendezvous, only to learn that the French had not yet crossed the Alps. Heavily outnumbered, he began to retreat, fighting off the Milanese troops until he reached the Adige River. There twin disasters awaited: news that the French forces had been routed, and visual proof that the dikes had been cut, flooding his route to safety. Hawkwood escaped only by abandoning everything – baggage, arms and artillery. Later in the year the two sides agreed to a truce. There was no victory, but no defeat, either.

When Hawkwood announced that he intended to pay a visit to England, he felt assured of immortality both at home and in Italy. In recognition of his services, Florence had voted to build him a magnificent tomb with an equestrian statue, located in a place of honour in the Duomo – the cathedral, Santa Maria del Fiore. He had married his elder daughters, aged fourteen and fifteen, to a Florentine nobleman and to one of his lieutenants, a German who was now replacing him in command. But Hawkwood did not live to see his green homeland again. He died unexpectedly in March of 1394.

Hawkwood's funeral was magnificent – Florentines loved spectacle and they were very, very good at it. But they were also very frugal. A bronze statue was far too expensive; the number of artists who had mastered the craft was small, their services were in high demand, and the materials were costly. Not that Florence could not have done it. The foremost experts in that craft lived in Florence. In the future Lorenzo Ghiberti (1378–1455) would cast the 'doors of Paradise' for the baptistery, and Donatello (1386–1466) would create the popular sexually ambiguous statue of David displayed today in the Bargello. But such craftsmen were expensive, the bronze even more highly priced, and Hawkwood was dead and gone. In the businesslike manner for which the city was justly famous, the city fathers decided that they could fulfill the essence of the agreement by having a fresco painted in the Duomo.

By that time Hawkwood no longer cared, nor did his men. At the request of King Richard II, his body was returned to England. Thus, there is no tomb to Giovanni Acuto in Florence. Uccello's fresco is his memorial. He rides through eternity – erect, proud, self-assured and *rich*.

Alas, his equestrian portrait is barely noticed by tourists who plod through the great building, too jaded from the superfluity of masterpieces to care much who the horseman is, and in summer heat they are even less inclined to ask. If they inquire, they seldom understand the answer. Why, they wonder, is an Englishman on the wall here? But, exhausted by the vain search for an affordable restaurant, they have little desire for further enlightenment.

From across the church the fading fresco remains impressive. A statue would probably not have survived. Frescos cannot be melted down and made into cannon, which was the fate of many a good statue in ensuing centuries. So there he is, still today, a powerful man mounted on a powerful steed, an expression of strength and pride far removed from Christian resignation and humility.

1494 THE PIVOTAL YEAR

Italian warfare changed forever when the French king, Charles VIII, invaded Italy at the head of a formidable army. Commanding trained royal infantry and cavalry, supported by many large cannon, Charles was able to reduce strongholds quickly. He was an exceptionally ugly man, but he was also very wealthy and faced by exceptionally incompetent opponents. On those few occasions he met resistance, he crushed it utterly. Guicciardini, the Florentine chronicler, described vividly the massacres and barbarities that terrorised his enemies, and the policy of killing citizens, but not mercenaries.

Sparing the mercenaries almost guaranteed that others would surrender in the future rather than fighting to the end; and the king would win their goodwill in case he needed to hire them later.

The only trouble, according to Guicciardini, came on Charles's march back north. Since he had left many troops to hold down his conquests, his force was much weaker, perhaps only 10,000 men. Also, he had to deal with the newly formed Italian League composed of small northern states that had traditionally opposed Milan. The Italian League raised a huge army, perhaps 25,000 men, many of whom were the best that could have been collected at any time. Francesco Gonzaga, the Venetian captain-general, took up a position at Fornovo to block Charles's army after it descended from the passes of the Apennines. The king, however, seeing the fortifications blocking the main road, crossed the small river to the narrower bank, then swung north, moving swiftly between the hills and the river in the direction of Milan. Gonzaga probably could not believe his eyes – he had not divided own men, because the royal forces, strung out along the narrow road, would be utterly vulnerable to an attack across the stream. It was the best opportunity he would ever have to crush Charles once and for all.

Gonzaga ordered his men to cross the river, a move that would have worked well if the weather had cooperated. But rain had made his artillery almost useless, and the river was rising. Gonzaga's first units were beaten off by the Swiss after many men had slipped off to plunder the French baggage train. Still, he had brought the French movement to a halt, had created disorder in the royal formation, and he could still well have routed the French if his mercenaries had been able to get at them. But the river continued to rise. Gonzaga could get only a few more units across, and was only able to make uncoordinated attacks that the French repulsed one after the other.

The next day, when the king marched off, Gonzaga let him go without a fight. By and large, the Italians also learned the wrong lessons from their defeat. Gonzaga claimed a victory. As far as he had captured the king's treasure – a magnificent collection of pornography – that was true. But Charles had escaped and he remained in control of much of Italy.

The battle was fatal not only to Italian unity, but also to the Italian reputation as soldiers. Tourists ignore the statues of tough condottieri in Venice and Padau and never think of Sylvester Stallone in *Rocky*. Fornovo cast a long shadow over Italian military pride.

THE LAST GREAT MERCENARY

Tourists wandering through the crowded stalls of Florentine vendors between the Central Market and the Medici palace may, if they look up, see an unprepossessing statue of a seated man. They will note that he is some kind of Medici, but not one they recognise, and pass on. Even if they read Italian, the inscription means little to them: *Giovanni de' Medici, delle bande nere* (Giovanni de' Medici of the black bands). That ignorance would not have been the case in 1540, when the statue was carved by Baccio Bandinelli, one of Michelangelo's contemporaries. Giovanni (1489–1526) was the second founder of the Medici fortunes. The rare close observer will note that the seated figure is dressed as an ancient warrior, with a broken spear in his hand. Giovanni was a mercenary soldier, the most famed commander of his age.

Giovanni was descended from a lesser line of the famous family that had ruled Florence so brilliantly through most of the fifteenth century. His father, for whom he was named, had met the notorious widow Caterina Sforza on a diplomatic mission to Milan and married her secretly. Caterina had been born illegitimate (which was no problem, really, since her grandfather, Francesco Sforza, had risen out of the ranks of the peasantry by his military skills to marry the last Visconti duke's illegitimate daughter), had married the extremely ugly son of Pope Sixtus IV at age fifteen (the pope presided at the wedding), then survived a conspiracy during which her husband was slain and her six children were held hostage. Caterina, safe on her battlements, after listening to her enemies' threats to cut the children's throats on the spot if she did not surrender, lifted her skirts to show that she was pregnant and taunted them with the joke that she still had the tools to make more children. Her enemies retreated without harming the hostages. Subsequently, after sampling a number of younger lovers, she selected one, the low-born son of one of her officials. When her eldest son joined a conspiracy which eliminated his new rival, she threw him into prison, then tortured the other conspirators and their families to death. A year later, at age thirty-seven, she met Giovanni de' Medici.

The marriage did not become public until three months after she delivered a son, little Giovanni, and only a couple months later the child's father was dead of natural causes. Few expected the child to live. Either poor health or jealous relatives would whisk him away. But he survived. His mother intended him to be both soldier and diplomat, with her fortresses and court as schoolrooms, but when Cesare Borgia attacked, she dispersed her children, sending Giovanni to an unmarried sister, who hid him in a country house; when Caterina was released from her papal prison, she reclaimed him and took refuge in Florence, only to hide him in a nunnery to keep him out of the hands of Lorenzo the Magnificent (1449–92). By the time Caterina finally felt safe, her son was nine, and she had only two more years to live.

Giovanni lived with the powerful Salviati family in Florence. That was fortunate, because he needed protection from himself as much as from his family's enemies. Giovanni loved hunting and fighting, not necessarily in that order; he excelled at swordmanship and society life. The Salviatis took him to Rome and Naples, perhaps mostly to keep him out of trouble in republican Florence, where noble-born toughs were kept in their place and Medici teenagers would be watched closer than other wild boys of noble ancestry. Then in 1512 the Florentine republic was crushed and his cousin, Giuliano de' Medici, became its ruler – this time not as a political boss, but as duke of Tuscany. Giovanni hurried home to enjoy the family's happy turn of fortunes. Soon afterward, another cousin, Cardinal Giovanni, became Pope Leo X (1513–21). Giovanni then rushed to Rome, where he was given his first military command at age eighteen.

His successes were immediate; and unpopular. He was adventurous and daring, and his superiors were experienced and cautious. They were professionals, and he was an amateur. If the war was over quickly, he would be famous and praised; while they would be unemployed. Worse, he even killed people! And his men did, too.

This was not proper behaviour for condottieri. Perhaps for Frenchmen and Spaniards, who were already beginning to think of Italy as theirs for the taking; but not for Italians, who understood that strategy, diplomacy and betrayal, even poison, were much safer and surer ways to success than clubbing people over the head or spilling their guts. Nor were the foreigners alone in thinking thus. Machiavelli, who had been important in the Florentine republic, was exiled from the city at this time. With nothing important to fill his leisure days, he began reflecting on the problems facing

Italy, then writing out his thoughts. The result was *The Prince*, one of the most important books ever written; one of his principal conclusions was that the condottieri were ruining Italy. National salvation could come only through citizen soldiers.

Giovanni de' Medici could not have agreed – such citizen soldiers could be used only in regional conflicts; they were useless for distant campaigns.

In 1515 the French and Spanish invaded Italy, each determined to frustrate the other's ambitions. Giovanni was involved in minor campaigns in the mountains, far from the scenes of the great combats, but he followed the war carefully. Like Machiavelli, he became persuaded that a new style of army was necessary, one built around soldiers who were properly drilled, well-led, and willing to risk their lives. He saw no place for the traditional mercenary – hurriedly recruited and quickly dismissed when the campaign was over. The new army had to have a proper mix of cavalry, infantry, artillery and engineers, all enrolled for life-time service. It had to be professional in every sense.

Giovanni was fortunate to have the Church's money to raise and train his men. He also had the Church's political resources. This made possible the Holy League – with most troops supplied by Charles V (1519–56), the Habsburg king of Spain and Holy Roman emperor – against the French. In the ensuing campaign in Lombardy, Giovanni acquired a reputation for invincibility. Victorious in numerous minor engagements, he drove the French back into Milan, then watched as they abandoned the city precipitously and fled.

At this point Leo X died. The war was ended and Giovanni was unemployed. He kept his army together, a feat that only a wealthy nobleman could afford, and continued its training; during this period the army acquired its famous name, the Black Bands, for his having attached mourning streamers to its banners in honour of the late pope. After a year and a half the unpopular, aged, reforming Dutch pope, Hadrian VI, died (and it would be four hundred years before another non-Italian was elected to that office). His successor was Giulio de' Medici, another of Giovanni's cousins, who chose the name Clement VII (1523–34) to indicate that the earlier Avignon pontiff had been an anti-pope. Clement had a disastrous reign. Dominated by Charles V, he failed to deal with Lutheran demands for reform or to respond satisfactorily to Henry VIII's request for a divorce, thus losing much of Germany and all of England to Protestantism; but he knew how to protect the Medici family; and he welcomed Giovanni back to Rome.

Giovanni married a Salviati daughter who was also a granddaughter of Lorenzo the Magnificent. He was not a faithful husband, but in those days such men were even rarer than courageous and intelligent commanders. Giovanni, having no war to keep him busy, made full use of the opportunities to make himself popular with the courtiers at the Vatican and in surrounding courts. This was important for his later career, and it was not fatal to his marriage.

War with France was inevitable once the pope's secret plots to join the French king against Charles V failed. Clement sent Giovanni north to drive the French out of Milan again, but without the authority or troops that were deemed necessary for success. Even so Giovanni forced the French to retreat. He was proclaimed the liberator of Italy!

Though not rewarded for his exploits, Giovanni continued to build up his army. He accepted only Italian and Albanian recruits, refusing to hire any of the traditional mercenaries from across the Alps. He knew that the French king was assembling a huge army, 40,000 men, many of whom were Swiss, who were counted as the finest fighters in all of Europe.

In the autumn of 1524 the French host crossed the Alps. Clement, persuaded that resistance was futile, agreed to join the invaders in attacking Charles V. Giovanni, now in French employ, discovered that his new masters mistrusted him and feared his impulsiveness. While looking over the opposing lines at Pavia a gunshot smashed Giovanni's leg. Everyone expected him to die, but after he was sent through the lines to Rome, medical treatment proved effective. Meanwhile, the Habsburg forces crushed the alliance's army and captured the French king, obtaining from him a renunciation of all claims to Italian soil.

Patriots were appalled. Machiavelli called for Italians to rally to Giovanni, and to assist him in driving the last foreigners from their lands (Italians still thought in the plural, not of a united nation). Soon even the pope had agreed. In 1526 he joined a league of Italian states (Florence and Venice) and the French to fight Charles V. Clement was not happy that Giovanni would command the army, but even he could not oppose such a popular hero. What he could do was refuse to give him authority over papal troops, and this was fatal.

First the commander of the papal forces refused to obey orders and then retreated; soon afterwards Clement faced an uprising in Rome that he quieted only by withdrawing from the league; his example was quickly followed by minor princes who held strategic fortresses in northern and central Italy. Meanwhile Charles V crossed the Alps with a new army that included a large number of German Protestants eager to fight the pope. All that stood between them and Rome were Giovanni's Black Bands.

On the Po, Giovanni watched the German mercenaries preparing to cross the swollen, ice-filled river. It was the opportunity he was waiting for! However, just as he was leading his men forward, out of nowhere a cannon ball came flying, hitting no one but Giovanni. Badly wounded in his still ailing leg, Giovanni called off the attack. A day later he was dead.

With Giovanni died the hopes of Italian liberty. There was no one with the talent to stop the imperial troops. The next spring German and Spanish forces captured Rome. After sacking the churches and palaces, they made the pope agree to follow the emperor's commands. Charles V saw that the Church was reformed, not immediately, but thoroughly, at the Council of Trent. The Counter-Reformation assured that no Medici could ever use the papacy to the benefit of his family again; no mercenary captain could ever again aspire to marrying into the exalted ranks of Italian nobility. Habsburgs thereafter ruled much of Italy, a fact that would change relatively little for three hundred years.

Giovanni's family did not suffer, however. At age seventeen, his son Cosimo seized power in Florence, establishing a Medici line that would preside over a rebirth of art, architecture, science, music and literature. Tourists visiting the Medici tombs in San Lorenzo should pause and reflect on Giovanni's accomplishments before dismissing the ornate stonework as bad taste and hurrying on to see Michelangelo's sacristy.

This was the man whose statue sits almost unrecognised at a corner of the marketplace between San Lorenzo and the Medici palace.

Obviously, successful politicians are more famous than successful mercenaries: they build lasting institutions, set states on roads to greatness, and establish dynasties. The examples of Giovanni Acuto and Giovanni delle bande nere suggest that leaders of armies must be extraordinarily lucky to be remembered by future generations; the most they get are obscure frescos and pigeon roosts.

11

THE BLACK GUARD

I F *The White Company* IMPLIES purity, honesty and patriotism, *The Black Guard* (*Die Schwarze Garde*) suggests exactly the opposite. While the Guard certainly deserved its evil reputation, its name probably had a more innocent derivation – from its uniforms. Black was a convenient colour for hiding the dirt and blood that were an unavoidable part of warfare. Troops in the field found regular bathing and washing impossible, and battle was a possibility at any moment. That was always dirty work. Commanders concerned about parade-ground appearances wanted uniforms that showed off the troops handsomely – this usually attracted girls, which attracted recruits – but commanders at war did not want troops distracted by the sight of blood. In addition, uniforms reduced the likelihood that soldiers would slaughter their colleagues in the heat of battle. Heat is the appropriate word, too. Even in northern Europe summers were warm, occasionally even hot. It was the time of year when civilians sat in the shade, drank fresh milk or beer, played board games and talked. It was the time of year when nobles liked to make war. Winter was an especially poor time for fighting in north Germany, not so much because of the cold as the wetness and wind. The Black Guard, a north German mercenary company, turned that reluctance to its advantage – the Guard was willing to fight when everyone else wanted to stay home. It was, in a sense, free enterprise at its best – the Guard saw a niche and filled it.

The late fifteenth century was a prosperous era for the Holy Roman Empire, but trade and commerce were hampered by regulations, taxes and petty wars. National union was one means of curing these problems, but few were willing to make the sacrifices necessary to create a German state.

Consequently, the empire was little more than a rag-tag collection of petty states; *the princes*, as historians often call the dukes, counts, bishops and abbots, met periodically at some major city to discuss national business – they called such assemblies the *Reichstag* – but they rarely achieved much. The emperor, living in far-away Vienna, would occasionally travel to Nuremberg and the Rhineland, but not to the north. The last emperor to cross the Elbe River had been insulted by the citizens of Lübeck, who suggested broadly that they were as good as he; and, truth to tell, they may have been right. Free cities, in fact, were a prominent part of the political landscape, and every territorial lord could see that the future would belong to those rulers who could subdue and tax their haughty and independent burghers.

MOUNTAINS AND MARSHES

There were free peasant communities in the north and south of Germany. The cantons of the Swiss Confederation are best known, but they were difficult to conquer. The Alps were a challenge to horsemen, but the Swiss themselves were formidable, too. They had proven their ability to dispatch Habsburg armies time and again, undermining the imperial family's efforts to provide national leadership. In fact, the Swiss had become such famous warriors that all the neighbouring rulers were recruiting them as mercenaries; one employer, in fact, still hires Swiss soldiers and dresses them in their traditional uniforms – the pope.

The Swiss preferred to fight in wealthy, warm lands, especially ones with wine and pretty women; if parts of France were less than warm all year round, the rest of the conditions were readily met. Warm, however, hardly applied to north Germany except perhaps to the women. Wine was lacking altogether. In addition, north Germany had swamps, which were impediments to Swiss tactics. Landsknechts marched in step like modern parade formations or American university bands; even worse, the cows that thrived on the watery pastures provided flying insects with soft, flat brown places for eggs, so that even today visitors are greeted by clouds of gnats, mites, flies and the dreaded *Mucke*, a horsefly which can bite through all but the stoutest of clothing.

The Frisians were once as free as the Swiss, but they were too scattered along the coast of the North Sea to be able to support one another militarily.

North Frisia had succumbed to Danish rule, while West Frisia, which ran to Holland, was dominated by local despots and threatened by Charles the Bold. In fact, Charles had once sternly ordered the Dithmarschers – an independent people living just north of the Elbe River where it ran into the North Sea – to surrender or else. The Dithmarschers ignored him. It was their tradition to ignore rulers, even when they did not also mock them.

The Dithmarschers – a mixed population of Saxons and Frisians who spoke Low German – could not be attacked easily by land, and the Hanseatic League prevented enemies from becoming a naval threat.

Nobles viewed free peasant communities with blind hatred – such republics were a violation of God's own precepts for properly ordered communities (God was a king); and a threat to the nobles themselves. What must other peasants think? Also, the existence of the Swiss Confederation, Dithmarschen and the Hanseatic League frustrated efforts at national unity. How could Germany have princes who could aid the emperor in governance and war, if it continued to permit people to live 'without a lord'?

MERCENARIES IN NORTH GERMANY

Of the various north German regional lords, only the Teutonic Order had relied on mercenary armies. By the late fifteenth century, however, it possessed only a shadow of its former power and glory, and it had little money. The grand master had lost his great castle at Marienburg to the Polish king, and West Prussia, too.

In 1497 the aged grand master, Gottfried von Tiefen, had taken a small force from East Prussia to far-away Moldavia. He had not done this by choice, though for a century his military order had been urged to help defend Christendom from the Turkish threat across the Danube River. He did it only because the king of Poland had ordered him to come. He had only a relative handful of knights, and he could afford only a few mercenaries. When he began the retreat back into Poland, panic set in – his units disintegrated, each man seeking to save himself. Tiefen, exhausted and ill, died shortly after reaching safety.

The kings of Denmark hired mercenaries for their wars against Swedish rivals. Because Danish nobles were unreliable, the churchmen corrupt and the farmers always on the verge of rebellion, the kings slept uneasily. Hamlet might well serve to remind us that having the ear of the king meant more than 'Something is rotten in Denmark'; one might even pour something in it.

King Hans (Johan, 1481–1513) ruled German lands, thanks to the complicated rules of inheritance that had made his father, the duke of Schleswig-Holstein, king of Denmark. For administrative purposes, he gave part the small but rich state of Holstein, the most northerly duchy in the Holy Roman Empire, to his younger brother, Friedrich; but his vassals had insisted that Schleswig-Holstein remain undivided. He would have liked to crush the Hanseatic League, but he did not dare attempt that without the cooperation of the nearest rulers – Lower Saxony (Hannover), Saxon-Lauenburg, Mecklenburg, Schwerin and West Frisia – and the approval of the emperor, who would be guided by his court and the Reichstag. It was better to start with a weaker and less popular opponent.

WAR ON DITHMARSCHEN

The Dithmarschers had been independent since 1227, when they had withdrawn from their assigned position in the Danish line facing an army of German princes, then attacked their erstwhile lord in the rear. Each generation thereafter Dithmarschers faced invasions, and each generation they had driven their foes away; sometimes they pursued a more aggressive policy, ravaging Holstein villages and towns, then bragging about their valour and fighting abilities. This won them no love among the neighbouring Saxon peasants and even Hanseatic merchants, who considered them pests and pirates. They saw themselves differently – under the constitution of 1447 they were a republic, like the Swiss, but one without any ecclesiastical or noble lords, one without serfs or knights.

Not all Dithmarschen farmers owned land, nor were all fishermen owners of boats, but all were free – a bit too free, their neighbours said. They thought themselves better than others, and were proud of their freedom. The notorious individualism of the Dithmarschers was moderated by the power of the clans, which directed the building of dikes and canals for their common benefit, and by the governing council, the regents. Their spears had a flat plate on the butt that could be put right into the mud, enabling the bearer to vault over any narrow water obstacle. In short, they were at home in water and had no fear of mud – situations avoided by men wearing heavy armour.

The Dithmarschers' fierce reputation was somewhat misleading, however. The peasant republic had warned off potential enemies so effectively for so long that none of the clansmen of military age in 1500 had experience in modern warfare; they had all studied contemporary practice at a distance, and many had been involved in the small-scale conflicts of fishermen and cattle-thieves, but drills after church services was not the same as actual battle.

King Hans had undoubtedly heard such assessments from visitors and exiles, who explained that the Dithmarschen military skills were out of date. Still, a campaign in north Germany, however, no matter how short or glorious it might promise to be, was not the prerogative of royal will – his was a modern kingdom, with influential churchmen and vassals; and his neighbours insisted on his giving at least lip-service to international law. Then there was the Reichstag, which had organised resistance to Charles the Bald at Neuss.

The more the king studied the situation, the more he recognised the obstacles to a successful campaign. First of all, there was geography. Dithmarschen was a coastal region with many swamps, forests, large areas reclaimed from the sea that could be easily flooded, the fortified towns of Meldorp (Meldorf) at the narrowest waist of the country and Brunsbüttel in the south, a large meeting area at Heide in the centre of the north, and forts covering the approaches from North Frisia and Holstein. Second was the Dithmarschers' clan system, which was the basis of the military organisation – each unit was composed of men who would rather die than be shamed before their relatives; each unit was well-equipped with spears, swords and halberds; in addition, the Dithmarschers possessed some modern cannon and matchlocks. Units practised regularly in Sunday exercises after church. Third, Dithmarschers were exceptionally pious and attributed their many military successes to the intervention of the Virgin Mary; Danes were Catholics, too, and many would scoff at the peasants' presumption of having a close relationship with God, but the king understood the power of religious faith. Fourth was the reluctance of the neighbouring rulers and the Reichstag to see any king of Denmark become stronger. Fifth was the low morale of his vassals. Every visit to their parish churches reminded them of ancestors who had fallen in combat against Dithmarschers; they had never seen action against these foes, but they knew their ancient war-cry: at the beginning of the battle, it was 'kill the horse, spare the rider'. That was to ensure that, in the event of defeat, as occasionally happened, the victor's relatives would not slaughter all the prisoners in revenge. But once victory was assured, they cried, 'kill the rider, spare the horse'. Horses might bring in more money than ransoms.

King Hans concluded that he could not invade the independent republic without a mercenary army. Money had to be set aside for wages, but also for bribes at the imperial court – he needed a ruling that the Dithmarschers had no lord, hence could be legally annexed by any lawful authority.

The Dithmarschers, well informed by friends in Lübeck and other Hanseatic cities, contested the Holstein case in the imperial court of Friedrich III and at the Reichstag. There were interesting technical problems, such as Denmark lying outside the Holy Roman Empire and thus having a weak case for attacking a German state, and the unexpectedly solid case presented by the farmers' lawyers, who called upon German patriotism and who reminded everyone that in 1474 the Danes had requested permission to annex Dithmarschen in 1474, only to be told NO. The Dithmarschers brought documents and affidavits to demonstrate that they were subjects of the archbishop of Hamburg–Bremen, who was once, long ago, the most important political figure of the region, and that they still paid him an annual tribute. The king and his brother complained that this payment was a ridiculously small fee of no significance. Most likely, the Dithmarschers obtained the archbishop's cooperation by playing on his jealousy of the king and paying him a bribe.

The Dithmarschers' lawyer managed to drag the case out for a long while, but in the end the royal case prevailed. Hans then began to work on the neighbouring rulers, to persuade them that they would benefit from the conquest and that they stood to lose much if they failed to cooperate. Eventually, the regional lords gave their consent – if the king was going ahead with his plans anyway, and seemed likely to succeed, why not get something for themselves, too?

THE BLACK GUARD

King Hans then approached the Black Guard, a mercenary army which had been in existence for several years, originally created to subdue rebellious peasant communities in Frisia. The leader was Thomas Slentz. Given the honorary title of 'Junker' Slentz, implying membership in the lower nobility, he was highly regarded as a military commander. Other contemporary mercenaries were more famous, but Slentz was a specialist in swamp warfare; everyone knew that if there was a stream to be crossed, his engineers could throw a bridge over it in minutes; if the van of his army encountered an enemy, he was at the spot, ready to make an swift study of the situation and give the orders best suited to overcoming the resistance. He paid his men regularly, which is a tribute to his ability to get money out of reluctant employers.

According to one Dithmarschen chronicler, Slentz came from Cologne, but the name suggests Silesian or Meissen origin. He had been the leader of the company since 1495, and a brother, Jürgen, was on his staff. The Dithmarschers loved poetry, especially poems about their past victories. One described Slentz thus:

He hadd einen Harnish aver sinen Liff getagen	He wore mail armour on his body
De schinede von Golde so rode,	That shone with gold so red
Daraver was ein Pantzer geschlagen	He wore a breastplate over it
Darup dede he sick vorlaten.	Upon which he could rely.

The Tøjhusmuseet in Copenhagen contains a suit of armour reputedly worn by Junker Slentz. It is the normal plate armour of a knight, rather elegant despite not being ornately decorated and suitable for fighting on either horse or foot. However, since the style was that of 1540, give or take a few years, it is unlikely that it was worn by Slentz in 1500.

Certainly a commander like Slentz would have worn plate armour. As Maurice Keen points out in *Chivalry*, nobles were willing to give up their horses, but not their plate armour. This was true even when fighting in swamps. The tradition of fighting on the defensive was giving way to the Swiss practice of forming a phalanx of bristling pikes backed by men bearing fearsome halberds. Artillery would soften the enemy position before the ranks of pikes advanced to sweep less disciplined or less determined units away. Officers, exposed more than the average soldier to marksmen, wore armour.

Slentz understood the prospects for social advancement, fame and good pay. A common soldier received four gulden a month, a cavalryman eight, an officer twelve or twenty-four, and Slentz fifty. At a time when a warhorse cost around forty gulden, a suit of armour ten and a sword three, Slentz was earning annually three times as much as a north German prince!

Slentz's 4,000 troops came from all parts of Europe and perhaps beyond. A good number came from Holland and France, but most were German. Many seem to have spoken Low German, the language of the states stretching from Westphalia across Saxony and as far east as Prussia and Livonia. It was not hard for him to persuade Saxons to fight against Frisians and Dithmarschers – there was no love between those communities. The Guard's evil reputation – earned in its campaigns against peasant communities – made peasants think carefully before offering resistance to lords' tax-collectors; they knew that revenge would be taken not only upon prisoners, but also upon their wives and children, and upon everyone in their communities and those round about.

THE CAMPAIGN

When the king announced that the Black Guard would be the spearhead of a gigantic force composed of Danish knights and infantry, Holstein knights and infantry, the royal artillery, and an immense wagon train for supplies, the neighbouring nobles quickly agreed to participate – as long as they were guaranteed a substantial portion of the booty. If the war came the next summer, it would be like a large picnic!

Unfortunately for those dreams, the king announced that he would attack in February of 1500. That would be after the season of the worst winter storms and before resistance could be organised.

We are fortunate in having excellent sources for the Danish invasion of 1500 – the poet Neocorus, then the detailed modern study by Walther Lammers, *Die Schlacht bei Hemmingstedt*. And lastly the folk memory of the Dithmarschers.

The king ordered his forces to assemble in western Holstein, immediately opposite that part of Dithmarschen which lay unprotected, east of the great forests and swamps. The Black Guard, being south of the Elbe River at the time, marched through the archbishopric of Bremen, eliminating a pocket of unruly peasants, then upstream to Winsen, where they met the cavalry from Brunswick and other northern states; this army then crossed the great river into Holstein, picking up units along the way to the royal camp, where Danish and Schleswig cavalry were waiting, along with Saxon, Frisian and

Jutland militia units. The numbers are difficult to calculate, but there were at least 2,000 cavalry (a total of 8,000 horse) and 5,000 militia, and an impressive number of artillery pieces (814 horses were brought to pull the guns and transport the ammunition). To carry supplies there were perhaps 1,500 wagons. This army alone should have been sufficient to crush a small state; the Black Guard made it invincible.

A summer campaign would have been more desirable, but the king could not bring all his forces and the Black Guard together earlier – and delay had its dangers, since Hans could not predict what the emperor or the Swedes would do if they had time to make trouble. In any case, the king did not expect the campaign to take too long; with luck, the Dithmarschers might realise how hopeless their situation was, and surrender. So confident of this was he that when his troops captured Dithmarschen spies, he had them escorted through his camp and then released to inform their fellow citizens of the strength of the royal array.

The king went to pains to assure the Dithmarschers that life under him would continue to be pleasant – he would make no sweeping changes, collect no outrageous taxes; he would perhaps even declare some clan leaders noble. But he would be unforgiving to those who did not see reason. Surrender meant peace and prosperity, war meant men slain and towns burned.

When the Dithmarschers heard from their scouts and spies, they met in the great public square in Heide to discuss their strategy. The almost universal feeling was that the Danish forces would march straight from the royal camp across the northern isthmus that ran from Holstein to Heide. That was the traditional invasion route. Consequently, the Dithmarschers took up their position behind earthen works at the narrowest point, with impassable forests and swamps to either side. The fortifications were formidable. Taking them by assault would be difficult, and flanking was impossible. The Dithmarschers would have welcomed battle in the swamps. Shallow water and mud were their natural elements.

King Hans, after consulting with his vassals and Junker Slentz, came to the same conclusion: an assault on the redoubts would be very costly, and success could not be guaranteed. Therefore, on 11 February 1500, he ordered a demonstration against the northern fortifications to fix the defenders' attention on that front, then made a night march down the narrow road of the southern isthmus to Meldorp. His lead elements arrived at dawn and attacked at once.

Meldorp's small garrison was composed of old men and boys. Although the attackers lost men in the first assaults, they quickly identified weak places in the defences, then swept over the walls. As women and children fled north along the dikes, the knights were close behind them, enjoying the sport. No doubt a few of the knights remembered grim stories of a battle 200 years earlier, when a rabbit ran between the two armies and the Dithmarschers began shouting 'lop, lop, lop', the traditional cry of a rabbit chase; that was sufficient to panic the Holstein militia into flight, leaving the nobles to fight to their death, by themselves. There was more than sport involved here. This was revenge.

The king arrived at daybreak, took possession of the town and began assigning quarters for his men and the mercenaries. The supply train arrived later, supplementing the food that had been found in the homes and taverns. He ordered the royal banner affixed to the pole atop the church. The ancient flag had fallen from heaven in 1219 in Reval (Tallinn), when Danish crusaders were hard-pressed by pagan Estonians. It was a symbol of God's favour and certain victory.

The king, his advisors and Junker Slentz then held a council of war. They had cut Dithmarschen in half. Should they wait there for a delegation to discuss the terms of surrender? Or march south, a relatively easy task now that the interior roads were in their possession? Or should they go north, to Heide and eventually the islands around Busum? From 14 to 16 February they considered their options.

Waiting in Meldorp had several disadvantages. First, the Dithmarschers gave no indications they were ready to negotiate. Second, even though the supply wagons were temporarily full and the city had been stocked with food, the huge army would quickly consume everything. Last, the king had hired the Black Guard for only one month; if the campaign lasted longer, he might not be able to pay them. The king had to move, either north or south. He could not stay put.

There was only one place of importance in the south – Brunsbüttel – a small town on the Elbe River protected by a formidable series of dikes. He would have to conduct a siege. If the river and marshes had frozen, there would be some hope of quick success, but the temperature hovered right above freezing. Unless the assault succeeded at the first try, the attackers would be too numb to try again, and many men would be lost to frostbite. Slentz could undoubtedly take the town, but he would have to warm and rest his men afterward; the time lost might prove fatal to the rest of the campaign.

Hans decided that it would be best to finish off the northern clans first. Victory there would lead to surrender elsewhere, it would shorten the number of days that he had to pay the Black Guard, and it would quiet those nobles who were already counting the remaining days of their required military service. The trouble was that the only road leading north toward Heide was very narrow, raised only slightly above the water table with earth dug from the ditches to either side; horsemen could be deployed in some of the fields and pastures along the road, but not in all, and in the dark of the short winter day, who knew how deep the water in the ditches was? Hans could, of course, retrace his steps and assault the northern fortifications, but that would leave him essentially where he had been at the beginning. He would have weakened Dithmarschen, but once he sent his army home, how would he hold his one conquest? Meldorp could be isolated by guerrilla bands, and sea communications were almost impossible until summer.

The king gave his orders: the army would begin its march north well before dawn of 17 February. Perhaps he hoped that the road would be frozen then, more suitable for heavy traffic; but more likely he was hoping to achieve surprise.

For the Dithmarschers the reasoning was very much the same. They had captured a scout who was tortured to tell what he knew. But could they believe him? Would the king really risk his army on a narrow road through the marshes? Moreover, could they stop the royal army there? There were no prepared defences. A few thought the situation hopeless – there were only 4,000 men in the militia army. But there was one man who was certain that the king would come straight at them, and that the Dithmarschers could turn him back. This was Wulf Isebrandt, a recent Dutch immigrant. He had lacked the prestige to speak up confidently before, and perhaps he had no reason to speak earlier, but he now argued forcefully that the Dithmarschers should put all their resources into an ambush along the road from Meldorp. Why the proud clansmen listened to him is a mystery. Perhaps he had military experience. Certainly no one else had.

Or was that the only suggestion that offered any hope for success?

Where should they take their stand? Isebrandt's suggestion was a hillock just south of Hemmingstedt, where earthen fortifications could be hastily erected. (Recent excavations suggest another, similar site about two miles away, but contemporaries had indicated this location.)

Patriotism burned high at this moment. One speaker was supposed to have said, 'Even those who are born serfs long to be free. Are we, who are born free, to subject ourselves to servitude without resisting? It is a shame to live under a regime where a farmer and a hunting dog fetch the same price.' Women volunteered; the scouts murdered royal emissaries who urged surrender and spies sent to locate the Dithmarscher army; the last militia units were summoned from distant guard duty.

The Dithmarschers marched south, determined that this would be their proudest moment. Perhaps their last, but proudest nevertheless, because they faced without flinching the consequences of fighting for their freedom.

THE BATTLE AT HEMMINGSTEDT

Isebrandt selected a slight elevation no more than eight or nine feet high near a bend in the road; this height would be sufficient to keep his force relatively dry when he flooded the ditches and the fields along the road – his proposal was to confine the royal army to the road, with the militia firing from right, left and straight ahead. Unfortunately, the hillock lay off the road, with only a shoulder extending over to it. That couldn't be helped now. Isebrandt ordered a redoubt built across the road, with a lesser fortification extending back over the rise. He put each unit into place as it arrived. The first task was to dig a shallow ditch across the road and throw the earth up to make the main redoubt's walls; water quickly filled the ditch. When that redoubt was ready, the troops lugged the cannon in place to face down the road. He put several hundred men there, and smaller units on the flanks; the rest he kept in reserve. The units to the east had the most difficult task – the elevation rose to their left and behind them, and their redoubt was less formidable; if the Guard could avoid the marsh at the bend in the road, they might be able to storm over the hillock and flank their position. The units to the west flooded the fields slightly and were ready to open the sluices more at the last moment, letting sea water rush in – but not too soon. Nothing should give away the ambush until the Danish forces were well into the trap.

Isebrandt had counted on the morning fog to hide the newly constructed fortifications and ditches, and Danish scouts were not likely to venture too far from the main forces. He must have been even more pleased when a strong wind from the north brought with it a combination of freezing rain and snow.

Junker Slentz must have been dismayed by the storm, but he may have hoped that it would disguise his approach. Who would imagine that an army would venture on to such a narrow road, with ditches and watery fields to either side and a huge wagon train separating his 4,000 landsknechts and the 2,000 cavalry from the rest of the army? Slentz knew that the wagon train was essential to support the artillery, but too much of it consisted of nobles' baggage and the paraphernalia necessary to housing the king comfortably. It was not as if this was serious war – the conquest of Meldorp had proven that their fears were exaggerated. But it was frightening to move out into a cold, wet windstorm and slog through mud that was deeper and more liquid for each following unit. Wagons sank almost to the axles. By the time the royal artillery came along, the road must have been nigh impassible.

Slentz was cautious, moving slowly, alert to danger; it was difficult to see far ahead, difficult even to keep one's face up – how much easier it was to slog forward, head down, hunkered under rain gear. His van, composed of landsknechts and engineers, were on the lookout for ambushes and efforts to destroy the road; they carried bridging materials to make the way quickly passable again. When the morning light first began to come through, his scouts saw the fresh mound of earth ahead. As Slentz rode out to look over the situation, his men began exchanging fire with the defenders.

It was a fight between nearly blind men at that distance – shadows in almost horizontal rain. Slentz could not see well, but he understood that his men would be an easy target on the road. He rode across the ditches on to the fields. That on the left, closest to the sea, was very low, almost a bog. Not suitable. The field on the right, to the east, was better – it was low but it rose upward behind the main redoubt. He ordered his men to form up on that field, just out of cannon range. The men with firearms stood off to one side. Their weapons were not always effective on this windy coast; with the cold wet wind now blowing into their faces, their matchlocks were essentially useless.

He ordered his gunners to move the cannon up the road into range. When they were sufficiently close, they opened fire; the Dithmarschers responded. If Slentz had hoped to gain an advantage from the fact that the Dithmarscher guns were smaller than his, and hence had a lesser range, he must have been disappointed – the few shells that were fired sank into the muddy walls of the redoubt and the powder was soon wet. Moreover, his guns were in the open, while the Dithmarschers' were behind shelter. The gunners sent to the rear for dry ammunition.

Slentz ordered the phalanx forward, toward the hillock on the right. He had little hope that many of the cavalry would join in. The nobles were not about to risk their fine horses and precious lives on an uncertain field, and the only area free for forming up behind the Guard phalanx was clearly a swamp; a few horsemen seem to have left the road and tried to form a line, but the rest preferred the role of spectators, no matter that the visibility was extremely poor.

As the landsknechts approached the flanking redoubt, they paused to yell, '*Wahr di, Bur, di Garr di kumt!*' (Defend yourselves, peasants, the Guard is coming). Then they stormed the barrier. Slipping in the mud, being pushed back by the farmers' spears and unable to get footing for a decent lunge themselves, they fell back, leaving a few comrades' bodies in front of the fortification. While they reformed their ranks, Slentz ordered moveable bridges brought up.

The engineers risked the defenders' musket fire to lay their bridges right on to the wall, then fell back to make way for the infantry attack.

Isebrandt, recognising that the decisive confrontation would be at this point, sent men to assist the units on the hillock. In weakening his right wing, he risked a Danish advance through the marsh that would bring horsemen into his rear; but, as he had hoped (but could not be certain was the case), the Holstein knights were unwilling to venture on to the low fields. Unable to see through the snow and fog, Isebrandt had no idea where the Holstein and Danish infantry was – he assumed that it was still on the road, but it could be forming up just out of sight. On the other hand, Slentz probably couldn't see troops moving, either. He knew that reinforcements should be on the way, but unless he could clear a space for them, how could he deploy them? He could end up with masses of confused troops milling around under the Dithmarschen guns. More than one military disaster had begun thus.

Isebrandt, too, had been concerned about the enemy cannon. He must have guessed that the rain had wetted the powder, but surely dry powder would be coming soon. Moreover, his own guns were having little effect on Slentz's batteries. Unless he could eliminate those weapons before they opened fire, he could expect that his main fortification would soon be under massive bombardment. His only hope was a sally to overturn the guns. That was a suicide mission if Slentz's gunners had fresh powder and could keep their wicks lit; and if they could train their fire on his troops. But he knew that wheeling the guns around in the mud and depressing the muzzles would be slow work. He ordered his men to attack.

Slentz, seeing the militiamen coming down the road, ordered a Guard unit forward to meet it. There was a fierce struggle in the narrow space, followed by the Dithmarschers retreating to their redoubt to reform. The Guard should perhaps have followed the retreating farmers, but they had been trained to maintain discipline and not pursue an enemy into an ambush. While this Guard unit was still realigning its ranks, Dithmarschen reinforcements stormed out of the redoubt and pushed them back. The gun crews, having no weapons, chose not to face an enemy armed with swords, spears and halberds; they fled. Without reserves instantly available to retake the cannon, Slentz could not prevent the Dithmarschers from tipping them off the road, into the ditches or on to their sides. Now, even if Slentz's men could be persuaded to return and set them right again, the muzzles would be filled with mud and water; they were useless until they could be cleaned.

Meanwhile, the Guard had formed up again, ready to surge forward. Slentz understood that this attack had to succeed – if his men couldn't take this position, there was no chance they could storm the main redoubt. He sent his phalanx forward, the men yelling wildly as they clambered up the bridges. There was a terrific struggle along the peak of the low ridge, then the landsknechts fell back again. As Slentz tried to organise his men for a third assault, the Dithmarschers began taking off their armour and clothing. No matter that the freezing, wet wind continued to blow, the farmers and fishermen were too exhausted to wear armour any longer; also, they could move more easily in the mud without it. Isebrandt moved all his infantry from the central redoubt to the eastern one and ordered a charge. The Guard stood firm. The landsknechts threw back the farmers, but their own momentum was stopped; they milled around, reforming their ranks and probably cursing the mud. Getting the clumsy pikes in the front ranks, the men with halberds and long doubled-handed swords behind them, could not be done instantly. The day had fully dawned by now, but the wind had picked up, carrying with it wet snow. Everyone was chilled to the bone, but those trudging into the gale suffered the most. Meanwhile, Isebrandt had gained precious moments for his artillery to fire into the Guard unit and for his reserves to come up. Sending every man he had to the endangered flank, he ordered an all-out attack. The Dithmarschers raised a cry, '*Wahr di Garr, di Bur die kumt!*' (Look out, Guard, the peasants are coming) and charged.

The Guard's ranks gave way. Slentz, vainly attempting to save the day, fell fighting. Some mercenaries ran for their lives, but most re-formed and kept their units together throughout the ensuing hurried retreat. That was their salvation.

To the west, the defenders opened the sluices in the dikes, pouring water across the fields that had previously had been little worse than dangerously soggy. The storm, meanwhile, was pushing the high tide even higher. Seawater rushed toward the slightly elevated road, where royal reinforcements had been pushing men, horses and wagons out of their way to get into the battle. When these units saw the water coming, their movement reversed itself – first the landsknechts who had not yet been involved in the combat fell back, then other units began to retreat, and finally everyone was hurrying away as fast as they could. Panic set in – jostling, confusion, rising water – and Dithmarschers coming down the road behind them, killing everyone they encountered.

The cavalry, thrust into fields that came to resemble a rapidly deepening lake, thrashed around, unable to move forward or backward. The nobles, unable to form a coherent unit, discovered themselves in one of those nightmares that they had heard about from childhood – they were in confused combat with a swarm of angry, stout farmers and fishermen. Dithmarschers came at them from all sides, moving swiftly across the rising water, wading through mud and easily crossing the drainage ditches that were causing the expensive warhorses to founder. While shouting 'Spare the horse, kill the man,' Dithmarschers were employing their spears to fly through the air, clearing ditches easily. The knights, fighting individually against gangs of militiamen, had no chance. A knight might pick out one enemy and move clumsily toward him, only to be pulled from his horse from behind by a cleverly placed halberd hook. If he didn't drown, he would be quickly stabbed to death.

Soon the entire column found itself in a perilous situation – the fleeing troops were pushing everyone and everything out of the way, forcing men and wagons into the ditches. Panic spread down the long line of the royal forces – everyone could see what was coming. There was no way to turn the wagons around; the drivers could only drop the reins and run. Run, that is, as best they could in the mud of a churned-up road with seawater sweeping in at an angle. The slaughter continued, the Dithmarschers following along behind the rabble, finishing off those too exhausted to run further, surrounding and wiping out scattered pockets of courageous but foolish resistance, slowing only to see if pockets or wagons contained coins.

The king was lucky in not having left Meldorp yet. Smart enough to leave generalship to a professional, he had stayed in the rear, out of the way. His instinct now was to rally the troops, but he quickly saw that the situation was beyond saving. Perhaps he could have held Meldorp with some of the units that had not yet disintegrated, but he could find no one willing to face the wrath of the Dithmarschers with him. Already there was talk that the road from Meldorp to Holstein could be cut easily, and whoever hoped to survive had better use it while it was still open. The king was persuaded that he and any followers loyal enough to risk dying with him would soon be trapped. Better to escape quickly than share the fate of Charles the Bold. King Hans led the way to safety, leaving his ancient banner still flying from the church.

The next day, when the casualties for the two sides were counted up and the booty collected to be distributed among the victors, everyone was amazed at the contrasting tolls. Over 4,000 men from the Danish army had perished. Surprisingly, only about 800 of these casualties were members of the Black Guard. Why? First of all, not all of Slentz's troops had gotten into the action. Second, their discipline held together through the retreat. Dithmarschers naturally chose to massacre the frightened and almost helpless militiamen and nobles who were seeking safety individually or in small groups. Why go up against determined bands of professional soldiers who were leaving anyway?

The losses among the nobles were staggering. 600 cavalrymen went into a mass grave; 150 Holstein nobles could be identified, so that their bodies could be ransomed for burial; how many drowned in failed efforts to escape across country cannot be estimated. The king left behind all his artillery, all his supplies, his jewellery, his gold and silver table settings, his money. Everything.

The Dithmarschers buried sixty of their own men.

Rebellions broke out across the Danish empire. King Hans never found it possible to seek revenge for Hemmingstedt.

THE AFTERMATH

Some units of Guard reformed under new leadership, but it was never as formidable as it had been before the battle of Hemmingstedt. Its aura of invincibility had been shattered. The soldiers were as good as before, but future enemies were less intimidated.

The Dithmarschers had almost another six decades of independence. It was not until 1559 that Denmark had a king, Friedrich II (1559–88) who understood that war was not a game played by amateurs. The army that he brought to Dithmarschen was truly modern, fully equipped with modern weapons, and led by the best general of his generation (a type of demi-mercenary, a noble, but one who had given his life to the service of arms) and supported by an impressive international coalition. Friedrich was intelligent enough not to interfere with his general or to expose his person to harm. The tactics were brilliant – a summer campaign, a lightning seizure of Meldorp, then, while the Dithmarschers waited at Hemmingstedt, a forced march around to the defenders' rear to seize the northern fortifications. The Danes advanced swiftly to Heide, then fended off the farmers' uncoordinated counter-attacks. The Dithmarschers succumbed, fighting desperately. As one motto put it, *Ditmarshia fuit libera*. That is, Dithmarschen *has been* free. It was no more.

Heroism was no match for professionalism.

12

MACHIAVELLI

T HE FINAL WORD ON MERCENARIES, as far as the medieval/
Renaissance world is concerned, was written by the Florentine
political philosopher, Niccolò Machiavelli. That word was not
favourable. The crisis provoked by the military defeats in 1494–95 caused
him to rethink traditional military strategies and tactics. His enforced
retirement from politics in 1512 and his humanist training allowed him to see
that situation in the broadest possible perspective, that is, typically for
Renaissance intellectuals, by the study of classical history. When he decided
that the disasters of the late Roman Empire came from the use of Germanic
recruits, it required only a little leap of the imagination to believe that Italy's
current problems lay in having hired foreigners.

However, since there were relatively few foreigners in the armies of the
many Italian states, the problem, he decided, might be in the use of *any*
mercenaries. Italians should return to the Roman Republic's practice of
enlisting their own young men. The decisive moment in the development of
his thought may have been at Pisa in 1509, when Florentine mercenaries had
refused to attack a breach in the walls.

Machiavelli had the standing to expect a hearing – education and
experience. In 1498, when a republican government ruled, he was second
chancellor, then secretary, to the Committee of Ten, in charge of military
preparations. In 1505 he began to organise a Florentine army of conscripted
soldiers. He did not supervise this force personally, however, since
diplomatic travel took him through Italy and even to France and Germany.

In 1512, after Medici partisans overthrew the republic, Machiavelli
composed *The Prince* as advice for Giuliano de' Medici, the brother of the

cardinal who would soon become Pope Leo X; but although both Medicis read the manuscript, they were not impressed. Meanwhile Machiavelli finished a second book, a more erudite study entitled *Discourses*, in which he argued for a democratic, republican form of government.

MACHIAVELLI'S COMMENTS ON MERCENARIES

Machiavelli's treatise was scholarly. When he discussed mercenaries in chapter twelve of *The Prince*, he began with a general premise: 'They do not fear God and do not keep faith with mankind'. So much for the condottieri. But Machiavelli was not intent of being fair. He even denied Hawkwood the claim of being the first great mercenary commander – he gave credit for that to Alberigo de Conto, whose lieutenants included Francesco Sforza, later the commander of Milanese mercenaries. He praised Sforza for taking the logical next step of a general with an army – taking over the country. But Sforza's descendents, relying on others to command their armies, 'began as dukes and ended as private citizens'.

Relying on foreign armies (auxiliaries), Machiavelli argued, was even worse – a ruler should rely only on his own citizens or subjects. From this flows a vast river of consequences – that a ruler has to be honest, just, respected. Exactly the opposite characteristics from those that a superficial reader might expect. But it was true that the prince was not to be a philosopher king – such an idealist would quickly fall to aggressive neighbours or internal plots. Above all, he had to be practical – it was good that citizens should both love and fear their prince; but it was essential that they should fear him.

Feared, but not hated. And if hated, then not simultaneously despised. Misplaced generosity and compassion would be perceived as weakness. But there had to be balance – other rulers should fear him, but not fear him so much that war became unavoidable. Statecraft was, in short, a craft, an art, a skill that could be mastered. Machiavelli offered himself as the teacher.

Alas, contemporaries laughed at his arguments that money was not essential for war, that a patriotic citizenry would fight without pay, that infantry was superior to cavalry, and that artillery was overrated.

The condottieri were better generals than Machiavelli indicated, and their men were strong and well trained, but he was right in saying that they instinctively shrank back from pitched battles in which a quarter or half of their force might be slaughtered.

There had to be a better way to face the well-financed French and Spanish armies than using mercenaries; traditional practices had failed and seemed ever less likely to be successful in the future. That was Machiavelli's great insight. National armies were practically invincible, he said, because a few determined men are always superior to a myriad of half-hearted ones. The French and Spanish were fighting for pride and their king, the Italians only for money. That had to change.

Machiavelli's proposals did make military strategists see the need to study history. He used his analysis of ancient Greek and Roman armies and politics to suggest parallels to modern politics; some examples he took from ancient Rome, some from Cesare Borgia (whose name alluded to the most successful of all the Roman generals, even though he was the son of a pope), but all were thought-provoking.

Machiavelli wisely did not spend much time condemning military popes. Julius II (1503–13) might have been safe – he was a true warrior – and Alexander Borgia (1492–1503) provided enough material for scandalous gossip for centuries. But with the Medici in control of the papacy, it was best to criticise popes as little as possible.

Contemporary clerics and secular rulers alike condemned Machiavelli's ideas as cynical, evil, and unsuitable for Christian readers – that was enough to guarantee him a large readership. They even popularised his name, Niccolò, as 'Old Nick', indicating that he was clearly in league with the devil. They did this while cynically lying and cheating themselves. The difference, they rationalised, was that they knew that they were doing wrong, and Machiavelli did not.

✕

MILITARY MATTERS

Machiavelli never commanded troops in the field. He lacked personal experience except in organisation and supply. He was an intellectual, a theorist. That was the most important reason that contemporaries did not heed his wisdom. One anecdote reported by Mallett illustrates the difference between the observer and the expert: Giovanni de' Medici is said to have allowed him to try out his proposed infantry drills on the Black Bands. Machiavelli explained the commands, then tried them on the parade ground.

As the morning passed into midday, the heat became intense; the soldiers, unaccustomed to the new drill, became confused and fell repeatedly into disorder. There must have been considerable heckling and laughter, and one doubts that the soldiers gave it their best effort. Finally Giovanni took over the command again, barked a few decisive commands and restored the formations to order. It was not a fair test, but Machiavelli was too wise to ask for another try with those men.

The story is probably apocryphal; that is, it wasn't true, but it should have been. In the long run Machiavelli was right, and that is why we still read him. Still, in the short run he was a failure. The immediate future still belonged to professional armies; and although these armies were no longer composed of short-term mercenaries, the French Revolution's introduction of mass armies of volunteers was still a long way off. Thus, in that odd way that history has of confounding us, Machiavelli was more important for future generations than he was for contemporaries.

Machiavelli wanted to revive the citizen-soldier, and with that also to revive the republican state. The citizen-soldier, knowing that the government's decisions would determine the chances of his living and dying, of prospering or paying taxes to foreigners, would insist on a role in the government. The ancient Roman republic could be restored, first in Florence, and then throughout Italy.

Although Machiavelli presented this as an original idea, it was not quite so. Every Italian city had once been defended by a citizen militia, and although these had become impractical as field troops, they were still useful for defending walls and forts. Indeed, the first use of revived civic militia – as envisioned by Florentine intellectuals between 1402 and 1420 – would be as garrison troops. But Florence was of several minds about arming the lower classes, and was definitely reluctant to give command to any member of any noble family. Giving command to a commoner, no matter how talented, was unthinkable.

There had been a major shift in the organisation of armies that began in the 1440s. The leading nation was France, but armies long remained small, rarely over 20,000 men. This was because of the difficulty of supplying a larger force, and also because once an army became too large, the general could not get an overview of the battlefield and his orders could not reach distant units in time to make any difference. There was also the lack of an experienced chain of command, with competent officers at each level of responsibility; and not only field officers, but commissary officials, paymasters, engineers, transport specialists, the staff responsible for the care and feeding of the commander and the courtiers necessary to entertain and advise him. But the final decision of an army's size was dictated by money.

As the mercenary tradition faded slowly into national armies, so too did the practice of living off the land – robbing, raping and burning. These were the hallmarks of the mercenary soldier, and there must have been many a disappointed young bully or old reprobate when the royal commander explained that their employer expected to win battles decisively, not stop to wait till his troops had finished with their pleasures. But whatever the troops lost in way of booty, they more than made up for in having guaranteed employment. Men and officers alike were becoming professionals, and like all professionals they were concerned with salaries, retirement benefits, and honours. Because kings and princes could provide these, their methods of war were those of the future. And because they could treat old-fashioned mercenaries as robber bands, they had a monopoly on war that allowed them to dictate the rules.

This did not mean the end of irregular troops, or plunder, or murder; those have survived to the present day and will surely last long into the future. But the rise of the national state and the national army marched a decisive change in the way western societies made war, and peace, and thus changed everything else. The Leviathan was coming – the modern state.

Machiavelli did not believe that the day of the modern army had already dawned – at least, not in the west. And it would not until Italy awoke. In chapter thirteen of *The Prince* he argued that the French were weaker than they should be because the king relied on Swiss mercenaries; in *The Discourses*, book three, he went further, to explain why the French are so ferocious at the beginning of a battle, then timid at the end (at first more courage than men, then less than women). It's a Celtic thing, he said, going back to the Gauls, to have more ardour than discipline.

He accused contemporary Italians of having neither ardour nor discipline. Italians, however, were descendants of Romans and hence had some hope of correcting their faults.

HIS EXHORTATION TO GIULIANO DE'MEDICI

Machiavelli concluded *The Prince* with a call to Giuliano de'Medici to take the lead in rescuing the nation from foreign barbarians. The Swiss must give way before infantry armed with swords, because infantrymen can slip beneath the pikes; such infantry, however, cannot withstand cavalry attacks; and cavalry cannot charge pikemen. The new Italian army must be a combination of arms. Most of all, it must have a leader who can inspire the troops:

> Let, therefore, your illustrious house take up this charge with that courage and hopes with which all just enterprises are undertaken; so that under its standard this our native country may be ennobled, and under its auspices may be verified that saying of Petrarch:

Virtú conra al Furore	Courage against rage
Prenderâ l'arme,	shall take up arms,
e fia il combatter corto:	and the battle will be brief
Che l'antico valore	because ancient valour
Negli italici cuor non è ancor morto	is not yet dead in Italian hearts.

13

MERCENARIES IN THE LATE MEDIEVAL BALTIC

TRANSFORMATION OF THE TEUTONIC ORDER

THE TEUTONIC ORDER'S catastrophe at Tannenberg (1410) was followed by decades of defeat and disorder. Polish armies ravaged Prussia again and again, depopulating some regions and reducing many others to penury. The grand masters' desperate efforts to collect taxes to led to revolts and, perhaps more important, to a significant shift away from relying on local forces and recruits in Germany to hiring mercenary troops, and even then only for emergencies. Whatever could be saved from supporting one knight in the lavish life-style of the past could be used to employ several professional horsemen.

Accompanying this was a shift away from recruiting knights from the lower nobility and ministeriales to knights with more impressive genealogies, that is, away from warriors to officers. This was, at least in part, an effort to reward German dynasties for their generous support in political matters, donations of money and land, and enlisting younger sons in the military order. To a certain degree, this was self-defeating, because these nobles were not inclined to live as simple monks; also, to the extent possible, they preferred to live in Germany on the estates contributed by their families.

No study has yet been made as to what percentage of these knights were not suited to warfare or administration. To what extent they were marriageable. To what extent they were just an embarrassment to the family. It may be that such a study is impossible, since all that one can do from the records is to wonder why a well-born knight was not promoted to positions of responsibility.

Knights served as officers of mercenary bands, commanded castles where mercenaries were stationed, and were responsible, as in the past, for collecting taxes, supervising justice and commerce, and maintaining the religious standards of the order. This latter duty was more difficult than ever, since the grand masters were insisting on pious behaviour more than ever before. Whether this reflected a belief that God had turned his back on the crusaders because their personal lives had been insufficiently holy can be debated, but hardly resolved to universal satisfaction.

The Livonian Knights went through tribulations, too – schism within the military order, war with the citizens of Riga, desperate quarrels with the archbishop of Riga and the other prelates – but the growing power of the grand dukes of Moscow served as a unifying stimulus. The Livonian Confederation was not a perfect instrument for governing the region, but it served all parties well in giving them excuses to forgo ancient quarrels and cooperate at least marginally in regional defence.

Livonia was too poor to permit the Livonian Order, the archbishops, the prelates, the abbots or the cities to hire many mercenaries. Therefore, in the years after 1490, when everyone knew that there would likely be war with Ivan III (the Great), the grand duke of Moscow, the Livonian master, Wolter von Plettenberg, was perplexed as to how he could raise a cavalry army to defend his lands. Or even how he could persuade all the members of the Livonian Confederation to support the war effort.

MERCENARIES IN PRUSSIA

Until relatively recently almost all information about medieval mercenaries came from Italian, French or English sources. Sven Ekdahl's research into the extensive manuscript collection of the Geheimes Staatsarchiv Preussischer Kulturbesitz has changed this significantly. Two documents proved to be especially important.

The first was a contract from 1413, when Grand Master Heinrich von Plauen (the heroic defender of Marienburg in 1410) raised a mercenary army to take revenge on the Polish king, Jagiełło. Peter Wilke, a mercenary commander from the Bohemian-Upper Silesian region, promised to bring a small force of horsemen, crossbowmen and squires – twenty-four horse in all. The contract listed all the animals by class, size and colour (wolf colour, brown, red-brown, bright red, black, white, etc.) and special marks (colour of feet, muzzle). The two warhorses were geldings; the carthorses were not specified. The price of the warhorses ran at twenty-six, twenty-eight, thirty and forty marks, fourteen others at ten to twenty marks, and three cart horses at five, seven and eight marks.

Only the six horsemen were named, not the twelve to fourteen crossbowmen and youths. An especially good suit of armour was valued at ten marks, the rest were lumped together – four suits of mail for twenty-four marks and so forth.

The list was especially detailed because the mercenaries considered the chances of defeat high. They would not sign up unless the promise to replace their losses would be honoured. A list of possessions was the first step in the process of claiming damages.

The second list, from 1431, was connected with a potential war with Poland. Grand Master Paul von Rusdorf had informed two officers in West Prussia and the Neumark that mercenaries would be coming. In late August 154 Silesian mercenaries under Friedrich von der Heyde appeared at Küstrin; On 1 September they were at Tuchel. The latter list was far the better.

The men were well suited for combat, properly mounted and well equipped. However, they had a smaller number of youths than customary, and some riders lacked armour, others iron helmets. These deficiencies they promised to make good as soon as they were paid. On the whole, only a third of the force reflected the ideal *Spieß* of horseman, archer and squire. There were forty horsemen, three men-at-arms, eighty-five crossbowmen (six without weapons) and twenty-six youths. The equipment was not described in detail, because the economically hard-strapped order made no promises to reimburse its men for their losses.

Not every company was so thoroughly described: 200 horsemen from the Mosel arrived at Küstrin, then absolutely refused to have their possessions inventoried. After hard negotiating, they were allowed to proceed to the grand master.

Mercenaries were especially important in this campaign because a severe drought had reduced the number of warhorses in Prussia. The grand master was not interested in provoking a battle, but only in tying down Polish forces which could otherwise be dispatched to tip the balance in Lithuania, where civil war raged. The grand master, through the Livonian Order, supported the grand duke – Jagiełło's younger brother – who was impulsive, tyrannical and Orthodox; the King Jagiełło backed a brother of the late Lithuanian grand duke, Vytautas, who was reliably Roman Catholic.

It was a matter of utmost importance to the future of Lithuania – would it return to its traditional orientation toward Russia or strengthen the more recent ties to Poland? The grand master hoped to split the Polish-Lithuanian alliance, but most of all he wanted revenge. The pope would not approve, but Paul von Rusdorf was not bothering to consult him.

The forces of the Teutonic Knights were divided into three armies, one from east Prussia to strike into Masovia, one with Livonian reinforcements to attack Kujavia from west Prussia, and a third body of mercenaries to operate out of the Neumark in Great Poland. The initial attacks were great successes, perhaps because the aged King Jagiełło could not believe the grand master would be so foolish as to challenge him. Events proved him right – the fine contingent of Livonian Knights and many mercenaries were ambushed in a West Prussian forest by Polish forces, then massacred as they retreated across bridges over the many branches of the Netze River.

Then a report came to Prussia that the grand master's Lithuanian ally had signed a truce with Jagiełło! The king had suggested to his younger brother that they might be able to resolve their dispute peacefully, and the mercurial grand duke, watching the royal forces march away, requested the grand master to withdraw his forces from Poland. There was little for Rusdorf to do but delay, to negotiate for the ransom of important officers, and to pray that God would not give more victories to Polish arms.

Prayers did little good. Not even hiring more mercenaries helped. Prussia had been worn down by repeated invasions; and the German convents of the Teutonic Order, which had once been enthusiastic supporters of the Hussite Wars, were now totally discouraged by their defeats at the hands of Czech heretics.

The Czechs had always been the foremost mercenaries of central Europe. Some 'Bohemians' were actually Germans, knightly immigrants given fiefs by past kings, but most were Czech speakers. During the Hussite wars (1419–34) – a combination of religious war and Czech rebellion against German domination – their skills had been honed to a fine edge. Their armies cut through superior forces with a sureness and efficiency that were the envy of all neighbouring peoples. Eventually their enemies began to flee when the Hussites broke into their war songs.

King Jagiełło was a master at diplomacy, even when – as his courtiers believed – he was in his dotage; they cited his forgetfulness, his love of the primeval forest, his slipping out at night to listen to the nightingale. He was not a man of passion – he neither drank nor sang, his love-life was so passive that many believed his young daughters had to be the bastard offspring of a prelate or some other low form of life. But his lethargy was brilliant. He wore down his hot-headed brother, the Orthodox claimant to the grand duchy, slowly stripping away his supporters until at last only the knights of the Livonian Order and a handful of Hussite exiles stood by him. He exhausted the grand master's resources by massing troops along the border, threatening attack, then signing a truce that allowed the grand master to release most of his mercenaries, and then again creating a war crisis. Approached by Hussites who wanted to cross Poland to strike at their most determined enemies, the Teutonic Knights, Jagiełło agreed – even promising to give them 600,000 groschen, equivalent to 15,000 marks. However, in this he had to move secretly, lest the pope object. Jagiełło played on the discouragement and failing health of the Holy Roman emperor, Sigismund – a devious sensualist who wanted victory over the Czechs – by warning him that if he assisted the Teutonic Order, Polish volunteers might come to the assistance of the Hussites. Then Jagiełło worked around the opposition of his own chief cleric, Archbishop Oleśnicki, who hated heretics even more than he did Germans. In 1433, while the king tied down Prussian forces on the Vistula, a Hussite army of 5,000 men, mostly infantry following twenty war wagons, and 900 cavalry, invaded west Prussia. The Hussites marched to the Baltic Sea unopposed except when they tried to storm well-fortified towns.

The king took many prisoners himself, delivering captured Czech mercenaries to their countrymen, who burned them alive. Two years later, Polish knights assisted in defeating the Orthodox Lithuanian grand duke and his Livonian allies. Roman Catholicism, Polish Catholicism, had triumphed.

Jagiełło had made Poland into the most powerful state in east central Europe. The way was made open for his adopted nation's climb to greatness in the next two centuries.

LIVONIA

Livonia was defended primarily by the order's knights, who were scattered among dozens of castles and frontier forts; the order also had many lower-class men-at-arms and mercenaries. A large number of knights were secular vassals of the archbishop of Riga, the bishops of Dorpat, Oesel-Wiek, Reval and Kurland; then there were city militias, well-drilled companies accompanied by musicians. All these groups were known later as Baltic Germans. Most spoke Low German – a language with some similarities to

Dutch and even English – but all believed that they were more connected to the Holy Roman Empire than was actually the case.

The native militias – Livs and Letts, Semgallians and Kurs (who all later merged to become Latvians) and Estonians – had no love for one another, but they realised what awaited them if Russians or Lithuanians invaded. They knew this because very often they had accompanied the Livonian Knights across the borders and been allowed to murder and loot to their hearts' content. They were fine troops – well drilled by German commanders and fighting under their own banners – as long as victory seemed likely, but they tended to melt away and head for home when faced with defeat, leaving the Livonian Knights to fend for themselves.

None of these forces – knights, civic militias or native militias – could be made into landsknechts, the type of soldier which had defeated Charles the Bold, or into artillerymen. The Livonian master was no more ready to abandon cavalry than the grand master in East Prussia, but he understood modern military theory.

MARX AND MERCENARIES

Marx stated that societal forms followed the evolution of economic systems. In saying this, he was saying that Marxist dialectic – the process of change – had its feet solidly on the ground, in the soil of the farmer and on the floor of the factory. This, he joked, turned Hegel on his head, because Hegel's dialectic had stressed competition between ideas, between ideologies.

The dominant class, Marx noted, was always able to buy support among those who should logically have been its enemies. There were the police, drawn exclusively from the working class, and the army, often forced into service by monarchs and parliaments who represented the enemies of all peasants and labourers.

According to Marxists, the mercenary sold his class interests for money. Why not? While the working classes, the *Proletariat*, could be expected to sense the importance of class solidarity, there was always a *Lumpenproletariat* that cared little about the common fate of ordinary people, not even about their friends and family. The German word that Marx invented, with his typical combination of pseudo-scientific exactness, sarcasm and invective, suggests a doughy lack of backbone. The Lumpenproletariat, composed of the unemployed and the unemployable, hated work. Its members were criminals, drunks or any lazy louts who would do anything for enough money to get through life. They were always counter-revolutionary. In short, the Lumpenproletariat was the class best suited to provide oppressive lords with mercenary armies.

In the Baltic mercenary armies appeared at a stage in society where the economic system was changing from individual peasant holdings to large estates raising grain for export. The Marxist analysis was that the land-owning class, suddenly having cash on hand, were able to hire soldiers to replace their less effective peasant militias. This opportunity combined nicely with their turning many tenants out on to an unfavourable labour market. Some of these unemployed men became mercenaries. Marxist analysis thus provided satisfactory reasons for the changes that scholars had noted in late medieval Europe – the rise of the national monarch, the enclosure of small fields into larger estates (a practice that prefigured capitalism's swallowing the artisan and small merchant), and appearance of well-organised mercenary armies.

Marxists were correct in assuming that there was a connection between economics and armies. But if changes in the economy should have come first, most explicitly the introduction of serfdom, that did not apply in Livonia; military theory seems to have changed first. Livonia could not be defended without mercenaries and cannons. Both cost money. How would the states of the Livonian Confederation raise the money to pay for them? The answer seems to be, first from the profits of traditional trade – grain, wax, wood, amber and furs – then through a greater emphasis on cash crops. Landlords, however, lacked the labour force to exploit their estates fully – and natives preferred to work their own small farms.

SERFDOM

Serfdom was spreading slowly in Livonia before 1500, just as it was in neigh-bouring Lithuania and Russia. England and France had moved into a cash economy and, therefore, could abandon serfdom, but in the east there was a great labour shortage. The only way that landowners could keep their labour force from leaving for better opportunities was to make their tenants into serfs.

One source of serfs was prisoners of war. From time out of mind the regional powers had stolen one another's peasants, selling them either to the long-distance slave traders or to landowners who would replace their own stolen labourers with serfs. Another source was bankrupt peasants or farmers' younger sons who were willing to accept the conditions of serfdom in order to acquire rental lands of their own. What prevented landowners from extending serfdom farther and faster was the awkward fact that the natives were armed.

The interplay of economics and military theory is more complicated than was once believed. Hegel may even have been right – ideas about military strategy and tactics may have been more important than landholding practices.

Since most knights of the Livonian Order were born in Germany, grew up there, and learned their military skills there, they were eager to bring to Livonia the knowledge and experience of the homeland – their understanding of the campaigns of Charles the Bold, for example. They believed that modern armies needed landsknechts and firearms. If the Livonian Order was to survive in a world of rapidly growing coalescing national states – Poland, Russia, Sweden, Denmark – it would have to have a modern army. They shared this belief with the other members of the Livonian Confederation, who, of course, had their own informants about military practices in the homeland.

What the Livonians did over time was to hire landsknechts, then convert the native militiamen into baggage handlers and haulers of cannon. In time these disarmed natives were converted into serfs. That did not occur quickly, of course, not becoming universal until the Livonian War of 1558–83, but this conversion of the native warriors into auxiliary troops had begun before Wolter van Plettenberg was elected master of the Livonian Order in 1494.

WOLTER VON PLETTENBERG AND IVAN THE GREAT

Wolter von Plettenberg was the greatest master of the Livonian Order ever. His family had come from Westphalia earlier in the fifteenth century. It was a common practice for families of the lower nobility to migrate in search of opportunities, and members of the Livonian Order from Westphalia had been urging their countrymen to come east, both as merchants and artisans and as proprietors of small estates. He had been marshal when the Livonian Order crushed Riga in a hard-fought civil war, but now he needed the assistance of all the order's former enemies.

Ivan III was an enemy worthy of Plettenberg's steel; he had reduced the number of Tatar raids, retaken territories lost earlier to Poland–Lithuania, made his country the centre of the Orthodox Christian world, and brought most of his notoriously independent boyars to heel. Most significantly for Livonia, he had conquered the powerful northern merchant state, Novgorod. Though Livonians would perhaps have said that their traditional Russian opponent was Pskov, which was often allied with either Moscow or Lithuania, they had always feared Novgorod more. After 1489, however, the year Ivan III became their new neighbour, many Livonians would have happily had their old foe back. Novgorod had been much weaker and less aggressive; it had also been a commercial partner. Ivan had little interest in trade, except for buying cannon.

Fear of Ivan would not have been so great if Poland–Lithuania could have been counted on as an ally. But Grand Duke Alexander had no sooner promised to stand by Livonia than his brother, the king of Poland, died. In early 1501 Alexander rushed off to Cracow to be elected and crowned.

This was very awkward timing for Plettenberg, who had hired lands-knechts and bought artillery to support his knights, then moved into the thinly settled borderlands to meet the expected Russian invasion. The Lithuanian general did not appear. Recriminations flew back and forth, but Plettenberg nevertheless took the war to the enemy, and after several artillery exchanges, he was pleased to see the Russians withdraw, abandoning wagons, weapons and supplies. When he learned that no troops stood between him Pskov, he faced a hard choice. Pskov had high stone walls and thus would have been difficult to capture with the forces at his disposal; he had counted on Lithuania for the necessary men and firepower. Making the best of his situation, he marched on Ostrov, a weaker, but still significant castle to the south on the overland route between Pskov and Lithuania. After capturing Ostov, a lack of provisions and an epidemic caused him to retreat.

In November of 1501 Ivan III invaded Livonia with a large army, perhaps 9,000 men; six weeks later, when he withdrew, he promised to be back soon, taking with him many thousands of peasants and thousands more head of cattle and horses. This helped Plettenberg persuade the grand master of the Teutonic Order to raise a special tax in Prussia, then to recruit 200 mercenaries to send to Livonia. This contribution was far less than in the past, when the grand master would send entire armies north. Prussia was no longer rich and the grand master no longer powerful.

The grand master did send an investigator to report on the situation. His written summary was grave: Plettenberg's officers had rejected his plan for a winter campaign; this came on top of their having hindered his operations again and again; and the plague had carried away two of his best commanders. To make matters worse, the bishops and abbots wanted Archbishop Michael Hildebrand, to seize this opportunity to humble the Livonian Knights; and the most rabid of all was the bishop of Dorpat, whose lands were most directly threatened by the Russians!

Although the archbishop chose to side with Plettenberg, it was difficult to raise mercenaries for the next campaign. After the Danish defeat at Hemmingstedt in 1500, the recently conquered Swedes rose in rebellion. This war drained off the supply of available men; it also caused the mercenaries already in Livonia to complain about not having been paid even the low wages promised.

The last straw was the rebellious attitude of the Estonian nobles, good horsemen who nursed grudges against the Livonian Knights over internal conflicts of recent decades. Dorpat's opposition to everything was taken for granted.

Serious observers believed that the Livonian Confederation was on the verge of collapse; the country was being held together by Wolter von Plettenberg alone. This was not a good sign. Plettenberg, facing one of the most powerful and capable rulers in Europe, had at his disposal totally inadequate forces. Also, his knights wanted to debate every strategy and approve every proposal; nor could he summon all to ride with him – some were too aged or infirm; many would have to be left as garrisons of castles – partly to guard against insurrection, partly to protect strategic strongholds against Christian neighbours. Thus Plettenberg could put only a relatively small number of horsemen into the field. To his knights Plettenberg could add the unhappy landsknechts, several bodies of knights from the various parts of Estonia and the vassals of the archbishop of Riga. Michael Hildebrand appeared in person to lead his forces, but that was still not enough. What Plettenberg really needed was massive reinforcements from the West. He had sent an appeal to the Holy Roman Empire for men and money, and the emperor, Maximilian (1493–1519), had promised help. Most likely he made a perfunctory prayer or two. But nothing more.

There was still the promise of Polish–Lithuanian help, but no troops had arrived by March 1502 when the first Russian forces appeared at Narva. When Plettenberg heard that the local commander had sought out that enemy and routed them, he made sure that the good news was proclaimed widely. Plettenberg was faced not only with the plague spreading throughout the countryside, but also with an epidemic of defeatism. When his mercenaries demanded that they be paid and dismissed, Plettenberg closed the ports to anyone wishing to leave the country.

Other than a few more troops from Prussia, there were no reinforcements arriving. New cannons had been ordered from France, but delivery was delayed by the Danish blockade of the straits; of the two cannons that did make it through, one exploded in a test firing.

Then a stroke of good luck. Spies reported that Ivan planned to invade Livonia in the late summer with 90,000 men and seek out a decisive battle. Actually, the plan was not much of a secret. It was probably part of a propaganda campaign intended to intimidate the Livonians. Plettenberg, in contrast to most of his countrymen, found this very encouraging. Ivan may have been planning a short campaign to avoid the severe supply problems that had hindered operations the past year, but Plettenberg's supply troubles were even greater – he certainly could not afford a long campaign. Yes, the Livonian Confederation could probably hold major fortresses for a few years, but the peasants would all be killed, carried away or scattered, and that would be fatal to the economy. Delay had not worked for Novgorod. It would probably not work for Livonia, either. Faith in God was good, but in the modern era God did not strike down His people's enemies as He once did. Orthodox believers seemed to have a monopoly on saints and angels coming to the rescue in the middle of combat; Catholics, though still superstitious, were practical – scepticism was an inseparable part of the education given to the northern Renaissance elite.

Plettenberg decided to risk everything on one great battle. He persuaded the Livonian Confederation that his plan was the best available, that in August he should put his army in motion toward Ivan's forces camped around Pskov and attack before the grand duke himself arrived. The assembly point was Dorpat.

THE BATTLE AT PSKOV

Plettenberg had 433 knights, men-at-arms and squires belonging to the Livonian Order, 1,500 to 2,500 secular knights from Estonia, the arch-bishopric of Riga and the dioceses of Dorpat and Oesel-Wiek, and 2,500 landsknechts. There were several hundred native militiamen and a small train of field artillery; also the natives employed to carry equipment. He moved so swiftly, taking only three days to move from Dorpat to Pskov, that his forward units almost reached the Russian camp before being detected.

Ivan's generals were disconcerted. Of their master's gigantic force, only 15,000 to 30,000 had arrived; and these were not his best units. The generals could only assume that the Lithuanian army would be right behind the Livonians. How else would such a small force dare cross the frontier?

Plettenberg encouraged this belief. When his men sacked the suburbs of Pskov, he told the people to surrender, warning that the Lithuanians would be there soon, and there would be no resisting them. The people of Pskov courageously refused to open their gates, but they passed on the information to the generals and their troops.

It was probably with considerable surprise that the Russian generals heard their scouts' reports that Plettenberg only had about 5,000 men. They themselves had 8,000 cavalry and a somewhat larger number of infantry. Other units were on the march, not far away – at least 3,000 cavalry were expected very soon. Although the generals could have withdrawn and waited for reinforcements, they probably worried that Plettenberg would use the delay to escape. Fearful of Ivan's anger, they remained in place, awaiting attack.

When it became clear that Ivan's generals were ready to offer battle, Plettenberg spoke to his troops, reminding them of the example of Judas Maccabaeus, whose tiny Jewish army had routed hordes of invincible Greeks. He took personal command of the right wing, gave the centre to Archbishop Michael, and the left wing to the marshal. He placed the knights to the front, with the landsknechts behind them so that the cavalry could re-group after a retreat, and also to thwart any effort to surround the horsemen. He put the artillery in the centre, but he expected little from it; he was relying on his heavily armoured knights to break up the Russian formations.

Plettenberg halted near the enemy camp, waiting until the 18,000 enemy had deployed, then his artillery cut loose, blowing large gaps in the massed formations. When the moment was right, he sent his knights forward. Desperate combat followed, especially in the centre where the Russians repulsed the archbishop's attack. The Russians then came forward themselves, actually reaching close enough to the main battle flag to cut off a part of it.

Elsewhere on the battlefield the Catholic forces were prevailing. As opposing units broke into panicked flight, there was a danger that the crusaders would repeat the error of Tannenberg and ride off the battlefield in pursuit. However, the marshal stopped his men from that folly, reorganised them and led a devastating charge into the flank of the main Russian force. There had been hard fighting for the landsknechts, who had held the Russian cavalry away from the artillery with their pikes, then taken on the Russian infantry in hand-to-hand combat; hundreds had fallen in the desperate struggle before the Russians realised that they were being attacked from all sides, then fled. The landsknechts and cavalry turned the desperate struggle into a massacre, then pursued the survivors until they were incapable of doing more.

The victorious Catholic army collapsed where it was, utterly spent. Plettenberg knew that there were other Russian armies nearby, but his men were too exhausted to get back to camp. He ordered the army to sleep on the battlefield and be ready to fight the next morning.

No Russian army appeared. Panic and defeatism spread even in armies whose commanders tolerate no excuses. The next day was devoted first to prayer, then to plundering the dead and burying 400 of their comrades. Plettenberg was informed that his men had counted 2,500 Russian corpses, but also that the actual losses were probably close to 8,000.

The total of Russian dead did not matter. Ivan had plenty of men. But his campaign had been disrupted. There was no way that he could invade Livonia this year. Peace talks began in early 1503. Perhaps God *was* intervening – Ivan's health was declining, and his troubles multiplying.

In negotiations among great powers, the interests of the minor states are often neglected. So it was now. Plettenberg informed his allies of Livonia's minimum needs for security, but his wishes were overruled by the representatives from Poland–Lithuania and the Holy Roman Empire. The great Catholic powers had ambitious plans for a grand alliance of all Christians against the Turks and, therefore, did not want Russia weakened. Ivan could tie down many Turks and Tatars along the Black Sea; moreover, unless he was committed to the war, Lithuanian troops would have to remain at home to guard against him. When no permanent peace agreement could be worked out, the Catholic representatives agreed to a short truce, only six years. The grand duke insisted on reimbursement for his wartime expenses and that Livonia pay tribute, but not even the Poles, Lithuanians and Germans could force that on Plettenberg. Nevertheless, they made it clear that Livonia was on its own. As a result, there was no permanent peace settlement. Only a truce.

It was not long before the Lithuanians could tolerate no more of Ivan's insults and threats. When King Alexander of Poland–Lithuania declared war, he assumed that Plettenberg would join him. Plettenberg, however, did nothing more than maintain a strong force on the eastern border. He lacked the resources for a long struggle and did not want to risk another great battle. Most of all, he did not trust Alexander.

Peace came when Ivan's death brought disorder into his nation. Plettenberg's victory gave Livonia five decades of peace and prosperity. When the Reformation threatened to divide the land into warring factions, Plettenberg presided over a peaceful transition – those wanting to become Protestant, did so, but those who did not, were not compelled to change; cities could establish Protestant churches, but the archbishop, bishops and abbots all remained Roman Catholic, together with most of the rural population.

THE FUTURE

Plettenberg had won his great battle with traditional knights, but future wars could not be fought without more landsknechts and artillery. Moreover, the Livonians were learning that Russian generals had come to the same conclusion. Moscow's armies were increasingly armed for modern warfare, with the traditional mercenary archers replaced by professional musketeers and backed by artillery. The Livonians had to copy the military reforms of Sweden and Denmark or go under in the next assault by the seemingly limitless manpower and superior weaponry of Russia.

To finance this professional army, the Livonian Confederation assisted the landowners in fastening serfdom around the necks of the rural population. The peasants still performed military service, but it was as porters and labourers – modern warfare required many supplies, heavy weapons and the construction of fortifications. The serfs could do these necessary jobs. For free.

The military classes deteriorated into idle rich; some secular nobles supervised their overseers and improved their estates, but most gave greater attention to hunting, wenching and boozing than to training for war. Protected by Plettenberg's fifty years of peace, their military skills atrophied. This made them ever more dependent on mercenaries.

As for the Livonian Knights, as the Protestant Reformation spread across their main recruiting areas, it became difficult to maintain their numbers. There was no alternative to hiring mercenaries.

14

SUMMARY

THE ORIGINS OF THE MEDIEVAL MERCENARY were in the exchange of services for pay. While there were freebooters who were often nothing more than wandering bands of organised robbers, these fall more in the category of pirate or outlaw than hired warrior.

No employer could stay in business without a source of revenue or the promise of one. This limited the hiring of mercenaries to governments or quasi-governments, whether legitimate, usurper, warlord or bandit-king. Governments that had no effective tax structure were limited in their ability to defend their lands at all, much less to hire anyone to fight for them. When William the Conqueror invited volunteers to participate in the invasion of Saxon England, he could only promise land and loot. Once he had the Saxon kingdom well in hand, he began to collect taxes. Not knowing how much of the tax structure had survived his many confiscations and depredations, he authorised an investigation into the financial status of all his subjects. This became the *Domesday Book*. With the revenues generated by taxation, English kings could exert an influence on Continental politics that neither their kingdom's population nor economy would have permitted, had it been organised on French, German or Italian models.

Perhaps mercenaries of a sort had always existed – bodyguards come to mind. But a significant difference in scale is discernable when the bodyguards become a military unit. Housecarls might be regarded as such a transition institution – they were the core of the Saxon army before being cut down at the battle of Hastings. Later, bodyguards became formal military units assigned to protect the monarch – the very name of some modern units (Horse Guards, Household Cavalry) betrays such origins. Technically, all British units are relatively modern, the earliest dating only from Cromwell's time or Charles II, and some trace their lineage no farther back than the late nineteenth century or even the Great War. But each Guards regiment understands the implications of its name and is usually stationed close to a royal residence.

Employing mercenaries as garrison troops became more common at the time of the crusades. The castles in the Holy Land, Spain and the Baltic could not be protected by local vassals each taking a turn at providing men to prowl the walls. To meet this need, military orders sprang up first, each providing essential services – hospital care, escorts for pilgrims, expert knowledge of the terrain and the enemy, garrisons and entertainment. The military orders, in time, hired mercenaries to supplement their numbers, especially to make up shortfalls of recruits for lower ranks; they also had networks of convents and hospitals which could serve as recruiting centres.

Mercenaries came to dominant the battlefield only in the Hundred Years War. Most were employed to supplement the feudal forces, but periodically the knights became *freelance operators* and the units free companies. This was most often in time of peace or during truces. Thus it happened that the ordinary person – farmer, artisan, cleric – was sometimes safer from attack during war than in peace!

Renaissance Italians made a science and an art out of warfare based on mercenary troops. War was no longer a business for amateurs, but became dominated by experienced and intelligent generals who demanded high pay and a flattering social status. Quickly, these professionals saw that pitched battles would result either in defeat, victory or a draw. Defeat or victory would put them out of a job, the first through death or disgrace, the latter through cutbacks in the employer's military budget. A bloody but indecisive battle would make employers look for another general and troops for another employer. Therefore, it was in the interest of all professionals to keep the wars as long and bloodless as could be managed.

This came to an end with the organisation of modern national armies. The French led the way in the fifteenth century, proceeding by fits and starts to make royal authority and the royal army ever more effective. These armies were slowly remodelled so that the soldiers did not wander off to rape and plunder. But, whatever their defects, these early modern armies were superior to their opponents, whether traditional feudal armies or freebooters.

The best of modern authors have recognised the dangers that mercenaries presented to everyone. Sharon Kay Penman, who bases her stories on original sources and the latest scholarship, concludes one battle in *When God and His Angels Slept* with an eyewitness to the slaughter saying, "It was even worse than you think, Uncle. Not only were some of the men seeking refuge in the church slain, but so were a few monks who tried to intervene.' Henry shook his head, in remembered anger, 'Breton mercenaries...all they know is killing."

Ellis Peters, whose Cadfael mysteries are set in that same dreary twelfth-century England, approaches mercenaries indirectly, assuming that readers will recognise a rough man by the merest suggestion of having fought for pay. In *A Rare Benedictine* she introduces a character who 'had seen, he said, Italy as far south as Rome, served once for a time under the Count of Flanders, crossed the mountain into Spain, never abiding anywhere for long. His feet still served him, but his mind grew weary of the road.' Cadfael himself had gone to war at fourteen – 'in Wales fourteen in manhood, and as I was a good lad with the short bow, and took kindly to the sword, I suppose I was worth my keep.' Both had taken the cross, and, as Cadfael said, 'So did many like me, all afire. I won't say what followed was all ash, but it burned very low at times.'

LITERATURE

No one can fully understand how we view our historical past without knowing literature. Authors sometimes only want to tell a story, but many also have a religious, political or patriotic agenda. Popular authors bring medieval history to life. One might ask whether it is better for non-professionals to read the tales of medieval writers who were more interested in telling a good story than in getting the facts right or to read modern fiction writers who do their best to base their stories on fact.

There is a place for 'dry as dust history'. But there is also a time to remember that history unread is history wasted. Popular history is, right now, well, extremely popular – books on medieval history sell better than ever. So do fictional accounts of those same events. This suggests that serious historians should be aware of serious fiction. Even of non-serious fiction.

A LESSON FOR OUR TIMES?

From all appearances mercenary soldiers will be with us for a time yet. It is a classic case of 'demand and supply' – in that order. That is, as long as there is an apparent need for trained warriors without any ideological or patriotic interest in the struggle at hand, states or revolutionaries will be hiring mercenaries.

Such organised groups are much preferable to relying on the hope that bandits or organised criminals will abandon their livelihoods and settle down as peaceable citizens. Intelligent employers can deal with mercenaries effectively without ruining either their reputation or credit rating (i.e., if the need arises to hire mercenaries again, they will want to have the appearance of having dealt honestly).

The most obvious means of ridding a state of mercenaries is to make them into part of the armed forces. Perhaps not as regular units – lower pay and higher discipline do not go well together – but as special units or, better yet, as instructors in a new and better national army.

The most practical is probably to pay them off in small groups, and to insure as best possible that they are not immediately hired by your enemies. Guaranteed pay for several years would do this. However, few countries which hire mercenaries or are liberated by them have any money to spare. International help for this? Not likely.

Trying to kill them is probably not going to work. Modern democratic states are adverse to casualties and expensive wars, and certainly not without some obvious national interest in the outcome.

Equally unlikely of success will be efforts to find mercenaries new employment. No one is likely to appreciate efforts to foist off unwanted hired soldiers on them or their neighbours. There is only a very slim chance that unemployed mercenaries could be hired by a group of nations – creating an international force somewhat similar to the French Foreign Legion. If Americans in the 1980s could become excited over the unlikely story that Belgian paratroopers were riding around the country on Amtrak (the national railroad system) as a rehearsal for a United Nations' takeover of the United States, imagine how they would react if they knew that the UN possessed a mercenary army! Or even a military force composed largely of idealists and only filled out with mercenary specialists – like some of the crusading armies. Many people want a more effective UN, but only the true believers are comfortable with the idea that the present politicised world body can be trusted with real weapons and real armies. Especially not bodies of well-trained mercenaries.

In the twentieth century we saw Leviathans greater than anything Hobbes ever imagined. And we managed to defeat them, or hold them off until they collapsed or evolved into more normal states. But what is the alternative to totalitarian megastates? A Hobbesean world of all against all? A secular pacifism that resists not evil? States failing under the weight of incompetence, corruption, disease, population growth, ethnic strife and a changing world economy – where new forms of free companies spring up and flourish?

The war on terror – or against political, ethnic and religious extremism – has brought forth new kinds of mercenaries. Call these bodyguards, security firms, or whatever, their faces are familiar and their profession easily recognised. We may recoil, but we cannot do without them.

So here we are. The lessons of our medieval experience may assist us in imagining various potential futures, some of which we should avoid. They might also assure us that this is a situation we can eventually overcome. But the problem is not the mercenaries. Mercenaries are merely the symptom of failed states or the failure of collective defence. It is like mosquitoes and swamps. We can swat gnats forever or drain the swamp.

SOURCES

Chapter 1 – Early Medieval Mercenaries

Frank Barlow, *William I and the Norman Conquest*. New York: MacMillan, 1965.

Brian Golding, *Conquest and Colonization, 1066–1100*. London: St. Martin's, 1994.

David Howarth, *1066. The Year of the Conquest*. New York: Dorset, 1977.

William Kapelle, *The Norman Conquest of the North. The Region and its Transformation, 1000–1135*. Chapel Hill: North Carolina, 1979.

Helen Nicholson, *Medieval warfare: theory and practice of war in Europe, 300–1500*. New York: Palgrave, 2004.

Magnus Magnusson and Hermann Pálsson, *King Harald's Saga. Harald Hardradi of Norway. From Snorri Sturluson's Heimkringla*. New York: Dorset, 1966.

Snorri Sturluson, *Heimskringla. History of the Kings of Norway*. Trans. Lee M. Hollander. Austin: University of Texas Press, 1964.

Chapter 2 – Early Italian Mercenaries

Philippe Contamine, *War in the Middle Ages*. Oxford: Blackwell, 1984.

Joseph Jay Diess, *Captains of Fortune. Profiles of Six Italian Condottieri*. New York: Thomas Crowell, 1967.

David Nicolle, *Italian Medieval Armies, 1300–1500*. London: Osprey, 1983.

Chapter 3 – The 'Classic' Medieval Mercenary

Sir John Froissart, *Chronicles of England, France, Spain, and the adjoining countries*. Trans. Thomas Johnes. New York: Leavitt, Trow and Co, 1848.

Johan Huizinga, *The Waning of the Middle Ages*. New York: St Martin, 1949.

John Schlight, *Monarchs and Mercenaries. A Reappraisal of the Importance of Knight Service in Norman and Early Angevin England*. New York: New York University Press, 1968.

Chapter 4 – Chivalry

Malcolm Barber, ed., *The Military Orders: Fighting for the Faith and Caring for the Sick*. Brookfield, Vermont: Ashgate, 1994.

Richard Barber, *The Knight and Chivalry*. Revised edition. Rochester, NY: The Boydell Press, 1995.

SOURCES

Mary Fischer, '*Di Himels Rote*', *The Idea of Christian Chivalry in the Chronicles of the Teutonic Order.*' Göppingen: Kümmerle, 1991.

Maurice Keen, *Chivalry*. New Haven and London: Yale, 1984.

William Urban, 'The Teutonic Knights and Baltic Chivalry.' *The Historian*, 56/3 (1994): 519–30.

Malcolm Vale, *War and Chivalry. Warfare and Aristocratic Culture in England, France and Burgundy at the End of the Middle Ages*. Athens, Georgia: University of Georgia Press, 1981.

Chapter 5 – The Hundred Years War: Part One

Andrian Bell, *War and the Soldier in the Fourteenth Century*. Woodbridge: Boydell, 2004.

Eric Christiansen, 'A Fine Life', *The New York Review of Books*, (30 November, 2000).

Anne Curry, *The Hundred Years War*. Blasingstock: MacMillan, 1993.

Kenneth Fowler, *Medieval Mercenaries. Vol. 1: The Great Companies*. Oxford: Blackwell, 2001.

Maurice Keen, *Nobles, Knights and Men-at-Arms in the Middle Ages*. London: Hamilton, 1996.

Jonathan Sumption, *The Hundred Years War*. 2 volumes. Philadelphia, University of Pennsylvania, 1999, 2000.

Barbara Tuchman, *A Distant Mirror: the calamitous fourteenth century*. Saddle Brook, New Jersey: Stratford Press, 1978.

Richard Venier, *The Flower of Chivalry. Bertrand du Guesclin and the Hundred Years War*. Woodbridge: Boydell, 2003.

Nicholas Wright, *Knights and Peasants in the Hundred Years War in the French Countryside*. Woodbridge: Boydell, 1998.

Chapter 6 – Forming the Victorian Imagination:
Chaucer's Knight and MarkTwain's Saint

Terry Jones, *Chaucer's Knight. The Portrait of a Medieval Mercenary*. New York: Methuen, 1985.

Mark Twain, *Historical Romances*. Vol. 3, Penguin Books, 1984.

Chapter 7 – Forming the Victorian Imagination: The White Company

John Dickson Carr, *The Life of Sir Arthur Conan Doyle*. New York: Harper, 1949.

Chapter 8 – The Crusades in the Baltic

The Chronicle of Henry of Livonia. Translated by James Brundage. 2nd edition. New York: Columbia, 2003.

Eric Christiansen, *The Northern Crusades: The Baltic and the Catholic Frontier 1100–1525*. New York: MacMillan Press Ltd, 1980.

Sven Ekdahl, 'Soldtruppen des Deutschen Ordens im Krieg gegen Polen 1409,' *Le Convoi Militaire, fasciculi archaelogiae historicae* Lodź, 2002, 47–64.

Helen Nicholson, ed. *The Military Orders: Welfare and Warfare*. Brookfield, Vermont: Ashgate, 1998.

Jerry C. Smith and William Urban, 'Peter von Suchenwirt.' *Lituanus*, 31/2 (1985), 5–26.

Stephen Turnbull, *Tannenberg 1410. Disaster for the Teutonic Knights*. London: Osprey, 2003.

William Urban, *The Baltic Crusade*. Chicago: Lithuanian Research and Studies Center, 1994.

William Urban, *The Livonian Crusade*. Chicago: Lithuanian Research and Studies Center, 2004.

Chapter 9 – The Hundred Years War: Part Two

Henry Stanley Bennett, 'Sir John Fastolf,' *Six Medieval Men and Women*. Cambridge, 1955.

Anne Curry and Michael Hughes, editors, *Arms, Armies and Fortifications in the Hundred Years War*. Woodbridge: Boydell, 1994.

Paul Murray Kendall, *Louis XI: The Universal Spider*. New York, W. W. Norton, 1971.

The Chronicle of Jean de Venette. Trans. Jean Birdsall. Edit Richard Newhall. New York: Columbia, 1953.

The Memoirs of Philippe de Commynes. Edited by Samuel Kinser. 2 vols. Translated by Isabelle Cazeaux. Columbia, South Carolina: University of South Carolina Press, 1969, 1973.

The Complete Works of William Shakespeare. Harvard Edition. Boston, 1886.

Richard Vaughan, *Charles the Bold, the Last Valois Duke of Burgundy*. New York: Harpers, 1973.

Chapter 10 – The Renaissance

Ernst Breisach, *Caterina Sforza. A Renaissance Virago*. Chicago and London: University of Chicago Press, 1967.

Francesco Guicciardini, *The History of Italy*. Translated by Sidney Alexander. London: Macmillan, 1969.

Michael Mallett, *Mercenaries and their Masters; warfare in Renaissance Italy*. Totowa: Rowman and Littlefield, 1974.

Chapter 11 – The Black Guard

William Urban, *Dithmarschen, a medieval peasant republic*. Lewiston: Mellen Press, 1991.

Walters Lammers, *Die Schlacht bei Hemmingstedt*. Heide: Boyens, 1982.

Chapter 12 – Machiavelli

Niccolò Machiavelli, *The Prince*. London & Toronto: J. M. Bent, 1908.

Niccolò Machiavelli, *The Discourses*. Numerous translations.

Chapter 13 – Mercenaries in the Late Medieval
Baltic

Sven Ekdahl, 'Zwei Musterungslisten von Deutschordens-Söldnern aus den Jahren 1413 und 1431.' *Arma et Ollae*, Lodź, 1992.

Juhan Kreem, 'The Business of War. Mercenary Market and Organisation in Reval in the Fifteenth and Early Sixteenth Centuries.' *Scandinavian Economic History Review*, 49/2 (2001) 26–42.

The Chronicle of Balthasar Russow. Translated by Jerry C. Smith and William Urban. Madison: Baltic Studies, 1988.

INDEX